5 Steps to a 5

AP English Literature

Other books in McGraw-Hill's *5 Steps to a 5 Series* include:

AP Biology
AP Calculus AB
AP English Language
AP Spanish Language
AP U.S. History

McGRAW-HILL

5 Steps to a 5

AP English Literature

Estelle M. Rankin
Barbara L. Murphy

McGRAW-HILL

New York   Chicago   San Francisco   Lisbon   London   Madrid   Mexico City
Milan   New Delhi   San Juan   Seoul   Singapore   Sydney   Toronto

Library of Congress Cataloging-in-Publication Data applied for.

McGraw-Hill

A Division of The McGraw·Hill Companies

7 8 9 10 QPD/QPD 0 9 8 7 6 5 4

ISBN 0-07-137719-0

From AS I LAY DYING by William Faulkner, copyright © 1930 and renewed 1958 by William Faulkner. Used by permission of Random House, Inc.

"To David, About His Education," by Howard Nemerov, from VOICES: THE 6th BOOK edited by Geoffrey Summerfield, published by Rand McNally and Company, Chicago, 1969. Used by permission of Margaret Nemerov.

"The End of the World," from COLLECTED POEMS, 1917–1982 by Archibald MacLeish. Copyright © 1985 by The Estate of Archibald MacLeish. Reprinted by permission of Houghton Mifflin Company. All rights reserved.

"The Flowers" from IN LOVE & TROUBLE: STORIES OF BLACK WOMEN, copyright © 1973 by Alice Walker, reprinted by permission of Harcourt, Inc.

"To a Friend Estranged from Me" by Edna St. Vincent Millay. From COLLECTED POEMS, HarperCollins. Copyright © 1928, 1955 by Edna St. Vincent Millay and Norma Millay Ellis. All rights reserved. Reprinted by permission of Elizabeth Barnett, literary executor.

From THE GOLD CELL by Sharon Olds, copyright © 1987 by Sharon Olds. Used by permission of Alfred A. Knopf, a division of Random House, Inc.

"Love Poem" by John Frederick Nims. From SELECTED POEMS BY JOHN F. NIMS, University of Chicago Press. Copyright © 1982 by John F. Nims. Reprinted by permission of Bonnie Larkin Nims.

"The Naked and the Nude," by Robert Graves from COMPLETE POEMS by Robert Graves. Used by permission of Carcanet Press Limited, Manchester England. On behalf of the Trustees of the Robert Graves Copyright Trust.

"Snake," from THE COMPLETE POEMS OF D. H. LAWRENCE by D. H. Lawrence, Viking Press, 1964. Used by permission of Laurence Pollinger Limited and the Estate of Frieda Lawrence Ravagli.

"The Writer" from THE MIND-HEALER, copyright © 1971 by Richard Wilbur, reprinted by permission of Harcourt, Inc.

The sponsoring editor for this book was Barbara Gilson, the series editor was Grace Freedson, the project editor was Don Reis, the editing supervisor was Maureen B. Walker, the designer was Azuretec Graphics, and the production supervisor was Clara Stanley.

Printed and bound by Quebecor/Dubuque.

♻ This book is printed on recycled, acid-free paper containing a minimum of 50% recycled, dc-inked fiber.

Contents

Preface / ix
Acknowledgments / xi

PART I   **HOW TO USE THIS BOOK / 1**

Chapter 1   **The Five-Step Program / 3**
Some Basics / 3
The Organization of the Book / 4
Introduction to the Five-Step Program / 5
Three Approaches to Preparing for the AP Literature Exam / 6
Introduction to the Graphics Used in the Book / 7
Calendars for Preparing for the AP Literature Exam / 9

PART II   **WHAT YOU NEED TO KNOW ABOUT THE AP LITERATURE EXAM / 13**

Chapter 2   **Introduction to the AP Literature Exam / 15**
Background on the Advanced Placement Exam / 15
Reasons for Taking the Advanced Placement Exam / 16
What You Need to Know about the AP Lit Exam / 17
A "Walk Through" the Diagnostic/Master Exam / 20
Advanced Placement Literature and Composition / 23

Chapter 3   **Section I of the Exam: The Multiple-Choice Questions / 34**
Introduction to the Multiple-Choice Section of the Exam / 34
Types of Multiple-Choice Questions / 37
Scoring the Multiple-Choice Section / 40
Strategies for Answering the Multiple-Choice Questions / 40
Answer Sheet for Diagnostic Multiple-Choice Questions / 45
The Multiple-Choice Section of the Diagnostic/Master Exam / 47
Explanation of Answers to the Multiple-Choice Questions of the
     Diagnostic/Master Exam / 54

Chapter 4   **The Prose Passage Essay / 59**
Introduction to the Prose Passage Essay / 59

Types of Prose Passage Essay Questions / 60
Rating the Prose Passage Essay / 61
Timing the Essay / 62
Working the Prompt / 62
Reading and Notating the Prose Passage / 64
Writing the Opening Paragraph / 66
Writing the Body of the Prose Passage Essay / 68
Sample Student Essays / 71
Rating the Student Essays / 74
Final Comments / 76
Rapid Review / 77

Chapter 5   The Poetry Essay / 78
Introduction to the Poetry Essay / 78
Types of Prompts Used in the Poetry Essay / 79
Timing and Planning the Poetry Essay / 79
Working the Prompt / 80
Writing the Opening Paragraph / 84
Writing the Body of the Poetry Essay / 86
Sample Student Essays / 88
Rating the Student Essays / 90
Rapid Review / 92

Chapter 6   The Free-Response Essay / 93
Introduction to the Free-Response Essay / 93
Types of Free-Response Prompts / 96
General Rubrics for the Free-Response Essay / 97
Timing and Planning the Free-Response Essay / 98
Working the Prompt from the Diagnostic/Master Exam / 98
Developing the Opening Paragraph / 101
Developing the Body of the Essay / 102
Sample Student Essays / 104
Rating the Student Essays / 107
Final Comments / 107
Rapid Review / 108

PART III   COMPREHENSIVE REVIEW: DEVELOPING THE KNOWLEDGE, SKILLS, AND STRATEGIES / 109
Introduction to Review Section / 111

Chapter 7   Prose Review / 113
Introduction to Prose / 113
Five Aspects of Every Narrative / 114
Types of Novels / 119
Literary Terminology / 120
Prose Analysis / 122

Final Comments / 124
Rapid Review / 125

Chapter 8   **Poetry Review / 126**
Introduction to Poetry / 126
The Structure of Poetry / 127
Types of Poetry / 130
Interpretation of Poetry / 142
Poems for Comparison and Contrast / 148
Rapid Review / 150

PART IV   **DEVELOPING CONFIDENCE BY APPLYING SKILLS / 151**

Chapter 9   **Practice Exam 1 / 153**
Section I / 155
Section II / 164
Answers to Multiple-Choice Questions / 166
Rating the Essay Section / 170

Chapter 10   **Practice Exam 2 / 181**
Section I / 183
Section II / 191
Answers to Multiple-Choice Questions / 194
Rating the Essay Section / 198

PART V   **"AFTER WORDS" / 209**

A Suggested Reading Guide / 211
Classicism / 211
Realism / 212
Romanticism / 213
Impressionism / 215
Expressionism / 215
Naturalism / 216

General Bibliography / 218

Glossary of Terms / 221

Websites Related to the Advanced Placement Exam / 224

Preface

Welcome to our AP Literature class. We are, first and foremost, teachers who have taught advanced placement to thousands of students who successfully took the AP exam. With this guide we hope to share with you what we know as well as what we have learned from our students.

We see you as a student in our class—only quieter! Our philosophy has always been *not* to teach only for the AP test. Instead, our goal has always been to develop appreciation and those insights and skills that lead to advanced levels of facility with literature and composition. These are the same skills that will enable you to do well on the AP literature exam. Our aim is to remove your nervousness and to improve your comfort level with the test. We believe that you are already motivated to succeed; otherwise, you would not have come this far. And, obviously, you would not have purchased this prep book.

Since you are already in an English class, this book is going to supplement your literature course readings, analysis, and writing. We are going to give you the opportunity to practice processes and techniques that we know from experience *really work!* We are confident that if you apply the techniques and processes presented in this book, you can succeed.

Let's begin.

Acknowledgments

Our love and appreciation to Allan and to Leah for their constant support and encouragement. Our very special thanks to our professional mentors who have guided us throughout our careers: Steven Piorkowski and Howard Damon. To the following for their support and suggestions: Diane Antonucci, Richard Andres, Mary Moran, Mike Thier, Mark Misthal, Dave Martin, and Edward Stern—thank you.

The authors wish to acknowledge the participation, insights, and feedback provided us by the following colleagues and students.

Jericho High School:
    Teachers: Diane Antonucci, Michael Hartnett
    Students: Tara Arschin, Samantha Brody, Jenna Butner,
                Julie Ivans, Grace Kwak, Ari Weiss, Erica Ross,
                David Swidler, and Sherli Yeroushalmi

Islip High School:
    Teacher: Marge Grossgold
    Students: Caitlin Rizzo and Katelyn Zawyrucha

Massapequa High School:
    Teachers: Sue Bruno and Rosemary Verade
    Student: Margaretta Dimos

Solomon Schechter School:
    Teachers: Dennis Young and Miriam Fischer
    Students: Yadin Duckstein, Ari Lucas, and Jonathan Kotter

Wantagh High School:
    Teachers: Sherry Skolnick and Pat Castellano
    Student: Lauren Manning

Also, our thanks to Danielle Tumminio and Andrew Brotman.

McGRAW-HILL

5 Steps to a 5

AP English Literature

PART I

HOW TO USE THIS BOOK

Chapter 1

The Five-Step Program

SOME BASICS

Consider Chapter 1 as a map of the new territory you are going to explore. We will provide the general directions, and you can decide when, where, and how you will follow this map.

Reading

We believe that reading should be an exciting interaction between you and the writer. You have to bring your own context to the experience, and you must feel comfortable reaching for and exploring ideas. You are an adventurer on a journey of exploration, and we will act as your guides. We will set the itinerary, but you will set your own pace. You can feel free to "stop and smell the roses" or to explore new territory.

The Journey

On any journey, each traveler sees something different on new horizons. So, too, each student is free to personalize his or her own literary experience, provided he or she tries at all times to strive for excellence and accuracy.

Critical Thinking

There are no tricks to critical thinking. Those who claim to guarantee you a score of 5 with gimmicks are doing you a disservice. No one can guarantee a 5; however, the reading and writing skills you will review, practice, and master will give you the very best chance to do your very best. You will have the opportunity to learn, to practice, and to master the critical thinking processes that can empower you to achieve your highest score.

The Beginning

It is our belief that if you focus on the beginning, the rest will fall into place. Once you purchase this book and decide to work your way through it, you are beginning your journey to the AP Literature exam. We will be with you every step of the way.

Why This Book?

We believe we have something unique to offer you. For over 25 years we have addressed the needs of AP students just like you. And we've been fortunate to learn from these students. Therefore, the content of this book reflects genuine student concerns and needs. This is a student-oriented book. We will not overwhelm you with pompous language, mislead you with inaccurate information and tasks, or lull you into a false sense of confidence with easy shortcuts. We stand behind every suggestion, process, and question we present. There is no "busy work" in this book.

We know you will not do every activity. Therefore, think of this book as a resource and guide to accompany you on your AP Literature journey throughout the year. This book is designed to serve many purposes. It will:

- Clarify requirements for the AP Literature exam.
- Provide you with test practice.
- Show you rubrics (grading standards) on which you can model and evaluate your own work.
- Anticipate and answer your questions.
- Enrich your understanding and appreciation of literature.
- Help you pace yourself.
- Make you aware of the Five Steps to Mastering the AP Literature Exam.

THE ORGANIZATION OF THE BOOK

We know that your primary concern is to obtain information about the AP Literature exam. So, we begin at the beginning with an overview of the AP exam in general. We then introduce you to our Diagnostic/Master exam which we use throughout the book to show you the ins and outs of an AP Literature test. In separate chapters you will become familiar with both sections of the exam. We will lead you through the multiple-choice questions and explain how you should answer them. Then we will take you through the essay questions and discuss approaches to writing these essays.

Because you must be fluent in the language and processes of literary analysis and composition, we provide a comprehensive review section in both prose and poetry. This review is not a mere listing of terms and concepts. Rather, it is a series of practices that will hone your analytical and writing skills. But, do not fear. You will find terms and concepts clearly delineated within their contexts. We also provide annotated suggestions for high-interest prose and poetry readings.

Part IV of the book is the practice-exam section. Here is where you will test your skills and knowledge. You may be sure that the prose and poetry selections included in each exam are on the AP level. The multiple-choice questions provide you with practice in responding to typical types of questions asked in past AP exams. The essay questions are designed to cover the techniques and terms required by the AP exam. The free-response essays are both challenging and specific, yet they are broad enough to suit all curricula. After taking each exam, you can check yourself against the explanations of every multiple-choice question and the ratings of the sample student essays.

The final section is one that you should not pass over. It contains a Glossary of Terms, a Bibliography of Works that may be of importance to you, and a list of Websites related to the AP Literature exam.

INTRODUCTION TO THE FIVE-STEP PROGRAM

The **Five-Step Program** is a powerful program designed to provide you with the best possible skills, strategies, and practice to help lead you to that perfect 5 on the Advanced Placement Literature exam that is administered each May to over 100,000 high school students. Each of the five steps will provide you with the opportunity to get closer and closer to the 5 which is the "Holy Grail" to all AP students.

STEP ONE leads you through a brief process that helps you determine which type of exam preparation you want to commit yourself to:

1. Month by month: September through May
2. The calendar year: January through May
3. Basic training: the 4–6 weeks prior to the exam

STEP TWO helps develop the knowledge you need to do well on the exam:

1. A comprehensive review of the exam
2. One "Diagnostic/Master exam" which you will go through step by step and question by question to build your confidence
3. Explanation of multiple-choice answers
4. A comprehensive review of literary analysis

5. A glossary of terms related to the AP Literature exam
6. A list of interesting and related Websites and a bibliography

STEP THREE helps develop the skills necessary for you to take the exam and do well:

1. Practice activities that will hone your skills in close reading
2. Practice activities in critical thinking
3. Practice activities in critical/analytical writing

STEP FOUR helps you develop strategies for taking the exam:

1. Learning about the test itself
2. Learning to read multiple-choice questions
3. Learning how to answer multiple-choice questions, including whether or not to guess
4. Learning how to deconstruct the essay prompts
5. Learning how to plan the essay

STEP FIVE will help you develop your confidence in using the skills required on the AP Literature exam:

1. The opportunity to take a Diagnostic/Master exam
2. Time management techniques and skills
3. Two practice exams that test how well-honed your skills are
4. Rubrics for self-evaluation

THREE APPROACHES TO PREPARING FOR THE AP LITERATURE EXAM

No one knows your study habits, likes, and dislikes better than you do. So you are the only one who can decide which approach you want and/or need to adopt to prepare for the Advanced Placement Literature Exam. Look at the brief profiles below. These may help you to place yourself in a particular prep mode.

You're a full-year prep student (Approach A) if:

1. You're the kind of person who likes to plan for a vacation or the prom a year in advance.
2. You'd never think of missing a practice session, whether it's your favorite sport, musical instrument, or activity.
3. You like detailed planning and everything in its place.
4. You feel you must be thoroughly prepared.
5. You hate surprises.
6. You're always early for appointments.

You're a one-semester prep student (Approach B) if:

1. You begin to plan for your vacation or the prom 4–5 months before the event.
2. You are willing to plan ahead so that you will feel comfortable in stressful situations, but you are okay with skipping some details.
3. You feel more comfortable when you know what to expect, but a surprise or two does not floor you.
4. You're always on time for appointments.

You're a 4–6 week prep student (Approach C) if:

1. You accept or find a date for the prom a week before the big day.
2. You work best under pressure and tight deadlines.
3. You feel very confident with the skills and background you've gained in your AP Literature class.
4. You decided late in the year to take the exam.
5. You like surprises.
6. You feel okay if you arrive 10–15 minutes late for an appointment.

INTRODUCTION TO THE GRAPHICS USED IN THE BOOK

To emphasize particular skills, strategies, and practice, we use seven sets of icons throughout this book. You will see these icons in the margins throughout the book.

The first icon is an hourglass. We've chosen this to indicate the passage of time during the school year. This hourglass icon is in the margin next to an item that may be of interest to one of the three types of students who are using this book.

For the student who plans to prepare for the AP Literature exam during the entire school year, September through May, we use an hourglass which is full on the top.

For the student who decides to begin preparing for the exam in January, we use an hourglass that is half full on the top and half full on the bottom.

For the student who wishes to prepare during the final 4–6 weeks before the exam, we use an hourglass that is almost empty on the top and almost full on the bottom.

The second icon is a footprint, indicating which one of the steps in the five-step program is being emphasized in a given analysis, technique, or practice activity.

Plan   Knowledge   Skills   Strategies   Confidence Building

The third icon is a clock that indicates a timed practice activity or a time management strategy. The face of the dial shows how much time to allow for a given exercise. The full dial will remind you that this is a strategy which can help you learn to manage your time on the test.

The fourth icon is an exclamation point that points to a very important idea, concept, or strategy that you should not pass over.

The fifth icon is a check that alerts you to pay close attention. This is an activity that will be most helpful if you go back and check your own work, your calendar, or your progress.

The sixth icon is the lightbulb that indicates strategies you may want to try.

The seventh icon is the sun that indicates a tip that you might find useful.

Boldfaced and _italicized_ words indicate terms that are included in the glossary.

Throughout the book you will find margin notes and boxes. We want you to pay close attention to these areas because they can provide tips, hints, strategies, and explanations that will help you reach your full potential.

CALENDARS FOR PREPARING
FOR THE AP LITERATURE EXAM

This is a personal journey, and each of you will have particular time constraints. Choose the calendar that will work best for you.

 ## Calendar for Approach A:
Year-long Preparation for the AP Literature Exam

Although its primary purpose is to prepare you for the AP Literature exam you will take in May, this book can enrich your study of literature, your analytical skills, and your writing skills.

SEPTEMBER–OCTOBER (Check off the activities as you complete them.)

_____ Determine student mode into which you place yourself.
_____ Carefully read Chapters 1 and 2.
_____ Pay close attention to the walk-through of the Diagnostic/Master exam.
_____ Get on the Web and take a look at the AP Website(s).
_____ Skim the Comprehensive Review section.
_____ Buy a highlighter.
_____ Flip through the entire book. Break the book in. Write in it. Highlight it.
_____ Get a clear picture of what your own school's AP Literature curriculum is.
_____ Review the Bibliography in Part V and establish a pattern of outside reading in the literary genres.
_____ Begin to use the book as a resource.

NOVEMBER (The first 10 weeks have elapsed.)

_____ Write the free-response essay in the Diagnostic/Master exam.
_____ Compare your essay with the sample student essays.
_____ Refer to the section in Chapter 8 on the free-response essay.

_____ Take five of our prompts and write solid, opening paragraphs.

DECEMBER

_____ Maintain notes on literary works you studied in and out of class.
_____ Refine your analytical skills (see Chapter 8).
_____ Write the prose passage or poetry essay in the Diagnostic/Master exam. (This will depend on the organization of your own curriculum.)
_____ Compare your essay with sample student essays.

JANUARY (20 weeks have elapsed.)

_____ Write the third essay in the Diagnostic/Master exam. (This will depend on the one you did previously.)
_____ Compare your essay with sample student essays.

FEBRUARY

_____ Take the multiple-choice section of the Diagnostic/Master exam.
_____ Carefully go over the explanations of the answers to the questions.

_____ Score yourself honestly.
_____ Make a note of terms, concepts, and types of questions that give you difficulty.
_____ Review troublesome terms in Chapter 8 or the Glossary.

MARCH (30 weeks have elapsed.)

_____ Form a study group.
_____ Outline or create a chart for full-length works that would be appropriate for the free-response essay.
_____ Choose a favorite poem and create an essay question to go with it, or use one of our suggested prompts.
_____ Choose a prose passage or essay and create an essay question to go with it, or choose one of our suggested prompts.
_____ Write the poetry essay.
_____ Write the prose essay.
_____ Compare essays and rate them with your study group. (Use our rubrics.)

APRIL

_____ Take Practice Exam 1 in the first week of April.
_____ Evaluate your strengths and weaknesses.

_____ Study appropriate chapters to correct your weaknesses.
_____ Practice creating multiple-choice questions of different types with your study group.
_____ Develop and review worksheets for and with your study group.

MAY—First 2 Weeks (THIS IS IT!)

_____ Highlight only those things in the Glossary you are still unsure of. Ask your teacher for clarification. Study!
_____ Thoroughly prepare three to five complete, full-length works; include several quotations that you can work into various responses.
_____ Write at least three times a week under timed conditions.
_____ Take Practice Exam 2.
_____ Score yourself.
_____ Give yourself a pat on the back for how much you have learned and improved over the past 9 months.
_____ Go to the movies. Call a friend.
_____ Get a good night's sleep. Fall asleep knowing you are well prepared.

GOOD LUCK ON THE TEST.

Calendar for Approach B:
Semester-Long Preparation for the AP Literature Exam

Working under the assumption that you've completed one semester of literature studies, apply those skills you've learned to prepare for the May exam. You have plenty of time to supplement your course work by taking our study recommendations, maintaining literary notations, doing outside readings, and so on. We divide the next 16 weeks into a workable program of preparation for you.

JANUARY–FEBRUARY (Check off the activities as you complete them.)

_____ Carefully read Chapters 1 and 2.
_____ Write the three essays in the Diagnostic/Master exam.
_____ Compare your essays with the sample student essays.
_____ Study Part III.
_____ Complete the multiple-choice section of the Diagnostic/Master exam.
_____ Carefully go over the answers and explanations of the answers.
_____ Take a close look at the Bibliography in Part V for suggestions on possible outside readings.

MARCH (10 weeks to go.)

_____ Form a study group.
_____ Outline or create a chart for full-length works that would be appropriate for the free-response essay.
_____ Choose a favorite poem and create an essay question to go with it, or use one of our suggested prompts.
_____ Choose a prose passage or essay and create an essay question to go with it, or choose one of our suggested prompts.
_____ Write the poetry essay.
_____ Write the prose essay.
_____ Compare essays and rate them with your study group. (Use our rubrics.)

APRIL

_____ Take Practice Exam 1 in the first week of April.
_____ Evaluate your strengths and weaknesses.
_____ Study appropriate chapters to correct your weaknesses.
_____ Practice creating multiple-choice questions of different types with your study group.
_____ Develop and review worksheets for and with your study group.

MAY—First 2 Weeks (THIS IS IT!)

_____ Highlight only those things in the Glossary you are still unsure of. Ask your teacher for clarification. Study!
_____ Thoroughly prepare at least three to five complete, full-length works, include several quotations that you can work into various questions.
_____ Write at least three times a week under timed conditions.
_____ Take Practice Exam 2.
_____ Score yourself.
_____ Give yourself a pat on the back for how much you have learned and improved over the past nine months.
_____ Go to the movies. Call a friend.
_____ Get a good night's sleep. Fall asleep knowing you are well prepared.

GOOD LUCK ON THE TEST.

Calendar for Approach C:
4–6 Week Preparation for the AP Literature Exam

At this point, we are going to assume that you have been developing your literary, analytical, and writing skills in your English class for more than 6 months. You will, therefore, use this book primarily as a specific guide to the AP Literature exam. Remember, there is a solid review section in this text to which you should refer. Given the time constraints, now is not the time to try to expand your AP Literature curriculum. Rather, it is the time to limit and refine what you already know.

APRIL

_____ Skim through Chapters 1 and 2.

_____ Carefully go over the "rapid review" sections of Chapters 3–6.

_____ Use Part III as a personal reference to strengthen, clarify, and correct areas you are weak in after taking the Diagnostic/Master exam.

_____ Write a minimum of three sample opening paragraphs for each of the three types of essays.

_____ Write a minimum of two timed essays for each type of essay on the exam.

_____ Complete Practice Exam 1.

_____ Score yourself and analyze your errors.

_____ Refer to Part III to correct your weaknesses.

_____ Refer to the Bibliography in Part V.

_____ If you feel unfamiliar with specific poetic forms, refer to Part V to see a list of suggested, appropriate works.

_____ Create review sheets for three to five solid, full-length works.

_____ Skim and highlight the glossary.

_____ Develop a weekly study group to hear each other's essays and to discuss literature.

MAY—First 2 Weeks (THIS IS IT!)

_____ Complete Practice Exam 2.

_____ Score yourself and analyze your errors.

_____ Refer to Part III to correct your weaknesses.

_____ Go to the movies. Call a friend.

_____ Get a good night's sleep. Fall asleep knowing you are well prepared.

GOOD LUCK ON THE TEST.

"One of the first steps to success on the AP exam is knowing your own study habits."
—Margaret R., AP Literature teacher

PART II

WHAT YOU NEED TO KNOW ABOUT THE AP LITERATURE EXAM

Chapter 2

Introduction to the AP Literature Exam

BACKGROUND ON THE ADVANCED PLACEMENT EXAM

"AP" does not stand for "Always Puzzling." The following should help lift the veil of mystery associated with the AP Exam.

What is the Advanced Placement Program?

The Advanced Placement program was begun by the College Board in 1955 to construct standard achievement exams that would allow highly motivated high school students the opportunity to be awarded advanced placement as freshmen in colleges and universities in the United States. Today, there are 33 courses and exams with more than a million students from every state in the nation, and from foreign countries, taking the annual exams in May.

As is obvious, the AP programs are designed for high school students who wish to take college-level courses. In our case, the AP Literature course and exam are designed to involve high school students in college-level English studies in both literature and composition.

Who writes the AP Literature exam?

According to the folks at the College Board, the AP Literature exam is created by college and high school English instructors called the AP Development Committee. The committee's job is to ensure that the annual AP Literature exam reflects what is being taught and studied in college-level English classes in high schools.

This committee writes a large number of multiple-choice questions which are pretested and evaluated for clarity, appropriateness, and range of possible answers. The committee also generates a pool of essay questions, pretests them, and chooses those questions that best represent the full range of the scoring scale which will allow the AP readers to evaluate the essays fairly.

It is important to remember that the AP Literature exam is thoroughly evaluated after it is administered each year. This way, the College Board can use the results to make course suggestions and to plan future tests.

What are the Advanced Placement grades, and who receives them?

Once you have taken the exam and it has been scored, your test will be assigned one of five numbers by the College Board:

- 5 indicates you are extremely well-qualified.
- 4 indicates you are well-qualified.
- 3 indicates you are qualified.
- 2 indicates you are possibly qualified.
- 1 indicates that you are not qualified to receive college credit.

A grade of 5, 4, 3, 2, or 1 will be reported to your college or university first, to your high school second, and to you third. All this reporting is usually completed by the middle to end of July.

REASONS FOR TAKING THE ADVANCED PLACEMENT EXAM

At some point during the year every AP student asks the ultimate question: Why am I taking this exam?

Good question. Why put yourself through a year of intensive study, pressure, stress, and preparation? To be honest, only you can answer that question. Over the years, our students have indicated to us that there are several primary reasons why they were willing to take the risk and to put in the effort:

- For personal satisfaction
- To compare themselves with other students across the nation
- Because colleges look favorably on the applications of students who elect to enroll in AP courses
- To receive college credit or advanced standing at their colleges or universities
- Because they love the subject
- So that their family will really be proud of them

There are plenty of other reasons, but no matter what the other reasons might be, the top reason for your enrolling in the AP Lit course and taking the exam in May is to feel good about yourself and the challenges you have met.

WHAT YOU NEED TO KNOW ABOUT THE AP LIT EXAM

Let's answer a few of the nitty-gritty questions about the exam and its scoring.

If I don't take an AP Lit Course, can I still take the AP Lit exam?

Yes. Even though the AP Lit exam is designed for the student who has had a year's course in AP Literature, there are high schools that do not offer this type of course, and the students in these high schools have done well on the exam. However, if your high school does offer an AP Lit course, by all means take advantage of it and the structured background it will provide you.

How is the Advanced Placement Literature exam organized?

The exam has two parts and is scheduled to last 3 hours. The first section is a set of multiple-choice questions based on a series of prose passages and poems. You will have 1 hour to complete this part of the test. The second section of the exam is a 2-hour essay writing segment consisting of three different essays: one on prose, one on poetry, and one free-response.

After you complete the multiple-choice section and hand in your test booklet and scan sheet, you will be given a brief break. Note that you will not be able to return to the multiple-choice questions when you return to the examination room.

Must I check the box at the end of the essay booklet that allows the AP people to use my essays as samples for research?

No. This is simply a way for the College Board to make certain that it has your permission if it decides to use one or more of your essays as a model. The readers of your essays pay no attention to whether or not that box is checked. Checking the box will not affect your grade.

How is my AP Lit exam scored?

Let's look at the basics first. The multiple-choice section counts for 45 percent of your total score, and the essay section counts for 55 percent. Next comes a four-part calculation: the raw scoring of the multiple-choice section, the raw scoring of the essay section, the calculation of the composite score, and the conversion of the composite score into the AP grade of 5, 4, 3, 2, or 1.

How is the multiple-choice section scored?

The scan sheet with your answers is run through a computer which counts the number of wrong answers and subtracts a fraction of that number from the number of correct answers. The AP Lit questions usually have five choices. Therefore, the fraction for a wrong answer would be one-fourth. A question left blank receives a zero. This is what the formula for this calculation looks like:

$$\text{number right} - (\text{number wrong} \times .25) = \text{raw score rounded up or down to nearest whole number}$$

How is my essay section scored?

Each of your essays is read by a different, trained AP reader called a faculty consultant. The AP/College Board people have developed a highly successful training program for its readers. This factor, together with many opportunities for checks and double checks of essays, ensures a fair and equitable reading of each essay.

The scoring guides are carefully developed by a chief faculty consultant, a question leader, table leaders, and content experts. All faculty consultants are then trained to read and score just *one* essay question on the exam. They actually become experts in that one essay question. No one knows the identity of any writer. The identification numbers and names are covered, and the exam booklets are randomly distributed to the readers in packets of 25 randomly chosen essays. Table leaders and the question leader review samples of each reader's scores to ensure that quality standards are consistent.

Each essay is scored as 9, 8, 7, 6, 5, 4, 3, 2, or 1, plus 0, with 9 the highest possible score. Once your essay is given a number from 9 to 1, the next set of calculations is completed. Here, if there are 27 possible points divided into 55 percent of the total possible score, each point awarded is given a value of 3.055. The formula looks something like this:

$$\underset{\text{Essay 1}}{(\text{pts.} \times 3.055)} + \underset{\text{Essay 2}}{(\text{pts.} \times 3.055)} + \underset{\text{Essay 3}}{(\text{pts.} \times 3.055)} = \text{essay raw score}$$

How is my composite score calculated?

The total composite score for the AP Lit test is 150. Of this score, 55 percent is the essay section; that equals 82.5 points. The multiple-choice section is 45 percent of the composite score, which equals 67.5 points. Each of your three essays is graded on a 9-point scale; therefore, each point is worth 3.055. Divide the number of multiple-choice questions by 67.5 For instance, if there were 55 questions, each point of the raw score would be multiplied by 1.227.

If you add together the raw scores of each of the two sections, you will have a composite score. We provide practice with this process in the two practice exams in this book.

How is my composite score turned into the grade that is reported to my college?

"Over the years, in comparison to students who fight the material, I've found students who receive the 4's and 5's are those who truly allow themselves to relate to the literature covered in the class."
—Pat K.
-AP teacher

Keep in mind that the total composite scores needed to earn a 5, 4, 3, 2, or 1 are different each year. This is determined by a committee of AP/College Board/Educational Testing Service directors, experts, and statisticians. The grading is based on items such as:

- AP distribution over the past three years
- Comparability studies
- Observations of the chief faculty consultant
- Frequency distributions of scores on each section and the essays
- Average scores on each exam section and essays

However, over the years a trend is apparent which indicates the number of points required to achieve a specific grade:

- 150–100 points = 5
- 99–86 = 4
- 85–67 = 3

Grades 2 and 1 fall below this range. You do not want to go there.

What should I bring to the exam?

You should bring:

- Several pencils with erasers
- Several *black* pens (black ink is easier to read than other colors)
- A watch
- Something to drink—water is best
- A quiet snack, like Lifesavers
- Tissues

Is there anything else I should be aware of?

You should be aware of the following:

- Allow plenty of time to get to the test site.
- Wear comfortable clothing.
- Eat a light breakfast or lunch.

- Remind yourself that you are well prepared and that the test is an enjoyable challenge and a chance to share your knowledge. Be proud of yourself! You worked hard all year. Now is your time to shine.

Is there anything special I should do the night before the exam?

We certainly don't advocate last minute cramming. If you've been following the guidelines, you won't have to cram. But there may be a slight value to some last minute review. Spend the night before the exam relaxing with family or friends. Watch a movie; play a game; gab on the phone. Then find a quiet spot. While you're unwinding, flip through your own notebook and review sheets. Recall some details from the full-length works you've prepared and think of your favorite scenes. By now, you're bound to be ready to drift off. Pleasant dreams.

2 "A WALK THROUGH" THE DIAGNOSTIC/MASTER EXAM

"You know, from my experience with AP exams, I've learned never to assume anything."
—Jeremy G., AP student

What follows is our version of an Advanced Placement Literature and Composition Exam which we use throughout this book to demonstrate processes, examples, terms, and so on. We call this the Diagnostic/Master exam. You will not be taking this exam at this point, but we would like you to "walk through" the exam with us, now.

The first part of this 3-hour exam is always the multiple-choice section which lasts 1 hour. It is related to both prose passages and poetry. The multiple-choice section of the Diagnostic/Master exam contains two prose passages from different time periods and of different styles. It also has two poems from different time periods and of different forms. The multiple-choice questions for each selection were developed to provide you with a wide range of question types and terminology that have been used in the actual AP Lit exams over the years.

To begin to know what the exam looks like, take some time now to look through the multiple-choice section of the Diagnostic/Master exam. Do not try to answer questions; just peruse the types of passages and questions.

- Take a turn through all of the pages of the test and familiarize yourself with the format.
- See where the longer and shorter readings are.
- See how many prose and poetry passages there are.
- Check the total number of questions and know what you are facing.
- Check out the essay prompts.

A Word about Our Sample Student Essays

We field-tested each of the essay questions in a variety of high schools, both public and private. We could have chosen to present essays that would have "knocked your socks off," but, we chose to present samples that are truly representative of the essays usually written within the time constraints of the exam.

These essays are indicative of a wide range of styles and levels of acceptability. We want you to recognize that there is not one model to which all essays must conform.

"To Thine Own Self Be True" (Polonius—*Hamlet*)

"Be true to yourself" is always the best advice and is especially appropriate for a writer. Listen to your teacher's advice; listen to our advice; listen to your own voice. Yours is the voice we want to "hear" in your writing. Use natural vocabulary and present honest observations. It is wonderful to read professional criticism, but you cannot adopt someone else's ideas and remain true to your own thoughts. Trust your brain—if you've prepared well, you'll do well.

ADVANCED PLACEMENT LITERATURE AND COMPOSITION

Section I

Total Time—1 hour

Carefully read the following passages and answer the questions which follow.

Questions 1–10 are based on the following passage.

Now Goes Under . . .
by Edna St. Vincent Millay

Now goes under, and I watch it go under, the sun
 That will not rise again.
Today has seen the setting, in your eyes cold
 and senseless as the sea,
Of friendship better than bread, and of bright charity   5
That lifts a man a little above the beasts that run.

That this could be!
That I should live to see
Most vulgar Pride, that stale obstreperous clown,
So fitted out with purple robe and crown   10
To stand among his betters! Face to face
With outraged me in this once holy place,
Where Wisdom was a favoured guest and hunted
Truth was harboured out of danger,
He bulks enthroned, a lewd, and insupportable stranger!   15

I would have sworn, indeed I swore it:
The hills may shift, the waters may decline,
Winter may twist the stem from the twig that bore it,
But never your love from me, your hand from mine.

Now goes under the sun, and I watch it go under.   20
Farewell, sweet light, great wonder!
You, too, farewell—but fare not well enough to dream
You have done wisely to invite the night before the darkness came.

1. The poem is an example of a(n)

 A. sonnet
 B. lyric
 C. ode
 D. ballad
 E. dramatic monologue

2. The setting of the sun is a symbol for

 A. the beginning of winter
 B. encountering danger
 C. the end of a relationship
 D. facing death
 E. the onset of night

3. The second stanza is developed primarily by

 A. metaphor
 B. simile
 C. personification
 D. hyperbole
 E. allusion

4. "He" in line 15 refers to

   A. Wisdom
   B. Truth
   C. I
   D. Pride
   E. charity

5. According to the speaker, what separates man from beast?

   A. love
   B. friendship
   C. charity
   D. truth
   E. wisdom

6. For the speaker, the relationship has been all of the following *except*

   A. honest
   B. dangerous
   C. spiritual
   D. ephemeral
   E. nourishing

7. The reader can infer from the play on words in the last stanza that the speaker is

   A. dying
   B. frantic
   C. wistful

   D. bitter
   E. capricious

8. "This holy place" (line 12) refers to

   A. the sunset
   B. the relationship
   C. the sea
   D. the circus
   E. the Church

9. The cause of the relationship's situation is

   A. a stranger coming between them
   B. the lover not taking the relationship seriously
   C. the lover feeling intellectually superior
   D. the lover's pride coming between them
   E. the lover being insensitive

10. The speaker acknowledges the finality of the relationship in line(s)

   A. 1–2
   B. 7
   C. 8
   D. 16
   E. 18–19

Questions 11–23 are based on the following passage.

The sea-reach of the Thames stretched before us like the beginning of an
interminable waterway. The air was dark above Gravesend, and farther back still
seemed condensed into a mournful gloom, brooding motionless over the biggest and
the greatest town on earth.
  "I was thinking of very old times, when the Romans first came here, nineteen   5
hundred years ago—the other day . . . Light came out of this river since—you say knights?
Yes; but it is like a running blaze on a plain, like a flash of lightning in the clouds. We live
in the flicker—may it last as long as the old earth keeps rolling! But darkness was here
yesterday. Imagine the feelings of a commander of a fine—what d'ye call 'em?—trireme
in the Mediterranean, ordered suddenly to the north; run overland across the Gauls in a   10
hurry; put in charge of one of these craft the legionnaires—a wonderful lot of handy men
they must have been, too—used to build, apparently by the hundred, in a month or two, if
we may believe what we read. Imagine him here—the very end of the world, a sea the color
of lead, a sky the color of smoke, a kind of ship about as rigid as a concertina—and going
up this river with stores, or orders, or what you like. Sandbanks, marshes, forests, savages—   15

precious little to eat for a civilized man, nothing but Thames water to drink. No Falernian wine here, no going ashore. Here and there a military camp lost in a wilderness, like a needle in a bundle of hay—cold, fog, tempests, disease, exile, and death—death skulking in the air, in the water, in the bush. They must have been dying like flies here. Oh yes—he did it. Did it very well, too, no doubt, and without thinking much about it either, except 20 afterwards to brag of what he had gone through in his time, perhaps. They were men enough to face darkness. And perhaps he was cheered by keeping his eye on a chance of promotion to the fleet at Ravenna by and by, if he had good friends in Rome and survived the awful climate. Or think of a decent young citizen in a toga—perhaps too much dice, you know— coming out here in the train of some prefect, or tax-gatherer, or trader even, to mend his 25 fortunes. Land in a swamp, march through the woods, and in some inland post feel the savagery, the utter savagery, had closed round him—all that mysterious life of the wilderness that stirs in the forest, in the jungles, in the hearts of wild men. There's no initiation either into such mysteries. He has to live in the midst of the incomprehensible, which is also detestable. And it has a fascination, too, that goes to work upon him. The fascination of the 30 abomination—you know, imagine the growing regrets, the longing to escape, the powerless disgust, the surrender, the hate."

He paused.

"Mind," he began again, lifting one arm from the elbow, the palm of the hand outwards, so that, with his legs folded before him, he had the pose of a Buddha preaching in 35 European clothes and without a lotus flower—"Mind, none of us would feel exactly like this. What saves us is efficiency—the devotion to efficiency. But these chaps were not much account, really. They were no colonists; their administration was merely a squeeze, and nothing more, I suspect. They were conquerors, and for that you want only brute force— nothing to boast of, when you have it, since your strength is just an accident arising from the 40 weakness of others. They grabbed what they could get for the sake of what was to be got. It was just robbery with violence, aggravated murder on a great scale, and men going at it blind— as is very proper for those who tackle a darkness. The conquest of the earth, which mostly means taking it away from those who have a different complexion or slightly flatter noses than ourselves, is not a pretty thing when you look at it too much. What redeems it is the idea 45 only. An idea at the back of it; not a sentimental pretense but an idea; and an unselfish belief in the idea—something you can set up, and bow down before, and offer a sacrifice to . . . "

11. In the passage, *darkness* implies all of the following except

    A. the unknown
    B. savagery
    C. ignorance
    D. death
    E. exploration

12. The setting of the passage is

    A. Africa
    B. Ancient Rome
    C. London
    D. the Mediterranean
    E. Italy

13. The tone of the passage is

    A. condescending
    B. indignant
    C. scornful
    D. pensive
    E. laudatory

14. Later events may be foreshadowed by all of the following phrases *except*

    A. ". . . imagine the feelings of a commander . . . "
    B. ". . . live in the midst of the incomprehensible . . . "

C. "... in some inland post feel the savagery ..."

D. "They must have been dying like flies here."

E. "The very end of the world ..."

15. The narrator draws a parallel between

A. light and dark
B. past and present
C. life and death
D. fascination and abomination
E. decency and savagery

16. In this passage, "We live in the flicker...." (lines 7–8) may be interpreted to mean

I. In the history of the world, humanity's span on earth is brief.
II. Future civilizations will learn from only a portion of the past.
III. Periods of enlightenment and vision appear only briefly.

A. I
B. II
C. III
D. II and III
E. I and III

17. One may conclude from the passage that the speaker

A. admires adventurers
B. longs to be a crusader
C. is a former military officer
D. recognizes and accepts the presence of evil in human experience
E. is prejudiced

18. In the context of the passage, which of the following phrases presents a paradox?

A. "The fascination of the abomination"
B. "In the hearts of wild men"
C. "There's no initiation ... into such mysteries ..."

D. "a flash of lightning in the clouds ..."

E. "Death skulking in the air ..."

19. The lines "Imagine him here ... concertina ..." (lines 13–15) contain examples of

A. hyperbole and personification
B. irony and metaphor
C. alliteration and personification
D. parallel structure and simile
E. allusion and simile

20. According to the speaker, the one trait which saves Europeans from savagery is

A. sentiment
B. a sense of mystery
C. brute force
D. religious zeal
E. efficiency

21. According to the speaker, the only justification for conquest is

A. the "weakness of others"
B. it's being "proper for those who tackle the darkness ..."
C. their grabbing "what they could get for the sake of what was to be got"
D. "... an unselfish belief in the idea ..."
E. "The fascination of the abomination"

22. In the statement by the speaker, "Mind, none of us would feel exactly like this" (line 36), "this" refers to

A. "... a Buddha preaching in European clothes ..." (lines 35–36)
B. "... imagine the growing regrets ... the hate." (lines 31–32)
C. "What redeems it is the idea only." (lines 45–46)
D. "... think of a decent young citizen in a toga ..." (line 24)
E. "I was thinking of very old times ..." (line 5)

23. The speaker presents all of the following reasons for exploration and conquest *except*

    A. military expeditions
    B. "... a chance of promotion"
    C. "... to mend his fortune ... "
    D. religious commitment
    E. punishment for a crime

Questions 24–35 are based on the following poem.

> That time of year thou mayst in me behold
> When yellow leaves, or none, or few, do hang
> Upon those boughs which shake against the cold,
> Bare ruin'd choirs, where late the sweet birds sang.
> In me thou see'st the twilight of such day   5
> As after sunset fadeth in the west;
> Which by and by black night doth take away,
> Death's second self, that seals up all in rest.
> In me thou see'st the glowing of such fire,
> That on the ashes of his youth doth lie,   10
> As the deathbed whereon it must expire,
> Consum'd with that which it was nourish'd by.
> This thou perceiv'st, which makes thy love more strong,
> To love that well which thou must leave ere long.

24. "That time of year" (line 1) refers to

    A. youth
    B. old age
    C. childhood
    D. senility
    E. maturity

25. "Death's second self" (line 8) refers to

    A. "That time of year"
    B. "sunset fadeth"
    C. "the west"
    D. "ruin'd choirs"
    E. "black night"

26. Line 12 is an example of

    A. paradox
    B. caesura
    C. parable
    D. hyperbole
    E. metonymy

27. "Twilight of such day" (line 5) is supported by all of the following images except

    A. "sunset fadeth"
    B. "the glowing of such fire"
    C. "west"
    D. "death's second self"
    E. "ashes of his youth"

28. "This thou perceiv'st" (line 13) refers to

    A. the beloved's deathbed
    B. the sorrow of unrequited love
    C. the passion of youth expiring
    D. the beloved's acknowledgment of the speaker's mortality
    E. the speaker sending the lover away

29. The poem is an example of a(n)

    A. elegy
    B. Spenserian sonnet
    C. Petrarchan sonnet
    D. Shakespearean sonnet
    E. sestina

30. The poem is primarily developed by means of

A. metaphor
B. argument
C. synecdoche
D. alternative choices
E. contradiction

A. Love Me or Leave Me
B. Death Be Not Proud
C. The End Justifies the Means
D. Love's Fall
E. Grow Old Along with Me

31. The irony of the poem is best expressed in line

    A. 5
    B. 7
    C. 10
    D. 11
    E. 14

34. The tone of the poem can best be described as

    A. contemplative
    B. defiant
    C. submissive
    D. arbitrary
    E. complaining

32. "It" in line 12 can best be interpreted to mean

    A. a funeral pyre
    B. spent youth
    C. the intensity of the speaker's love
    D. the impending departure of his beloved
    E. the immortality of the relationship

35. The speaker most likely is

    A jealous of the beloved's youth
    B. pleased that the lover will leave
    C. unable to keep up with the young lover
    D. unwilling to face his own mortality
    E. responsive to the beloved's constancy

33. An apt title for the poem could be

Questions 36–47 are based on the following passage.

Poets and Language
by Percy Bysshe Shelley

Poets, according to the circumstances of the age and nation in which they appeared, were called, in the earlier epochs of the world, legislators, or prophets: a poet essentially comprises and unites both these characters. For he not only beholds intensely the present as it is, and discovers those laws according to which present things ought to be ordered, but he beholds the future in the present, and his thoughts are the germs of the flower and the fruit of latest time. Not that I assert poets to be prophets in the gross sense of the word, or that they can foretell the form as surely as they foreknow the spirit of events; such is the pretense of superstition, which would make poetry an attribute of prophesy, rather than prophecy an attribute of poetry. A poet participates in the eternal, the infinite, and the one; as far as relates to his conceptions, time and place and number are not. The grammatical forms which express the moods of time, and the difference of persons, and the distinction of place, are convertible with respect to the highest poetry without injuring it as poetry; and the choruses of Aeschylus, and the book of Job, and Dante's Paradise, would afford, more than any other writings, examples of this fact, if the limits of this essay did not forbid citation. The creations of sculpture, painting, and music, are illustrations still more decisive.

Language, colour, form, and religious and civil habits of action, are all the instruments and materials of poetry; they may be called poetry by that figure of speech which considers

the effect as a synonym for a cause. But poetry in a more restricted sense expresses those
arrangements of language, and especially metrical language, which are created by that
imperial faculty, whose throne is curtained within the invisible nature of man. And this   20
springs from the nature itself of language, which is a more direct representation of the actions
and passions of our internal being, and is susceptible of more various and delicate
combinations, than colour, form, or motion, and is more plastic and obedient to the control
of that faculty of which it is the creation. For Language is arbitrarily produced by the
imagination, and has relation to thoughts alone; but all other materials, instruments, and   25
conditions of art, have relations among each other, which limit and interpose between
conception and expression. The former is a mirror which reflects the latter as a cloud which
enfeebles, the light of which both are mediums of communication . . .

Poets are the hierophants* of an unapprehended inspiration; the mirrors of the
gigantic shadows which futurity casts upon the present, the words which express what they   30
understand not; the trumpets which sing to battle, and feel not what they inspire; the
influence which is moved not, but moves. Poets are the unacknowledged legislators of the world.

*Hierophants: chief priests, advocates.

36. The passage is an example of

   A. the opening of a novel
   B. the opening of an autobiography
   C. an essay
   D. an ode
   E. a dramatic monologue

37. According to Shelley, a poet is a combination of

   A. historical figure and patriot
   B. artist and priest
   C. grammarian and poet
   D. sculptor and musician
   E. lawmaker and seer

38. In lines 5 and 6 "the germs of the flower and the fruit of latest time" can best be interpreted to mean

   A. the guardian of the future
   B. that the poet's thoughts destroy conventional thinking
   C. that the poet is clairvoyant
   D. that the poet is the gardener of thought
   E. that the current thoughts of the poet presage the future

39. According to Shelley, "the pretense of superstition" (lines 7–9) is

   A. the ability to foreknow events
   B. the ability to control the future
   C. to grant immortality to the poet
   D. to be a legislator
   E. the ability to change the future

40. Shelley asserts that grammatical forms (lines 10–15) serve all the following purposes *except*

   A. to indicate verb tense
   B. to clarify pronoun agreement
   C. to solidify relative pronouns
   D. to forbid citation
   E. to enhance poetry

41. The reader may infer that the Bible, the works of Aeschylus and Dante

   A. are too far in the past to be of value today
   B. are examples of Shelley's theories
   C. have injured poetry
   D. deal with superstition
   E. are more decisive than art

42. According to Shelley, poetry, sculpture, music, and painting have what characteristic in common?

   A. They are dependent on one another.
   B. They rely on grammatical forms.

C. They are at odds with one another.
D. They are eternal.
E. They can only relate to a specific time and place.

43. In lines 18–20, the phrase "that imperial faculty, whose throne . . . " refers to

    A. legislators
    B. language
    C. synonyms
    D. nature
    E. poetry

44. According to Shelley, which of the following is not part of the nature of language?

    A. It is imaginative.
    B. It is a reflection of passion.
    C. It causes civil habits of action.
    D. It deals with the eternal self.
    E. It is connected only to thought.

45. In line 27, if the word "Former" refers to language, then "Latter" refers to

    A. art
    B. motion
    C. limits
    D. imagination
    E. metrics

46. Lines 27–28, beginning with "The former . . . " contain which of the following literary devices?

    I.   parallel structure
    II. simile
    III. personification
        A. I only
        B. II only
        C. III only
        D. I and II
        E. I, II, and III

47. According to the final paragraph, the greatest attribute of the poet is his

    A. sensitivity to light and dark
    B. depiction of fantasy and reality
    C. perception of others
    D. ability to reflect the future
    E. creation of art

END OF SECTION I

The second part of the test is the 2-hour essay-writing section. You take this part of the exam after the break following your completion of the multiple-choice section. You will be required to write three different essays. In all likelihood, one of the questions will be based on a prose passage, one on a poem or two, and one will be what is called the free-response essay.

Do not write any essays at this time. Just take a careful look at each of the questions to get an idea of the types of writing assignments you are expected to be able to handle. Essay questions are called "prompts" by the AP.

Section II

Total time—2 hours

Question 1

(Suggested time—40 minutes. This question counts
as one-third of the total score for Section II.)

In the following passage from the short story "The Dead," James Joyce
presents an insight into the character of Gabriel. Write a well-organized essay
in which you discuss how Joyce reveals aspects of Gabriel's character
to the reader and to Gabriel himself. Refer to such techniques and devices
as imagery, point of view, motif, diction, and syntax.

The Dead

She was fast asleep.

Gabriel, leaning on his elbow, looked for a few moments
unresentfully on her tangled hair and half-open mouth, listening to her
deep-drawn breath. So she had had that romance in her life: a man had
died for her sake. It hardly pained him now to think how poor a part   5
he, her husband, had played in her life. He watched her while she slept
as though he and she had never lived together as man and wife. His
curious eyes rested long upon her face and on her hair and, as he thought
of what she must have been then, in that time of her first girlish beauty,
a strange friendly pity for her entered his soul. He did not like to say   10
even to himself that her face was no longer beautiful but he knew that it
was no longer the face for which Michael Furey had braved death.

Perhaps she had not told him all the story. His eyes moved to the
chair over which she had thrown some of her clothes. A petticoat string
dangled to the floor. One boot stood upright, its limp upper fallen down: 15
the fellow of it lay upon its side. He wondered at his riot of emotions of
an hour before. From what had it proceeded? From his aunt's supper,
from his own foolish speech, from the wine and dancing, the merry-making
when saying good-night in the hall, the pleasure of the walk along the river
in the snow. Poor Aunt Julia! She, too, would soon be a shade with the   20
shade of Patrick Morkan and his horse. He had caught that haggard look
upon her face for a moment when she was singing *Arrayed for the Bridal*.
Soon, perhaps, he would be sitting in the same drawing-room dressed in
black, his silk hat on his knees. The blinds would be drawn down and
Aunt Kate would be sitting beside him, crying and blowing her nose and   25
telling him how Julia had died. He would cast about in his mind for some
words that might console her, and would find only lame and useless ones.
Yes, yes: that would happen very soon.

Question 2

(Suggested time—40 minutes. This question counts
as one-third of the total score for Section II.)

In "On the Subway," Sharon Olds brings two worlds into close proximity.
Identify the contrasts that develop both portraits in the poem and
discuss the insights the narrator comes to as a result of the experience.
Refer to such literary techniques as tone, poetic devices, imagery, and organization.

On the Subway
by Sharon Olds

The boy and I face each other
His feet are huge, in black sneakers
laced with white in a complex pattern like a
set of intentional scars. We are stuck on
opposite sides of the car, a couple of   5
molecules stuck in a rod of light
rapidly moving through darkness.
He has the casual cold look of a mugger,
alert under hooded lids. He is wearing
red, like the inside of the body   10
exposed. I am wearing dark fur, the
whole skin of an animal taken and
used. I look at his raw face,
he looks at my fur coat, and I don't
know if I am in his power—   15
he could take my coat so easily, my
briefcase, my life—
or if he is in my power, the way I am
living off his life, eating the steak
he does not eat, as if I am taking   20
the food from his mouth. And he is black
and I am white, and without meaning or
trying to I must profit from his darkness,
the way he absorbs the murderous beams of the
nation's heart, as black cotton   25
absorbs the heat of the sun and holds it. There is
no way to know how easy this
white skin makes my life, this
life he could take so easily and
break across his knee like a stick the way his   30
own back is being broken, the
rod of his soul that at birth was dark and
fluid and rich as the heart of a seedling
ready to thrust up into any available light

Question 3

(Suggested time—40 minutes. This question counts
as one-third of the total score for Section II.)

Often in literature, a literal or figurative journey is a significant factor in the development of a character or the meaning of the work. Choose a full-length work and write a well-organized essay in which you discuss the literal and/or figurative nature of the journey and how it affects characterization and theme. You may choose a work from the list below or another play or novel of literary merit.

As I Lay Dying	*Tom Jones*
Jane Eyre	*Heart of Darkness*
The Odyssey	*Moby Dick*
Don Quixote	*The Sun Also Rises*
Candide	*The Grapes of Wrath*
A Streetcar Named Desire	*The Stranger*
A Passage to India	*Ulysses*
Gulliver's Travels	*Their Eyes Were Watching God*
No Exit	*Obasan*

END OF SECTION II

So, that's what the Advanced Placement Literature and Composition exam looks like. If you're being honest with yourself, you're probably feeling a bit overwhelmed at this point. Good! This is primarily why we are going to deconstruct this entire Diagnostic/Master exam for you and with you throughout this book. By the time you reach Part IV and Practice Exams 1 and 2, you should be feeling much more confident and comfortable about doing well on the AP Literature exam.

As you progress through this book you will:

!

- Take each section of the Diagnostic/Master exam.
- Read the explanations for the answers to the multiple-choice questions.
- Read sample student essays written in response to each of the three prompts.
- Read the rubrics and ratings of the student essays.
- Evaluate your own performance in light of this information.

Chapter 3

Section I of the Exam: The Multiple-Choice Questions

4 INTRODUCTION TO THE MULTIPLE-CHOICE SECTION OF THE EXAM

Multiple choice? Multiple guess? Multiple anxiety? The day after the exam students often bemoan the difficulties and uncertainties of Section I of the AP Literature exam.

"It's unfair."

"It's crazy."

"Was that in English?"

"Did you get four Ds in a row for the second poem?"

"I just closed my eyes and pointed."

Is it really possible to avoid these and other exam woes? We hope that by following along with us in this chapter you will begin to feel a bit more familiar with the world of multiple-choice questions and, thus, become a little more comfortable with the multiple-choice section of the exam.

What is it about the multiple-choice questions that causes such anxiety?

Basically, a multiple-choice literature question is a flawed method of gauging understanding because, by its very nature, it forces you to play a cat-and-mouse game with the test maker who demands that you concentrate on items that are incorrect before you can choose what is correct. We know, however, that complex literature has a richness that allows for ambiguity. When you are taking the exam, you are expected to match someone else's take on a work with the answers you choose. This is what often causes the student to feel that the multiple-choice section is unfair. And maybe, to a degree, it is. However, the test is designed to allow you to shine, *not* to be humiliated. To that end, you will not find "cutesy" questions, and the test writers will not play games with you. What they will do is to present several valid options as a response to a challenging and appropriate question. These questions are designed to separate the perceptive and thoughtful reader from the superficial and impulsive one.

This said, it's wise to develop a strategy for success. Practice is the key to this success. You've been confronted with all types of multiple-choice questions during your career as a student. The test-taking skills you have learned in your social studies, math, and science classes may also apply to the AP Literature exam.

What should I expect in Section I?

For this first section of the AP Literature exam, you are allotted 1 hour to answer between 45 and 60 objective questions on four or five prose and poetry selections. The prose passages may come from works of fiction or nonfiction. You can expect the poems to be complete and from different time periods and of different styles and forms. In other words, you will not find two Shakespearean sonnets on the same exam.

These are *not* easy readings. They are representative of the college-level work you have been doing throughout the year. You will be expected to

- Follow sophisticated syntax
- Respond to diction
- Be comfortable with upper-level vocabulary
- Be familiar with literary terminology
- Make inferences
- Be sensitive to irony and tone
- Recognize components of style

The good news is that the selection is self-contained. This means that if it is about the Irish Potato Famine, you will not be at a disadvantage if you know nothing about it prior to the exam. Frequently there will be biblical references in a selection. This is especially true of works from an earlier time period. You are expected to be aware of basic allusions to biblical and mythological works often found in literature, but the passage will never require you to have any specific religious background.

Do not let the subject matter of a passage throw you. Strong analytical skills will work on any passage.

How should I begin to work with Section I?

Take no more than a minute and thumb through the exam, looking for the following:

- The length of the selections
- The time periods or writing styles, if you can recognize them
- The number of questions asked
- A quick idea of the type of questions

This brief skimming of the test will put your mind into gear because you will be aware of what is expected of you.

How should I proceed through this section of the exam?

Timing is important. Always maintain an awareness of the time. Wear a watch. (Some students like to put it directly in front of them on the desk.) Remember, this will not be your first encounter with the multiple-choice section of the test. You've probably been practicing timed exams in class; in addition, this book provides you with three timed experiences. We're sure you will notice improvements as you progress through the timed practice activities.

Although the test naturally breaks into 15 minute sections, you may take less or more time on a particular passage, but you must know when to move on. The test *does not* become more difficult as it progresses. So, you will want to give yourself the opportunity to answer each set of questions.

"Creating my own multiple-choice questions was a terrific help to me when it came to doing close readings and correctly answering multiple-choice questions on the exam."
—Bill N.
-AP student

Work at a pace of about one question per minute. Every question is worth the same number of points, so don't get bogged down on those that involve multiple tasks. Don't panic if a question is beyond you. Remember, it will probably be beyond a great number of other students as well. There has to be a bar that determines the 5's and 4's for this exam. Just do your best.

Reading the text carefully is a must. Begin at the beginning and work your way through. Do not waste time reading questions before you read the selection.

Most people read just with their eyes. We want you to slow down and read with your senses of sight, sound, and touch.

- Underline, circle, highlight the text.
- Read closely, paying attention to punctuation and rhythms of the lines or sentences.
- Read as if you were reading the passage aloud to an audience emphasizing meaning and intent.
- As corny as it may seem, hear those words in your head.
- This technique may seem childish, but it works. Using your finger as a pointer, underscore the line as you are reading it aloud in your head. This forces you to slow down and to really notice the text. This will be helpful when you have to refer to the passage.
- Use all the information given to you about the passage, such as title, author, date of publication, and footnotes.

- Be aware of foreshadowing.
- Be aware of thematic lines and be sensitive to details that will obviously be material for multiple-choice questions.
- When reading poetry, pay particular attention to enjambment and end-stopped lines because they carry meaning.
- With poetry, it's often helpful to paraphrase a stanza, especially if the order of the lines has been inverted.

> Tip: You can practice these techniques any time. Take any work and read it aloud. Time yourself. A good rate is about 1½ minutes per page.

TYPES OF MULTIPLE-CHOICE QUESTIONS

Multiple-choice questions are not written randomly. There are certain formats you will encounter. The answers to the following questions should clarify some of the mystery.

Is the structure the same for all of the multiple-choice questions?

No. There are several basic patterns that the AP test makers employ:

1. **The straightforward question,** such as:
   - The poem is an example of a

     C. lyric
   - The word "smooth" refers to

     B. his skin

2. **The question that refers you to specific lines and asks you to draw a conclusion or to interpret.**
   - Lines 52–57 serve to

     A. reinforce the author's thesis

3. **The "all . . . except" question** requires extra time because it demands that you consider every possibility.
   - The AP Literature exam is all of the following *except*:

     A. It is given in May of each year.
     B. It is open to high school seniors.
     C. It is published in *The New York Times*.

    D. It is used as a qualifier for college credit.
    E. It is a 3-hour test.

4. **The question that asks you to make an inference or to abstract a concept that is not directly stated in the passage.**

   • In the poem "My Last Duchess," the reader can infer that the speaker is

     E. arrogant

5. Here is the killer question. It uses **Roman Numerals,** no less! The question employing Roman numerals is problematic and time-consuming. You can be certain that each exam will have several of these questions.

   • In the poem, "night" refers to

     I.   the death of the maiden
     II. a pun on Sir Lancelot's title
     III. the end of the affair

        A. I only
        B. I and II
        C. I and III
        D. II and III
        E. I, II, and III

This is the type of question to skip if it causes you problems and/or you are short on time. Remember, it will cost you a quarter of a point if you are wrong and 0 if you skip it. (An explanation of how the exam is scored appears later in this chapter.)

What kinds of questions should I expect on the exam?

The multiple-choice questions center around form and content. The test makers want to assess your understanding of the meaning of the selection as well as your ability to draw inferences and perceive implications based on it. They also want to know whether you understand *how* a writer develops his or her ideas.

The questions, therefore, will be factual, technical, analytical, and inferential. The two tables below illustrate the types of key words and phrases in these four categories that you can expect to find in questions for both the prose and poetry selections.

Note: Do not memorize these tables. Also, do not panic if a word or phrase is not familiar to you. You may or may not encounter any or all of these words or phrases on any given exam. You can, however, count on meeting up with many of these in the practice exams in this book.

Prose: Key Words and Phrases found in Multiple-Choice Questions

Factual	Technical	Analytical	Inferential
words refer to	sentence structure	rhetorical strategy	effect of diction
allusions	style	shift in development	tone
antecedents	grammatical purpose	rhetorical stance	inferences
pronoun referents	dominant technique	style	effect of description
genre	imagery	metaphor	effect of last paragraph
setting	point of view	contrast	effect on reader
	organization of passage	comparison	narrator's attitude
	narrative progress of passage	cause/effect	image suggests
	conflict	argument	effect of detail
	irony	description	author implies
	function of	narration	author most concerned with
		specific-general	symbol
		how something is characterized	
		imagery	
		passage is primarily concerned with	
		function of	

Poetry: Key Words and Phrases found in Multiple-Choice Questions

Factual	Technical	Analytical	Inferential
all except	imagery	character portrayal	mood
definition	literary devices	imagery	attitude of
thesis	paradox	literary devices	poet's attitude
sequence of events	organizational pattern	paradox	purpose of
the object of ___ is ___	syntax	purpose of	tone of the poem
allusion	metrics	rhetorical shifts	theme of the poem
the subject of dramatic situation	parallel structure	ironies presented	reader may infer
	rhetorical shifts	least important	best interpreted as
paraphrasing	ironies presented	most important	effect of diction
subject	function of diction		speaker implies
references	dramatic moment		___ is associated with ___
	meaning conveyed by		context
			symbol

Note: A word about Jargon. Jargon refers to words that are unique to a specific subject. A common language is important for communication, and there must be agreement on the basic meanings of terms. Even though it is important to know the universal language of a subject, it is also important that you *not* limit the scope of your thinking to a brief definition. All the terms used in the tables are interwoven in literature. They are categorized only for easy reference. They also work in many other contexts. *In other words, think beyond the box.*

SCORING THE MULTIPLE-CHOICE SECTION

It may be an English Exam, but Math is a necessary evil when it comes to tabulating the score.

How does the scoring of the multiple-choice section work?

The scan sheet containing your answers is run through a computer that counts the number of wrong answers and subtracts a fraction of that number from the number of correct answers. The AP Lit questions always have five choices. Therefore, the fraction would be one-fourth. A question left blank receives a zero. The following is what the formula for this calculation looks like:

number right – (number wrong × .25) = raw score rounded up or down
to nearest whole number

Let's work with a fictional scoring situation. Assume there were 55 multiple-choice questions, and you answered 40 correctly and 15 incorrectly. You did not leave any question blank.

$$40 - (15 \times .25) = 40 - 3.75 = 36.25 = 36$$

Thus 36 is your raw score for the multiple-choice section of the exam. This raw score, which is 45 percent of the total, is combined with that of the essay section to make up a composite score. This is then manipulated to form a scale on which the final AP grade is based. For each of the practice multiple-choice sections in this book you will have a chance to practice this formula on your score.

4 STRATEGIES FOR ANSWERING THE MULTIPLE-CHOICE QUESTIONS

You've been answering multiple-choice questions most of your academic life, and you've probably figured out ways to deal with them. However, there may be some points you have not considered that will be helpful for this particular exam.

GENERAL GUIDELINES

- Work in order. This is a good approach for several reasons:
  - It's clear.
  - You will not lose your place on the scan sheet.
  - There may be a logic to working sequentially that will help you answer previous questions. But, this is your call. If you are more comfortable moving around the exam, do so.
- Write on the exam booklet. Mark it up. Make it yours. Interact with the test.
- Do not spend too much time on any one question.
- Focus on your strengths. If you are more comfortable working with poetry, answer the poetry questions first.

- Don't be misled by the length or appearance of a selection. There is no correlation between length or appearance and the difficulty of the questions.
- Don't fight the question or the passage. You may know other information about the subject of the text or a question. It's irrelevant. Work within the given context.
- Consider all the choices in a given question. This will keep you from jumping to a false conclusion. It helps you to slow down and to really look at each possibility. You may find that your first choice is not the best or most appropriate one.
- Maintain an open mind as you answer subsequent questions in a series. Sometimes the answer to a later question will contradict your answer to a previous one. Reconsider both answers. Also, the phrasing of a question may point to an answer in a previous question.
- Remember that all parts of an answer must be correct.
- When in doubt, go to the text.

SPECIFIC TECHNIQUES

- *Process of elimination*: This is your primary tool, except for direct knowledge of the answer.

  1. Read the five choices.
  2. If no choice immediately strikes you as correct, you can

  - Eliminate those that are obviously wrong
  - Eliminate those choices that are too narrow or too broad
  - Eliminate illogical choices
  - Eliminate answers that are synonymous
  - Eliminate answers that cancel each other out

  3. If two answers are close, do one *or* the other of the following:

  - Find the one that is general enough to cover all aspects of the question

- Find the one that is limited enough to be the detail the question is looking for

- *Substitution/fill in the blank*

  1. Rephrase the question, leaving a blank where the answer should go.
  2. Use each of the choices to fill in the blank until you find the one that is the best fit.

- *Using context*

  1. Consider the context when the question directs you to specific lines, words, or phrases.
  2. Locate the given word, phrase, sentence, or poetic line and read the sentence or line before and after the section of the text to which the question refers. Often this provides the information or clues you need to make your choice.

- *Anticipation*: As you read the passage for the first time, mark any details and ideas that you would ask a question about. You may be able to anticipate the test makers this way.

- *Intuition or the educated guess*: You have a wealth of skills and knowledge in your literary subconscious. A question or a choice may trigger a "remembrance of things past." This can be the basis for your educated guess. Have the confidence to use the educated guess as a valid technique. Trust your own resources.

A Survival Tip

If time is running out and you haven't finished the fourth selection:

1. Scan the remaining questions and look for:
   - The shortest questions
   - The questions that direct you to a specific line.
2. Look for specific detail/definition questions.
3. Look for self-contained questions. For example: "The sea slid silently from the shore" is an example of C. alliteration. You did not have to go to the passage to answer this question.

If I don't know an answer, should I guess?

If you do the math, you will see that a wrong answer is worth ¼ of a point. Thus, you would have to miss four questions to lose a full point. THEREFORE, WE AND THE AP TEST MAKERS URGE YOU TO TRY TO ANSWER EVERY QUESTION. You can't be seriously hurt by making *educated guesses* based on a careful reading of the selection.

Be smart. Understand that you need to come to this exam well prepared. You must have a foundation of knowledge and skills. You cannot guess through the entire exam and expect to do well.

This is not lotto. This book is not about how to "beat the exam." We want to maximize the skills you already have. There is an inherent integrity in this exam and your participation in it. With this in mind, when there is no other direction open to you, it is perfectly fine to make an educated guess.

3 Is there anything special I should know about preparing for the prose multiple-choice questions?

After you have finished with the Diagnostic/Master exam, you will be familiar with the format and types of questions asked on the AP Lit exam. However, just practicing answering multiple-choice questions on specific works will not give you a complete understanding of this questioning process. We suggest the following to help you hone your multiple-choice answering skills with prose multiple-choice questions:

- Choose a challenging passage from a full-length prose work.
- Read the selection a couple of times and create several multiple-choice questions about specific sections of the selection.
  - Make certain the section is self-contained and complex.
  - Choose a dialogue, monologue, introductory setting, set description, stage directions, philosophical passage, significant event, or a moment of conflict.

- Refer to the prose table given earlier in this chapter for suggested language and type.
- Administer your miniquiz to a classmate, study group, or class.
- Evaluate your results.
- Repeat this process through several different full-length works during your preparation for the exam. The works can certainly come from those you are studying in class.
- Create a variety of question types.

"One of my biggest challenges in preparing for the exam was to learn not to jump to conclusions when I was doing the multiple-choice questions."
—Samantha S.
–AP student

Here's what should happen as a result of your using this process.

- Your expectation level for the selections in the actual test will be more realistic.
- You will become familiar with the language of multiple-choice questions.
- Your understanding of the process of choosing answers will be heightened.
- Questions you write that you find less than satisfactory will trigger your analytical skills as you attempt to figure out "what went wrong."
- Terminology will become more accurate.
- *Bonus*: If you continue to do this work throughout your preparation for the AP exam, you will have created a mental storehouse of literary information. So when you are presented with a prose or free-response essay in Section II, you will have an extra resource at your disposal.

Is there anything special I should do to prepare for the poetry questions?

The points made about prose hold true for the poetry multiple-choice questions as well. But there are a few specific pointers that may prove helpful:

- Choose thoughtful and interesting poems of some length. (See our suggested reading list.)
- Read the poem several times. Practice reading the poems aloud.
- The greatest benefit will be that as you read any poem, you will automatically begin to respond to areas of the poem that would lend themselves to a multiple-choice question.
- Here is a list of suitable poets you may want to read.

  - Shakespeare
  - John Donne
  - Philip Larkin
  - Emily Dickinson
  - Sylvia Plath
  - Dylan Thomas
  - May Swenson
  - Theodore Roethke

  - Richard Wilbur
  - Adrienne Rich
  - Edmund Spenser
  - W. H. Auden
  - W. B. Yeats
  - Gwendolyn Brooks
  - Elizabeth Bishop
  - Langston Hughes

> Tip: You might want to utilize this process throughout the year with major works studied in and out of class and keep track of your progress. See the Bibliography in Part V of this book.

The Time is at Hand

It is now time to try the Diagnostic/Master exam, Section I. Do this section in *one* sitting. Time yourself! Be honest with yourself when you score your answers.

Note: If the 1 hour passes before you finish all the questions, stop where you are and score what you have done up to this point. Afterwards, answer the remaining questions, but do not count the answers as part of your score.

When you have completed all the multiple-choice questions in this Diagnostic/Master exam, carefully read the explanations of the answers. Spend time here and assess which types of questions give you trouble. Use this book to learn from your mistakes.

ANSWER SHEET FOR
DIAGNOSTIC MULTIPLE-CHOICE QUESTIONS

1. _____	17. _____	33. _____
2. _____	18. _____	34. _____
3. _____	19. _____	35. _____
4. _____	20. _____	36. _____
5. _____	21. _____	37. _____
6. _____	22. _____	38. _____
7. _____	23. _____	39. _____
8. _____	24. _____	40. _____
9. _____	25. _____	41. _____
10. _____	26. _____	42. _____
11. _____	27. _____	43. _____
12. _____	28. _____	44. _____
13. _____	29. _____	45. _____
14. _____	30. _____	46. _____
15. _____	31. _____	47. _____
16. _____	32. _____	

I ____ did ____ did not finish all the questions in the allotted 1 hour.

I had ____ correct answers. I had ____ incorrect answers. I left ____ questions blank.

Scoring Formula:

$$\underline{\hspace{3cm}} - \underline{\hspace{4cm}} = \underline{\hspace{2.5cm}}$$

number right − (number wrong × .25) = raw score

I have carefully reviewed the explanations of the answers, and I think I need to work on the following types of questions:

THE MULTIPLE-CHOICE SECTION OF THE DIAGNOSTIC/MASTER EXAM

The multiple-choice section of the Diagnostic/Master exam follows. You have seen the questions in the "Walk through" in Chapter 2.

ADVANCED PLACEMENT LITERATURE AND COMPOSITION

Section 1

Total Time — 1 hour

Carefully read the following passages and answer the accompanying questions.

Questions 1–10 are based on the following poem.

Now Goes Under . . .
by Edna St. Vincent Millay

Now goes under, and I watch it go under, the sun
  That will not rise again.
Today has seen the setting, in your eyes cold
  and senseless as the sea,
Of friendship better than bread, and of bright charity   5
That lifts a man a little above the beasts that run.

That this could be!
That I should live to see
Most vulgar Pride, that stale obstreperous clown,
So fitted out with purple robe and crown   10
To stand among his betters! Face to face
With outraged me in this once holy place,
Where Wisdom was a favoured guest and hunted
Truth was harboured out of danger,
He bulks enthroned, a lewd, and insupportable stranger!   15

I would have sworn, indeed I swore it:
The hills may shift, the waters may decline,
Winter may twist the stem from the twig that bore it,
But never your love from me, your hand from mine.

Now goes under the sun, and I watch it go under.   20
Farewell, sweet light, great wonder!
You, too, farewell—but fare not well enough to dream
You have done wisely to invite the night before the darkness came.

1. The poem is an example of a(n)

   A. sonnet
   B. lyric
   C. ode
   D. ballad
   E. dramatic monologue

2. The setting of the sun is a symbol for

   A. the beginning of winter
   B. encountering danger
   C. the end of a relationship
   D. facing death
   E. the onset of night

3. The second stanza is developed primarily by

   A. metaphor
   B. simile
   C. personification
   D. hyperbole
   E. allusion

4. "He" in line 15 refers to

   A. Wisdom
   B. Truth
   C. I
   D. Pride
   E. charity

5. According to the speaker, what separates man from beast?

   A. love
   B. friendship
   C. charity
   D. truth
   E. wisdom

6. For the speaker, the relationship has been all of the following *except*

   A. honest
   B. dangerous
   C. spiritual
   D. ephemeral
   E. nourishing

7. The reader can infer from the play on words in the last stanza that the speaker is

   A. dying
   B. frantic
   C. wistful
   D. bitter
   E. capricous

8. "this holy place" (line 12) refers to

   A. the sunset
   B. the relationship
   C. the sea
   D. the circus
   E. the Church

9. The cause of the relationship's situation is

   A. a stranger coming between them
   B. the lover not taking the relationship seriously
   C. the lover feeling intellectually superior
   D. the lover's pride coming between them
   E. the lover being insensitive

10. The speaker acknowledges the finality of the relationship in line(s)

    A. 1–2
    B. 7
    C. 8
    D. 16
    E. 18–19

Questions 11–23 are based on the following passage.

The sea-reach of the Thames stretched before us like the beginning of an interminable waterway. The air was dark above Gravesend, and farther back still seemed condensed into a mournful gloom, brooding motionless over the biggest and the greatest town on earth.

"I was thinking of very old times, when the Romans first came here, nineteen 5
hundred years ago—the other day . . . Light came out of this river since—you say knights?
Yes; but it is like a running blaze on a plain, like a flash of lightning in the clouds. We live
in the flicker—may it last as long as the old earth keeps rolling! But darkness was here
yesterday. Imagine the feelings of a commander of a fine—what d'ye call 'em?—trireme
in the Mediterranean, ordered suddenly to the north; run overland across the Gauls in a 10
hurry; put in charge of one of these craft the legionnaires—a wonderful lot of handy men
they must have been, too—used to build, apparently by the hundred, in a month or two, if
we may believe what we read. Imagine him here—the very end of the world, a sea the color
of lead, a sky the color of smoke, a kind of ship about as rigid as a concertina—and going
up this river with stores, or orders, or what you like. Sandbanks, marshes, forests, savages— 15
precious little to eat for a civilized man, nothing but Thames water to drink. No Falernian
wine here, no going ashore. Here and there a military camp lost in a wilderness, like a
needle in a bundle of hay—cold, fog, tempests, disease, exile, and death—death skulking in
the air, in the water, in the bush. They must have been dying like flies here. Oh yes—he
did it. Did it very well, too, no doubt, and without thinking much about it either, except 20
afterwards to brag of what he had gone through in his time, perhaps. They were men enough
to face darkness. And perhaps he was cheered by keeping his eye on a chance of promotion
to the fleet at Ravenna by and by, if he had good friends in Rome and survived the awful
climate. Or think of a decent young citizen in a toga—perhaps too much dice, you know—
coming out here in the train of some prefect, or tax-gatherer, or trader even, to mend his 25
fortunes. Land in a swamp, march through the woods, and in some inland post feel the
savagery, the utter savagery, had closed round him—all that mysterious life of the wilderness
that stirs in the forest, in the jungles, in the hearts of wild men. There's no initiation either
into such mysteries. He has to live in the midst of the incomprehensible, which is also
detestable. And it has a fascination, too, that goes to work upon him. The fascination of the 30
abomination—you know, imagine the growing regrets, the longing to escape, the powerless
disgust, the surrender, the hate."

He paused.

"Mind," he began again, lifting one arm from the elbow, the palm of the hand
outwards, so that, with his legs folded before him, he had the pose of a Buddha preaching in 35
European clothes and without a lotus flower—"Mind, none of us would feel exactly like this.
What saves us is efficiency—the devotion to efficiency. But these chaps were not much
account, really. They were no colonists; their administration was merely a squeeze, and
nothing more, I suspect. They were conquerors, and for that you want only brute force—
nothing to boast of, when you have it, since your strength is just an accident arising from the 40
weakness of others. They grabbed what they could get for the sake of what was to be got. It
was just robbery with violence, aggravated murder on a great scale, and men going at it blind—
as is very proper for those who tackle a darkness. The conquest of the earth, which mostly
means taking it away from those who have a different complexion or slightly flatter noses
than ourselves, is not a pretty thing when you look at it too much. What redeems it is the idea 45
only. An idea at the back of it; not a sentimental pretense but an idea; and an unselfish belief
in the idea—something you can set up, and bow down before, and offer a sacrifice to . . . "

11. In the passage, *darkness* implies all of
the following except

    A. the unknown
    B. savagery
    C. ignorance

    D. death
    E. exploration

12. The setting of the passage is

    A. Africa

B. Ancient Rome
C. London
D. the Mediterranean
E. Italy

13. The tone of the passage is

A. condescending
B. indignant
C. scornful
D. pensive
E. laudatory

14. Later events may be foreshadowed by all of the following phrases *except*

A. "... imagine the feelings of a commander ..."
B. "... live in the midst of the incomprehensible ..."
C. "... in some inland post feel the savagery ..."
D. "They must have been dying like flies here."
E. "The very end of the world ..."

15. The narrator draws a parallel between

A. light and dark
B. past and present
C. life and death
D. fascination and abomination
E. decency and savagery

16. In this passage, "We live in the flicker ..." (lines 7–8) may be interpreted to mean

I. In the history of the world, humanity's span on earth is brief.
II. Future civilizations will learn from only a portion of the past.
III. Periods of enlightenment and vision appear only briefly.

A. I
B. II
C. III
D. II and III
E. I and III

17. One may conclude from the passage that the speaker

A. admires adventurers
B. longs to be a crusader
C. is a former military officer
D. recognizes and accepts the presence of evil in human experience
E. is prejudiced

18. In the context of the passage, which of the following phrases presents a paradox?

A. "The fascination of the abomination"
B. "In the hearts of wild men"
C. "There's no initiation ... into such mysteries ..."
D. "a flash of lightning in the clouds ..."
E. "Death skulking in the air ..."

19. The lines "Imagine him here ... concertina ..." (lines 13–15) contain examples of

A. hyperbole and personification
B. irony and metaphor
C. alliteration and personification
D. parallel structure and simile
E. allusion and simile

20. According to the speaker, the one trait which saves Europeans from savagery is

A. sentiment
B. a sense of mystery
C. brute force
D. religious zeal
E. efficiency

21. According to the speaker, the only justification for conquest is

A. the "weakness of others"
B. it's being "proper for those who tackle the darkness ..."
C. their grabbing "what they could get for the sake of what was to be got"
D. "... an unselfish belief in the idea ..."
E. "The fascination of the abomination"

22. In the statement by the speaker, "Mind none of us would feel exactly like this" (line 36), "this" refers to

A. "...a Buddha preaching in European clothes..." (lines 35–36)
B. "...imagine the growing regrets... the hate." (lines 31–32)
C. "What redeems it is the idea only." (lines 45–46)
D. "...think of a decent young citizen in a toga..." (line 24)
E. "I was thinking of very old times..." (line 5)

23. The speaker presents all of the following reasons for exploration and conquest *except*

A. military expeditions
B. "...a chance of promotion"
C. "...to mend his fortune..."
D. religious commitment
E. punishment for a crime

Questions 24–35 are based on the following poem.

That time of year thou mayst in me behold
When yellow leaves, or none, or few, do hang
Upon those boughs which shake against the cold,
Bare ruin'd choirs, where late the sweet birds sang.
In me thou see'st the twilight of such day   5
As after sunset fadeth in the west;
Which by and by black night doth take away,
Death's second self, that seals up all in rest.
In me thou see'st the glowing of such fire,
That on the ashes of his youth doth lie,   10
As the deathbed whereon it must expire,
Consum'd with that which it was nourish'd by.
This thou perceiv'st, which makes thy love more strong,
To love that well which thou must leave ere long.

24. "That time of year" (line 1) refers to

A. youth
B. old age
C. childhood
D. senility
E. maturity

25. "Death's second self" (line 8) refers to

A. "That time of year"
B. "sunset fadeth"
C. "the west"
D. "ruin'd choirs"
E. "black night"

26. Line 12 is an example of

A. paradox
B. caesura
C. parable
D. hyperbole
E. metonymy

27. "Twilight of such day" (line 5) is supported by all of the following images except

A. "sunset fadeth"
B. "the glowing of such fire"
C. "west"
D. "death's second self"
E. "ashes of his youth"

28. "This thou perceiv'st" (line 13) refers to

A. the beloved's deathbed

B. the sorrow of unrequited love
C. the passion of youth expiring
D. the beloved's acknowledgement of the speaker's mortality
E. the speaker sending the lover away

29. The poem is an example of a(n)

   A. elegy
   B. Spenserian sonnet
   C. Petrarchan sonnet
   D. Shakespearean sonnet
   E. sestina

30. The poem is primarily developed by means of

   A. metaphor
   B. argument
   C. synecdoche
   D. alternative choices
   E. contradiction

31. The irony of the poem is best expressed in line

   A. 5
   B. 7
   C. 10
   D. 11
   E. 14

32. "It" in line 12 can best be interpreted to mean

A. a funeral pyre
B. spent youth
C. the intensity of the speaker's love
D. the impending departure of his beloved
E. the immortality of the relationship

33. An apt title for the poem could be

   A. Love Me or Leave Me
   B. Death Be Not Proud
   C. The End Justifies the Means
   D. Love's Fall
   E. Grow Old Along with Me

34. The tone of the poem can best be described as

   A. contemplative
   B. defiant
   C. submissive
   D. arbitrary
   E. complaining

35. The speaker most likely is

   A. jealous of the beloved's youth
   B. pleased that the lover will leave
   C. unable to keep up with the young lover
   D. unwilling to face his own mortality
   E. responsive to the beloved's constancy

Questions 36–47 are based on the following passage.

Poets and Language
by Percy Bysshe Shelley

Poets, according to the circumstances of the age and nation in which they appeared, were called, in the earlier epochs of the world, legislators, or prophets: a poet essentially comprises and unites both these characters. For he not only beholds intensely the present as it is, and discovers those laws according to which present things ought to be ordered, but he beholds the future in the present, and his thoughts are the germs of the flower and the fruit of latest time. Not that I assert poets to be prophets in the gross sense of the word, or that they can foretell the form as surely as they foreknow the spirit of events; such is the pretense of superstition, which would make poetry an attribute of prophesy, rather than prophecy an attribute of poetry. A poet participates in the eternal, the infinite, and the one; as far as relates to his conceptions, time and place and number are not. The grammatical 10 forms which express the moods of time, and the difference of persons, and the distinction of place, are convertible with respect to the highest poetry without injuring it as poetry; and the choruses of Aeschylus, and the book of Job, and Dante's Paradise, would afford, more than any other writings, examples of this fact, if the limits of this essay did not forbid citation. The creations of sculpture, painting, and music, are illustrations still more decisive. 15

    Language, colour, form, and religious and civil habits of action, are all the instruments and materials of poetry; they may be called poetry by that figure of speech which considers the effect as a synonym for a cause. But poetry in a more restricted sense expresses those arrangements of language, and especially metrical language, which are created by that imperial faculty, whose throne is curtained within the invisible nature of man. And this 20 springs from the nature itself of language, which is a more direct representation of the actions and passions of our internal being, and is susceptible of more various and delicate combinations, than colour, form, or motion, and is more plastic and obedient to the control of that faculty of which it is the creation. For Language is arbitrarily produced by the imagination, and has relation to thoughts alone; but all other materials, instruments, and 25 conditions of art, have relations among each other, which limit and interpose between conception and expression. The former is a mirror which reflects the latter as a cloud which enfeebles, the light of which both are mediums of communication . . .

    Poets are the hierophants* of an unapprehended inspiration; the mirrors of the gigantic shadows which futurity casts upon the present, the words which express what they 30 understand not; the trumpets which sing to battle, and feel not what they inspire; the influence which is moved not, but moves. Poets are the unacknowledged legislators of the world.

*Hierophants: chief priests, advocates

36. The passage is an example of
    A. the opening of a novel
    B. the opening of an autobiography
    C. an essay
    D. an ode
    E. a dramatic monologue

37. According to Shelley, a poet is a combination of

    A. historical figure and patriot
    B. artist and priest
    C. grammarian and poet
    D. sculptor and musician
    E. lawmaker and seer

38. In lines 5 and 6 "the germs of the flower and the fruit of latest time" can best be interpreted to mean

    A. the guardian of the future
    B. that the poet's thoughts destroy conventional thinking
    C. that the poet is clairvoyant

    D. that the poet is the gardener of thought
    E. that the current thoughts of the poet presage the future

39. According to Shelley, "the pretense of superstition" (lines 7–9) is

    A. the ability to foreknow events
    B. the ability to control the future
    C. to grant immortality to the poet
    D. to be a legislator
    E. the ability to change the future

40. Shelley asserts that grammatical forms (lines 10–15) serve all the following purposes *except*

    A. to indicate verb tense
    B. to clarify pronoun agreement
    C. to solidify relative pronouns
    D. to forbid citation
    E. to enhance poetry

41. The reader may infer that the Bible, the works of Aeschylus and Dante

    A. are too far in the past to be of value today
    B. are examples of Shelley's theories
    C. have injured poetry
    D. deal with superstition
    E. are more decisive than art

42. According to Shelley, poetry, sculpture, music, and painting have what characteristic in common?

    A. They are dependent on one another.
    B. They rely on grammatical forms.
    C. They are at odds with one another.
    D. They are eternal.
    E. They can only relate to a specific time and place.

43. In lines 18–20, the phrase "that imperial faculty, whose throne . . . " refers to

    A. legislators
    B. language
    C. synonyms
    D. nature
    E. poetry

44. According to Shelley, which of the following is not part of the nature of language?

    A. It is imaginative.

B. It is a reflection of passion.
C. It causes civil habits of action.
D. It deals with the eternal self.
E. It is connected only to thought.

45. In line 27, if the word "Former" refers to language, then "Latter" refers to

    A. art
    B. motion
    C. limits
    D. imagination
    E. metrics

46. Lines 27–28, beginning with "The former . . . " contain which of the following literary devices?

    I.   parallel structure
    II. simile
    III. personification

    A. I only
    B. II only
    C. III only
    D. I and II
    E. I, II, and III

47. According to the final paragraph, the greatest attribute of the poet is his

    A. sensitivity to light and dark
    B. depiction of fantasy and reality
    C. perception of others
    D. ability to reflect the future
    E. creation of art

2 EXPLANATION OF ANSWERS TO THE MULTIPLE-CHOICE QUESTIONS OF THE DIAGNOSTIC/MASTER EXAM

Explanation of answers to *Now Goes Under . . .* by Edna St. Vincent Millay

1. **B.** This question requires the student to know the characteristics of various poetic forms. (See Chapter 8.) Using the process of elimination, the correct answer B is readily confirmed. Lyric poetry is emotional and personal.

2. **C.** Although the setting sun is often associated with winter, death, and darkness, these answers are not symbolic of the literal topic of the poem—the end of the love relationship.

3. **C.** The poet uses personification in lines 8–15: "vulgar Pride," "favored Wisdom," "hunted Truth" as characters to develop the conflicts apparent in the poem. [TIP: Capitalization of nouns often indicates personification.]

4. **D.** This is an antecedent question. The student must retrace the reference "He" back to its origins to locate the correct answer. Try asking "who is enthroned, lewd and unsupportable?" Since truth, charity, and wisdom are described positively, only *vulgar* pride qualifies as the answer.

5. **C.** This question requires you to find the antecedent. Ask yourself, "Who or what lifts man?" The answer, *charity*, should be obvious.

6. **B.** Sometimes you can find information from a previous question. In question 2, "danger" was eliminated as a choice; therefore, it probably wouldn't be suitable for this question either. Try finding proof of the others. Truth = honest; holy = spiritual; bread = nourishment. Therefore, *dangerous* has to be the answer.

7. **D.** This is a tone question based on a repetitive contradictory phrase. She does *not* wish him well; therefore, she is bitter and resigned. There is nothing playful, wistful, or frantic in the conclusion.

8. **B.** This is a relationship question. You should realize this by the intensity of the opposing lewd force, pride, which destroyed the sanctity of the love. (If you see this, you could validate your answer to question 9.)

9. **D.** The cause is developed in the longest stanza, lines 7–15. Find the proof for your answer in lines 7–12.

10. **A.** Interestingly enough, the speaker reveals the conclusion in the first two lines of the poem. "The sun that will not rise again" establishes the totality of the circumstances.

Explanation of questions for passage from *Heart of Darkness* by Joseph Conrad

11. **E.** Here's an easy question to start you off. For years you heard your English teachers and your classmates discussing all the elements that could be associated with *darkness*. All the choices given in this question would qualify except for *exploration*.

12. **C.** Line 1 gives you the answer. The Thames is the river that runs through the heart of London.

13. **D.** A careful reading of the passage will introduce you to a speaker who is *thinking* about the past, *thinking* about exploration and conquest, and *thinking* about the conqueror and the conquered.

14. **A.** Here, the speaker is asking his listeners to picture the past. Therefore, it is *not* pointing to the future. The feelings of a commander have nothing to do with a future event; whereas, each of the other choices hints at a future concept.

15. **B.** The first paragraph is about ancient Rome and its conquests. The second paragraph has the speaker considering "us" and what saves "us." This is past and present.

16. **D.** The first ten lines support the inclusion of I. Choice III is supported in the second paragraph. Choice II is *not* part of the speaker's conversation.

17. **D.** Lines 26–30 and 39–45 indicate the speaker's attitude toward the human condition. There is no evidence in the passage to support any of the other choices.

18. **A.** The question assumes you know the definition of paradox. Therefore, you should be able to see that to be fascinated by that which is repulsive, awful, and horrible is a paradox.

19. **D.** "a sea," "a sky," "a kind," "or orders," "or what" are examples of parallel structure. The simile is "ship about as rigid as a concertina."

20. **E.** This is a straightforward, factual question. The answer is found in line 37.

21. **D.** In lines 45–47 the speaker is philosophizing about what it is that "redeems" the "conquest of the earth." It is the *idea*.

22. **B.** This question asks you to locate the antecedent of "this." You could use the substitution method here. Just replace "this" with the word or phrase. Or, you could look carefully at the text itself. The omniscient narrator is describing the speaker as a Buddha. Lines 45–46 come after "this." D and E are not real possibilities. Also, they are too far away from the pronoun.

23. **E.** A careful reading of the passage allows you to find references to A and D and to locate the quoted phrases in B and C. What you will *not* find are any references to "punishment for a crime."

Explanations for questions based on *Sonnet 73* by William Shakespeare

24. **B.** The difficulty with this question lies in the similarity between B and E. However, it should be apparent by the numerous references to death and the contrast to youth that the poet is speaking of a literal time period in life and not of a state of emotional development.

25. **E.** Use the process of substitution and work backward in the poem to find the antecedent. Recognize the appositive phrase, which is set off by commas, to spot the previous image—"black night." Another trick is to recast the line into a directly stated sentence instead of the poetic inversion. Asking "who or what is Death's second self" will help you locate the subject of the line.

26. **A.** Once again you are being tested on terminology and your ability to recognize an example. Deconstruct the line and find its essence; here it is obvious that "consumed" and "nourished" are contradictory.

27. **B.** Even without returning to the poem, you should notice that A, C, D, and E suggest death or diminishment. The only image of intensity and life appears in choice B.

28. **D.** The keys to this question can be found in lines 10–12 and line 14, which restate the irony of the beloved's devotion and the speaker's mortality. A good technique is to always check the previous and subsequent lines in order to clarify your answer. Also, careful reading would eliminate A and B. Passion is not mentioned in the poem.

29. **D.** For the prepared student, this question is a giveaway. Definitions of these terms in Chapter 8 clarify the differences among the types of sonnets. The rhyme scheme should lead you to choose D.

30. **A.** The sonnet depends on several extended comparisons with nature—the seasons, day and night, and fire. Although there may be a contradiction in the final three lines, the primary means of development is metaphor. (See Chapter 8 for examples of synecdoche.)

31. **E.** Since contradiction and paradox are techniques that create irony, you should be able to see that choice E restates the essential opposing forces in the sonnet.

32. **C.** You must reread and interpret the entire third quatrain to clearly figure out this question. You need to decode the metaphor and realize that fires must be fed and that they expire when they exhaust the source of fuel.

33. **D.** Even though E is a lovely thought, the speaker never expresses the desire to have the beloved age along with him. This answer depends on the pun in the title of choice D—fall. Here it may refer to the season of age as well as to the decline of the speaker and the relationship. No other choice is supported in the sonnet.

34. **A.** At first glance, one might think the speaker is submissive to the greater force of death; however, at no time does he acquiesce to the demands of mortality. The speaker thinks about and reflects on his circumstances.

35. **E.** You should notice that three of the five choices are negative. If you have read carefully, you will be aware that the poem is laudatory and positive with regard to the depth of the beloved's love. And, at no time is the speaker looking forward to his lover's departure.

Explanation of answers to *Poets and Language* by Percy Bysshe Shelley

36. **C.** This question is an example of how important the knowledge of definitions of literary terms is if you hope to do well on the AP Lit exam. Using your knowledge and experience, you would obviously choose C after reading just a few of the opening lines.

37. **E.** Lines 2–3 give you the answer to this factual question. You simply have to know a couple of synonyms for "legislators" and "prophets."

38. **E.** Here, you are being asked to make some serious associations with germination and flowering of buds and plants that lead to the future production of fruit. Also, the word "latest" should lead you to choose E.

39. **A.** This question centers around a literary definition and requires you to look at the words preceding and following the given phrase. "Foreknow the spirit of events" and "attribute of prophecy" point only to A.

40. **D.** A careful reading of lines 10–15 will lead you to conclude that all choices *except* "forbid citation" can be seen as a function of grammatical forms. Citation is associated with the limits of the essay.

41. **B.** In line 14, "examples of this fact" refers to Aeschylus, the Bible, and Dante. The word "examples" must lead you to choose B.

42. **D.** This is a rather difficult question. In lines 9–10, the reader is told that the poet participates in the eternal. Lines 11–12 state that grammatical forms will not injure poetry, and the reader is given examples of this. At the end of the paragraph, Shelley states that sculpture, etc. is even "more decisive," meaning indicative of the eternal.

43. **E.** Simply, the antecedent of "that" is "poetry." If in doubt, use substitution.

44. **C.** Lines 21–24 indicate all the characteristics given except for C.

45. **A.** This question demands nothing more than knowing the meanings of two words and locating an antecedent. To find the answer, you must go to the preceding sentence. In line 26, you will see the *last* item is "art."

46. **D.** Notice the use of "which" in the construction of the sentence and "reflects the latter as a cloud . . . ." Here are both parallel structure and simile.

47. **D.** Carefully read the words in lines 29–30, beginning with "the mirrors" and ending with "upon the present." Here, Shelley compares poets to mirrors of the future. Mirrors reflect.

Chapter 4

The Prose Passage Essay

INTRODUCTION TO THE PROSE PASSAGE ESSAY

This section of the exam gives you an opportunity to read and analyze a prose piece of literature. This is your chance to become personally involved in the text and to demonstrate your literary skills.

What is an AP Literature prose passage?

Generally, it is a one-page excerpt from a work of fiction or nonfiction. More often than not, the selection will be from a novel or short story. The nonfiction selection may include essays, biographies, autobiographies, and articles from periodicals.

What is the purpose in writing an essay about a prose piece?

First, the people at the College Board want to determine your facility in reading and interpreting a sustained piece of literature. It requires you to understand the text and to analyze those techniques and devices the author uses to achieve his or her purpose.

Second, the AP exam is designed to allow you to demonstrate your ease and fluency with terminology, interpretation, and criticism. Also, the level of your writing should be a direct reflection of your critical thinking.

Third, the AP exam determines your ability to make connections between analysis and interpretation. For example, when you find a metaphor, you should identify and connect it to the author's intended purpose or meaning. You should not just list items as you locate them. You must connect them to your interpretation.

Tip: Before beginning to work with an actual prose essay, read the review of processes and terms in the Comprehensive Review section of this book. You should also have completed some of the activities in that section.

TYPES OF PROSE PASSAGE ESSAY QUESTIONS

Let's look at a few prose passage questions that have been asked on the AP Literature exam in the past:

- Analyze narrative and literary techniques and other resources of language used for characterization.
- How does a narrator reveal character? (i.e., tone, diction, syntax, point of view)
- How does the author reveal a character's predicament? (i.e., diction, imagery, point of view)
- Explain the effect of the passage on the reader.
- Compare/contrast two passages concerning diction and details for effect on reader.
- How does the passage provide characterization and evaluation of one character over another? (i.e., diction, syntax, imagery, tone)
- What is the attitude of the speaker toward a particular subject?
- Analyze the effect of revision when given both the original and the revised version of a text.
- Analyze style and tone and how they are used to explore the author's attitudes toward his or her subject.
- How is the reader prepared for the conclusion of the piece?

You should be prepared to write an essay based on any of these prompts. (In Chapter 2, "prompt" was defined as the essay question.) Practice. Practice. Practice anticipating questions. Keep a running list of the kinds of questions your teacher asks.

Tip: Don't be thrown by the complexity of a passage. Generally, the more difficult the reading, the more basic the question. You choose the references you wish to incorporate into your essay. So, even if you haven't understood everything, you are still able to write an intelligent essay—*as long as you address the prompt* and refer to the parts of the passage you do understand.

Watch out for overconfidence when you see what you believe to be an easy question with an easy passage. You are going to have to work extra hard to find the nuances in the text that will allow you to write a mature essay.

RATING THE PROSE PASSAGE ESSAY

You will be relieved to know that the rating of your essay is *not* based on whether or not the reader likes you or agrees with your point-of-view.

How do the test readers evaluate my essay?

It's important to understand just what it is that goes into rating your essay. This is called a *rubric*, but don't let that word throw you. A rubric is a word that simply refers to the <u>rating standards that are set and used by the people who read the essays</u>. These standards are fairly consistent, no matter what the prompt might be. The primary change is in the citing of the specifics in a particular prompt.

Let us assure you that, as experienced readers of the AP English Exams, we know that the readers are trained to reward those things you do well in addressing the question. They are *not* looking to punish you. They are aware of the time constraints, and they read your essay just as your own instructor would read the first draft of an essay you wrote on a 40-minute exam. <u>These readers look forward to an interesting, insightful, and well-constructed essay</u>.

So, let's take a look at the following rubrics:

- <u>A 9 essay</u> has all the qualities of an 8 essay, *and* the writing style is especially <u>impressive</u>, as is the analysis and/or discussion of the specifics related to the prompt and the text.
- <u>An 8 essay</u> will <u>effectively</u> and <u>cohesively</u> address the prompt. It will analyze and/or discuss the stylistic elements called for in the question. And it will do so using appropriate evidence from the given text. The essay will also show the writer's ability to control language well.
- <u>A 7 essay</u> has all the properties of a 6, only with a <u>more complete and well-developed</u> analysis/discussion or a more mature writing style.
- <u>A 6 essay adequately</u> addresses the prompt. The analysis and/or discussion is on target and makes use of appropriate specifics from the text. However, these elements are less fully developed than scores in the 7, 8, and 9 range. The essay writer's ideas are expressed with clarity, but the writing may have a few errors in syntax and/or diction.
- <u>A 5 essay</u> demonstrates that the writer <u>understands the prompt</u>. The analysis/discussion is generally understandable, but the analysis/discussion is limited or uneven. The writer's ideas are expressed clearly with a few errors in syntax or diction.
- <u>A 4 essay</u> is <u>not an adequate response</u> to the prompt. The writer's analysis/discussion of the text indicates a misunderstanding, an over-simplification, or a misrepresentation of the given passage. The writer may use evidence that is not appropriate or not sufficient to support the analysis/discussion.

- <u>A 3 essay</u> is a lower 4 because it is <u>even less effective</u> in addressing the prompt. It is also less mature in its syntax and organization.
- <u>A 2 essay</u> indicates <u>little success in speaking to the prompt</u>. The writer may misread the question, only summarize the passage, never develop the required analysis/discussion, or simply ignore the prompt and write about another topic altogether. The writing may also lack organization and control of language and syntax. (*Note*: No matter how good a summary may be, it will never rate more than a 2.)
- <u>A 1 essay</u> is a lower 2 because it is <u>even more simplistic</u>, <u>disorganized, and lacking in control of language</u>.

> Tip: Remember, this essay is really a first draft. The test readers know this and approach each essay with this in mind.

 **TIMING THE ESSAY**

Remember, timing is crucial. With that in mind, here's a workable strategy:

- 1–3 minutes reading and "working the prompt."
- 5 minutes reading and making marginal notes about the passage. Try to isolate 2 quotations that strike you. This may give you your opening and closing.
- 10 minutes preparing to write. (Choose one or two of the following methods that you feel comfortable with.)
  - Highlighting
  - Marginal notations
  - Charts or key word/one word/line number outlining
- 20 minutes to write your essay, based on your preparation.
- 3 minutes for proofreading.

WORKING THE PROMPT

You can't write clearly unless you know *Why* you are writing and *What's Expected* of you. When you "Work the Prompt," you are maximizing both of these areas.

How should I go about reading the prose prompt?

To bring the answer home to you, we will deconstruct a prompt for you now. (This is the same question that is in the Diagnostic/Master exam in Chapter 2.) Plan to spend 1–3 minutes carefully reading the question. This will give you time to really digest what the question is asking you to do.

Here's the prompt:

In the following passage from the short story "The Dead," James Joyce presents an insight into the character of Gabriel. Write a well-organized essay in which you discuss various aspects of Gabriel's character that Joyce reveals to the reader and to Gabriel himself. Refer to such techniques and devices as imagery, point of view, motif, diction, and syntax.

Tip: In the margin, note what time you should be finished with this essay. For example, the test starts at 1 p.m. You write 1:40 in the margin. Time to move on.

Here are three reasons why you should do a 1–3 minute careful analysis of the prompt.

1. Once you know what is expected, you will read in a more directed manner.
2. Once you internalize the question, you will be sensitive to those details that will apply.
3. Once you know all the facets that need to be addressed, you will be able to write a complete essay demonstrating adherence to the topic.

Tip: Topic adherence, which means sticking to the question, is a key strategy for achieving a high score.

Do this now. Highlight, circle, or underline the essential terms and elements in the prompt. Time yourself. How long did it take you? _____ Don't worry if it took you longer than 1–3 minutes in this first attempt. You will be practicing this technique throughout this review, and it will become almost second nature to you.
Compare our highlighting of the prompt with yours.

In the following passage from the <u>short story</u>, <u>"The Dead,"</u> <u>James Joyce</u> presents an <u>insight</u> into the character of Gabriel. Write a well-organized essay in which you <u>discuss</u> various <u>aspects of Gabriel's character</u> that Joyce <u>reveals to the reader and to Gabriel himself.</u> Refer to such <u>techniques</u> and devices as <u>imagery, point of view, motif, diction,</u> and <u>syntax.</u>

In this prompt, anything else you may have highlighted is extraneous.

Note: When the question uses the expression "such as," you are *not* required to use only those ideas presented; you are free to use your own selection of techniques and devices. Notice that the prompt requires more than one technique. One will not be enough. You *must* use more than one. If you fail to use more than one technique, no matter how well you present your answer, your essay will be incomplete.

3 READING AND NOTATING THE PROSE PASSAGE

Depending on your style and comfort level, choose one of these approaches to your reading:

1. A. Read quickly to get the gist of the passage.
   B. Reread, using the highlighting and marginal notes approach.
2. A. Read slowly, using highlighting and making marginal notes.
   B. Reread to confirm that you understand the full impact of the passage.

Note: In both approaches, you *must* highlight and make marginal notes. There is no way to avoid this. Ignore what you don't immediately understand. It may become clear to you after you finish reading the passage. Practice. Practice. Concentrate on those parts of the passage that apply to what you highlighted in the prompt.

There are many ways to read and interpret any given passage. You have to choose which one to use and which specifics to include for support. Don't be rattled if there is leftover material.

We've reproduced the passage for you below so that you can practice both the reading and the process of deconstructing the text. Use highlighting, arrows, circles, underlining, notes, numbers, and whatever you need to make the connections clear to you.

Do this now. Spend between 8–10 minutes working the material. *Do not skip this step.* It is time well spent and is a key to the high score essay.

The Dead

She was fast asleep.

Gabriel, leaning on his elbow, looked for a few moments unresentfully on her tangled hair and half-open mouth, listening to her deep-drawn breath. So she had had that romance in her life: a man had died for her sake. It hardly pained him now to think how poor a part   5
he, her husband, had played in her life. He watched her while she slept as though he and she had never lived together as man and wife. His curious eyes rested long upon her face and on her hair and, as he thought of what she must have been then, in that time of her first girlish beauty, a strange friendly pity for her entered his soul. He did not like to say   10
even to himself that her face was no longer beautiful but he knew that it was no longer the face for which Michael Furey had braved death.

Perhaps she had not told him all the story. His eyes moved to the chair over which she had thrown some of her clothes. A petticoat string dangled to the floor. One boot stood upright, its limp upper fallen down: 15
the fellow of it lay upon the side. He wondered at his riot of emotions of an hour before. From what had it proceeded? From his aunt's supper, from his own foolish speech, from the wine and dancing, the merry-making when saying good-night in the hall, the pleasure of the walk along the river in the snow. Poor Aunt Julia! She, too, would soon be a shade with the   20
shade of Patrick Morkan and his horse. He had caught that haggard look upon her face for a moment when she was singing *Arrayed for the Bridal.*
Soon, perhaps, he would be sitting in the same drawing-room dressed in

black, his silk hat on his knees. The blinds would be drawn down and
Aunt Kate would be sitting beside him, crying and blowing her nose and   25
telling him how Julia had died. He would cast about in his mind for some
words that might console her, and would find only lame and useless ones.
Yes, yes: that would happen very soon.

Now, compare your reading notes with what we've done below.
Yours may vary from ours, but the results of your note-taking should be
similar in scope.

who?

The Dead

alike?

Bible?
angel?
death?

She was fast asleep. ———— *short sentence*   *time*

Gabriel, leaning on his elbow, looked for a few moments   *he hears*

unresentfully on her tangled hair and half-open mouth, listening to her   *not him*

last? —— deep-drawn breath. So she had had that romance in her life: a man had   *he thinks*

died for her sake. It hardly pained him now to think how poor a part   *he sees*

detached? —— he, her husband, had played in her life. He watched her while she slept   *death-like?*

death as though he and she had never lived together as man and wife. His

curious eyes rested long upon her face and on her hair and, as he thought   *time-again*

of what she must have been then, in that time of her first girlish beauty,   *back to death*

he's kind? —— a strange friendly pity for her entered his soul. He did not like to say   *time*

weak
coward? —— even to himself that her face was no longer beautiful but he knew that it   *fury?*

self-image *time* —— was no longer the face for which Michael Furey had braved death.   *not a coward*

Perhaps she had not told him all the story. His eyes moved to the

chair over which she had thrown some of her clothes. A petticoat string   *weak?*
lack of
dangled to the floor. One boot stood upright, its limp upper fallen down: *control?*
afraid to
time —— the fellow of it lay upon the side. He wondered at his riot of emotions of   *let go?*

self-image —— an hour before. From what had it proceeded? From his aunt's supper,

death? —— from his own foolish speech, from the wine and dancing, the merry-making

cold death? —— when saying good-night in the hall, the pleasure of the walk along the river   *time*

ghost?
cold in the snow. Poor Aunt Julia! She, too, would soon be a shade with the   *cold*

time —— shade of Patrick Morkan and his horse. He had caught that haggard look

time —— upon her face for a moment when she was singing *Arrayed for the Bridal.*

Soon, perhaps, he would be sitting in the same drawing-room dressed in *mourning*
closed off
death —— black, his silk hat on his knees. The blinds would be drawn down and   *mourning*

Aunt Kate would be sitting beside him, crying and blowing her nose and   *self-image*

death —— *detached*

weak? telling him how Julia had died. He would cast about in his mind for some

uncertain? —— words that might console her, and would find only lame and useless ones.

Yes, yes: that would happen very soon. ——— *time*   *weakness*

After you have marked the passage, review the prompt. When you look at your notes, certain categories will begin to pop out at you. These can be the basis for the development of the body of your essay. For example:

- Death
- Insecurity
- Time
- Passivity
- Short sentences
- Detachment

Notice that we have ignored notes that did not apply to the prompt.

Now choose the techniques you are able to explore and defend that reveal Gabriel's character.

In response to the prompt, we have decided that the techniques/devices we will analyze are:

- Imagery
- Style
- Diction
- Motif

 If you expand the above techniques/devices and the above categories into interpretive statements and support those statements with appropriate details that you've already isolated, you will be writing a defended essay.

WRITING THE OPENING PARAGRAPH

Your opening statement is the one that sets the tone of your essay and possibly raises the expectations of the reader. Spend time on your first paragraph to maximize your score.

Make certain that your topic is very clear. This reinforces the idea that you fully understand what is expected of you and what you will communicate to the reader. Generally, identify both the text and its author in this first paragraph.

A suggested approach is to relate a direct quotation from the passage to the topic.

Tip: Consider the "philosophy of firsts." It is a crucial strategy to spend focused time on the first part of the question and on the first paragraph of the essay because:

1. It establishes the direction and tone of your essay.

2. It gives you the guidelines for what to develop in your essay.

3. It connects you to the reader.

Remember our philosophy: **In the Beginning:** if you focus on the beginning, the rest will fall into place. A wonderful thing happens after much practice, highlighting, and note-taking. Your mind starts to focus automatically. Trust us on this. It is the winning edge that can take an average essay and raise it to a higher level.

Do this now. Take 5 minutes to write your opening paragraph for "The Dead" prompt. Write quickly, referring to your notes.

Let's check what you've written:

Highlight these points to see if you've done them. You may be surprised at what is actually there.

- Have you included author and title?
- Have you addressed the character of Gabriel?
- Have you specifically mentioned the techniques you will refer to in your essay?

Here are four sample opening paragraphs that address all of the criteria:

A

In "The Dead" by James Joyce, the character Gabriel is revealed through diction, point of view, and imagery as he watches his wife sleep.

B

Poor Gabriel! Who would have thought he knew so little about himself and his life. And yet, in "The Dead," James Joyce, through diction, point of view, and imagery, makes it clear to the reader and to Gabriel that there is much to reveal about his character.

C

"Yes, yes: this would happen very soon." And, yes, very soon the reader of the excerpt from Joyce's "The Dead" gets to know the character of Gabriel. Through diction, point of view, and imagery, we are introduced to Gabriel and what he thinks of himself.

D

"The Dead." How apt a title. James Joyce turns his reader into a fly on the wall as Gabriel is about to realize the many losses in his life. Death pervades the passage, from his sleeping wife to his dying aunt.

Each of these opening paragraphs is an acceptable beginning to an AP Literature exam essay. Note what each of these paragraphs has:

- Each has identified the title and author.
- Each has stated which technique/devices will be used.
- Each has stated the purpose of analyzing these techniques/devices.

Now, note what is different about each opening paragraph.

- Sample **A** restates the question without anything extra. It is to the point, so much so that it does nothing more than repeat the question. It's correct, but it does not really pique the reader's interest. (Use this type of opening if you feel unsure of or uncomfortable with the prompt.)

- Sample **B** reveals the writer's attitude toward the subject. The writer has already determined that Gabriel is flawed and indicates an understanding of how Gabriel's character is revealed in the passage.
- Sample **C**, with its direct quotation, places the reader immediately into the passage. The reader quickly begins to hear the writer's voice through his or her choice of words (diction).
- Sample **D**, at first glance, reveals a mature, confident writer who is not afraid to *imply* the prompt's criteria.

Note: There are many other types of opening paragraphs that could do the job as well. The paragraphs above are just a few samples.

Into which of the above samples would you classify your opening paragraph?

WRITING THE BODY OF THE PROSE PASSAGE ESSAY

When you write the body of your essay, take only 15–20 minutes. Time yourself and try your best to finish within that time frame.

Since this is practice, don't panic if you can't complete the essay within the allotted time. You will become more and more comfortable with the tasks presented to you as you gain experience with this type of question.

What should I include in the body of the prose passage essay?

1. Obviously, this is where you present your interpretation and the points you wish to make that are related to the prompt.
2. Use specific references and details from the passage.
    - Don't always paraphrase the original; refer directly to it.
    - Place quotation marks around those words and phrases that you extract from the passage.

Adhere to the question

3. Use "connective tissue" in your essay to establish adherence to the question.
    - Use the repetition of key ideas from your opening paragraph.
    - Try using "echo words" (i.e., synonyms, such as death/loss/passing or character/persona/personality).
    - Create transitions from one paragraph to the next.

To understand the process, carefully read the following sample paragraphs. Each develops one of the categories and techniques/devices asked for in the prompt. Notice the specific references and the "connective tissue." Also, notice that details that do no apply to the prompt have been ignored.

A
This paragraph develops **imagery**.

Joyce creates imagery to lead his reader to sense the cloud of death that pervades Gabriel's world. From its very title "The Dead," the reader is prepared for loss. Just what has Gabriel lost: his wife, his confidence, his job, a friend, a relative, what? As his "wife slept," Gabriel sees her "half-open mouth" and "listens" to her "deep-drawn breath." The reader almost senses this to be a death watch. The images about the room reinforce this sense of doom. One boot is "limp" and the other is "fallen down." Picturing the future, Gabriel sees a "drawing-room dressed in black" with blinds "drawn down" and his Aunt Kate "crying" and "telling him how Julia had died." And to underscore his own feelings of internal lifelessness, he can only find "lame and useless" words of comfort.

B
This paragraph develops the **motif of time**.

Time is a constant from the beginning to the end of the passage. In the first paragraph, Gabriel is in the present while thinking of the past. He is an observer, watching his wife as he, himself, is observed by the narrator, and as we, as readers, observe the entire scene. Time moves the reader and Gabriel through the experience. Immediately, we spend a "few moments" with Gabriel as he goes back and forth in time assessing his relationship with his wife. He recognizes she "had had romance in the past." But, "it hardly pains him now." He thinks of what she had been "then" in her "girlish" beauty, which may indicate his own aging. His "strange, friendly pity," because she is "no longer beautiful," may be self-pity, as well. In the next paragraph, we are with Gabriel as he reflects on his emotional "riot" only an hour before. However, he jumps to the future because he can't sustain self-examination. He chooses to allow himself to jump to this future and a new subject—Aunt Julia's death. In this future, he continues to see only his inability and incompetence. For Gabriel, all this will happen "very soon."

C
This passage develops **diction**.

Gabriel appears to be a man who is on the outside of his life. Joyce's diction reveals his passive nature. Gabriel "looked on" and "watched" his wife sleeping. He spent time "listening to her breath" and was "hardly pained by his role in her life." His eyes "rest" on her, and he "thinks of the past." All of Gabriel's actions are as weak as a "limp" and "fallen down" boot, "inert in the face of life." He is in direct contrast to Michael Furey, who has "braved death." And he knows this about himself. The narrator's diction reveals that Gabriel "did not like to say even to himself," implying that he is too weak to face the truth.

Later in the text, Gabriel's word choice further indicates his insecurity. He is troubled by his "riot of emotions," his "foolish speech." It is obvious that Gabriel will not take such risks again.

D
This passage develops **style**.

Joyce's very straightforward writing style supports the conclusions he wishes the reader to draw about the character of Gabriel. Most sentences are in the subject/verb, simple sentence form, reflecting the plain, uncomplicated character of Gabriel.

Joyce employs a third person narrator to further reinforce Gabriel's detachment from his own circumstances. We watch him observing his own life with little or no connection on his part. He wonders at his "riot of emotions." All this is presented without Joyce using obvious poetic devices. This punctuates the lack of "romance" in Gabriel's life when compared with that of Michael Furey.

Tip: Start a study group. Approach an essay as a team. After you've deconstructed the prompt, have each person write a paragraph on a separate area of the question. Then come together and discuss what was written. You'll be amazed at how much fun this is because the work will carry you away. This is a chance to explore exciting ideas.

We urge you to spend more time developing the body paragraphs than worrying about a concluding paragraph, especially one that begins with "In conclusion," or "In summary." In such a brief essay, the reader will have no problem remembering what you have already stated. It is not necessary to repeat yourself in a summary-type final paragraph.

If you want to make a final statement, try to link your ideas to a particularly effective line or image from the passage.

Note: Look at the last line of Sample **B** on motif. For Gabriel, all this will happen "very soon." This final sentence would be fine as the conclusion to the essay. A conclusion does not have to be a paragraph. It can be the writer's final remark or observation presented in a sentence or two.

Do this now. Write the body of your essay. Time yourself. Allow 15–20 minutes to complete this task.

Tip: Again, sharing your writing with members of your class or study group will allow you to gain experience and find a comfort zone with requirements and possibilities.

SAMPLE STUDENT ESSAYS

Following are two actual student essays followed by a rubric and comments on each. Read both of the samples in sequence to clarify the differences between "high" and "mid-range" essays.

Student Essay A

A picture is worth a thousand words, but James Joyce manages to paint a pretty vivid one in only two short paragraphs. Joyce offers tremendous insight into the character of Gabriel in the short story "The Dead." He captures the essence of a scene laden with death and laced with tones of despair and hopelessness. By employing third person narration alternating with a stream of consciousness, Joyce demonstrates his abilities to delve deep into Gabriel's mind, illustrating this somewhat detached disposition and low self-image.

The passage takes us through Gabriel's reflections upon past, present, and future events while his inner character unfolds. Joyce's careful use of diction suggests that Gabriel has emotionally closed himself off to the world as he tries to cope with some aforementioned incident. He was "hardly pained" to think about a situation which caused a "riot of emotions" just a little earlier on that evening. Here, Joyce is emphasizing Gabriel's way of coping with an unfavorable event by blocking it out. He continues to "unresentfully" reflect upon what had occurred, closing himself off from any pain he obviously experienced a short while ago.

With the powerful omniscience of a third-person narrator, Joyce is able to describe the workings of Gabriel's inner consciousness without writing from the first-person point of view. Gabriel further detaches himself as he thinks about his wife. He watches her from the point of view of an outsider, as if they were never married. The mere fact that Gabriel is able to do this suggests that he and his wife do not have a truly loving relationship. This assertion is underscored by the "friendly" pity Gabriel feels for his wife, emphasizing the lack of true love in their relationship. Gabriel later questions his wife's honesty, further emphasizing a troubled relationship. The reader may be inclined to infer that Gabriel is completely devoid of compassion; however, this idea is refuted. Gabriel proceeds to express an element of sorrow when he thinks back to his wife's youth and beauty.

The evening's events had evidently triggered some type of emotional outburst which Gabriel cannot stop thinking about. His mental state is paralleled by the chaotic state of disorder in the room he is in. With a masterful control of language and syntax, Joyce describes in short, choppy sentences the array of clothing strewn around the room. This is followed by one of the longest sentences in the passage. Joyce reveals this series of events all at once, paralleling Gabriel's release of a multitude of emotions at once.

Joyce weaves a motif of darkness and death into the story. His aunt's "haggard" appearance ironically catches Gabriel's attention during the recitation of *Arrayed for the Bridal*, a seemingly happy song. This image of happiness and marriage is further contrasted with images of the woman's funeral and a detailed description of how Gabriel will mourn for her. Joyce also takes time to underscore Gabriel's low self-esteem, in that he will only think of "lame and useless" words at a time when comforting tones are necessary. He is essentially describing himself, since it has been established that he failed as a husband and that he is emotionally distraught even though he blocks out the pain he feels. "The blinds would be drawn down," Gabriel says, as he describes both the room at his aunt's funeral and his mental state of affairs.

The true originator of "stream-of-consciousness" techniques, Joyce delves deep into Gabriel's mind, describing his wide range of emotions and state of mind. His powerful diction reveals a great deal about Gabriel's character while his implied insights penetrate into the reader's mind, reinforcing the abstract meanings behind the actions and events that transpire throughout the course of his story.

Student Essay B

In the excerpt from the short story "The Dead" from *Dubliners* by James Joyce, the author describes some personality traits of the character Gabriel as he sits watching a sleeping woman. The point of view from which this excerpt is expressed helps the reader to get to know Gabriel because the narrator is omniscient and knows how Gabriel perceives things and what he is thinking. With the use of many literary devices such as imagery, diction, and syntax, the reader is able to see that Gabriel is an observant and a reflective person, but he is also detached.

Gabriel comes across as observant, because throughout the entire passage he is observing a woman, his wife, sleeping. He scans the room looking over everything and taking note of everything. An example of this is looking at "her tangled hair and half-open mouth, listening to her deep drawn breath." The author uses the technique of syntax ("deep-drawn breath" and "half-open mouth") in the above quotation to show us exactly what Gabriel is seeing. Gabriel notices many details, and they are described so that the reader can clearly formulate a picture of what he is gazing at. This imagery can be seen in lines such as the one where the woman's boots are being described. "One boot stood upright, its limp upper fallen down; the fellow of it lay upon the side." The diction used such as "limp" and "upright," are concrete words that create clear pictures. Another reason that Gabriel comes across as observant is because he catches and notices little things. For example, he "caught" the "haggard look" on his Aunt Julia's face.

Resulting from the fact that Gabriel is observant, he is also reflective. He thinks over past events that had happened and wonders what caused them and why he did what he did. In the first paragraph he reflects on his wife's "fading beauty," what she used to look like, and the story of the death of Michael Furey. He realizes

that it is a possibility that she had not told him the entire story concerning the boy's 25
death. He further reflects when he is thinking about his emotional outburst. He asks himself many questions including "From what had it preceded?"

A feeling of detachment is also present. The way he looks at his wife "as though he and she had never lived together as man and wife" shows that he is viewing his own life from an objective standpoint. He is able to look at his own life 30 as though it wasn't his. The sentence that reads "it hardly pained him now to think how poor a part he, her husband, had played in her life," further exemplifies this feeling of detachment. Feelings that he used to feel no longer even touched him. He was able to recognize them, yet remain separate. In the second paragraph Gabriel continues to come across as remote. He is able to picture and describe in great detail the 35 death and funeral of his Aunt Julia. He narrates the future drastic event in a matter-of-fact way. Gabriel goes so far as to describe what he will be thinking at the time of his Aunt Julia's death which is "he would cast about in his mind for some words that might console her (his Aunt Kate), and would find only lame and useless ones". This statement finalizes the idea that Gabriel is a person who is, at least to 40 some degree, detached from his own life.

Even though the passage is fairly short, the author is able to impart a fair amount of information concerning the character Gabriel. It becomes apparent that he possesses the qualities of observance, reflection, and detachment. These qualities are all interconnected because of the fact that he is observant leading to 45 his ability to reflect on his actions and actions of others. This in turn leads to his detachment, because when he reflects on his life he does it from the standpoint of a third-person narrator. The author's use of literary techniques helps to convey these personality traits of Gabriel to a reader.

 Let's take a look at a set of rubrics for this prose passage essay. (If you want to see actual AP rubrics as used in a recent AP Lit exam, log on to the College Board Website: <www.collegeboard.org/ap>.) As you probably know, essays are rated on a 9–1 scale, with 9 the highest and 1 the lowest. Since we are not with you to personally rate your essay and to respond to your style and approach, we will, instead, list the criteria for high-, middle-, and low-range papers. These criteria are based on our experience with rubrics and reading AP Literature exam essays.

A *high* range essay can be a 9 or an 8. *Middle* refers to essays in the 7, 6, 5 range. And the *low* scoring essays are rated 4, 3, 2, 1.

After reading the following rubrics, evaluate the two essays that you have just read.

> Tip: Let's be honest with each other. We all can recognize a 9 essay. It sings, and we wish we had written it. It's wonderful that the essays don't all have to sing the same song with the same words and rhythm. Conversely, we can, unfortunately, recognize the 1 or 2 paper which is off key, and we are relieved not to have written one like it.

RATING THE STUDENT ESSAYS

High-Range Essay (9–8)

- Indicates complete understanding of the prompt.
- Distinguishes between what Gabriel acknowledges about himself and what the reader comes to know about him.
- Explores the complexity of Gabriel's character.
- Identifies and analyzes Joyce's literary techniques, such as imagery, diction, point of view, motif, and style.
- Cites specific references to the passage.
- Illustrates and supports the points being made.
- Is clear, well-organized, and coherent.
- Reflects the ability to manipulate language at an advanced level.
- Contains only minor errors or flaws, if any.

Tip: Rarely, a 7 essay can make the jump into the high range because of its more mature style and perception.

Middle-Range Essay (7–6–5)

- Refers accurately to the prompt.
- Refers accurately to the literary devices used by Joyce.
- Provides a less thorough analysis of Gabriel's character than the higher-rated paper.
- Is less adept at linking techniques to the purpose of the passage.
- Demonstrates writing that is adequate to convey the writer's intent.
- May not be sensitive to the implications about Gabriel's character.

Tip: The 7 paper demonstrates a more consistent command of college-level writing than does the 5 or 6 paper.
A 5 paper does the minimum required by the prompt. It relies on generalizations and sketchy analysis. It is often sidetracked by plot, and the references may be limited or simplistic.

Low-Range Essay (4–3–2–1)

- Does not respond adequately to the prompt.
- Demonstrates insufficient and/or inaccurate understanding of the passage.
- Does not link literary devices to Gabriel's character.
- Underdevelops and/or inaccurately analyzes literary techniques.
- Fails to demonstrate an understanding of Gabriel's character.
- Demonstrates weak control of the elements of diction, syntax, and organization.

> Tip: A 4 or 3 essay may do no more than paraphrase sections of the passage rather than analyze Gabriel's character.
>
> A 2 essay may merely summarize the passage. *(No matter how well written, a summary can never earn more than a 2.)*
>
> A 1–2 essay indicates a major lack of understanding and control. It fails to comprehend the prompt and/or the passage. It may also indicate severe writing problems.

Now, compare your evaluation of the two student essays with ours.

Student Essay A

This is a high-range paper for the following reasons:

- Is on task.
- Shows complete understanding of the prompt and the passage.
- Indicates perceptive, subtle analysis (line 8).
- Maintains excellent topic adherence (lines 9, 17, 28, 39).
- Uses good "connective tissue" (repetition of key words).
- Chooses good specific references (lines 11, 12, 21, 35).
- Knows how to distinguish between the author and the narrator.
- Understands point of view well.
- Makes suggestions and inferences (lines 7, 20).
- Demonstrates good critical thinking.
- Is perceptive about syntax and the style of author (lines 27–33).
- Links techniques with character (line 34).
- Demonstrates mature language manipulation (line 34).
- Understands function of diction and motif (lines 40–44).

> Tip: It's best to omit extraneous judgmental words from your essay (line 45).

This is obviously a mature, critical reader and writer. Using subtle inferences and implications, the writer demonstrates an understanding of the character of Gabriel as both Joyce presents him and as Gabriel views himself. There is nothing extraneous or repetitious in this essay. Each point leads directly and compellingly to the next aspect of Gabriel's character.

This is definitely a strong, high-range essay.

Student Essay B

This is a middle-range essay for the following reasons:

- Sets up an introduction which indicates the techniques that will be developed, but neglects to clearly set up the required discussion of how Gabriel views himself.

- Immediately establishes that the essay will address Gabriel's character as drawn by the narrator and seen by the reader.
- Addresses three aspects of Gabriel's character without fully developing the analysis of literary techniques.
- Adheres to the essay's topic.
- Uses "connective tissue" (lines 21, 28).
- Uses "echo words" (lines 8, 9, 10).
- Uses citations from the passages.
- Isolates some details to illustrate Gabriel's character (lines 31–32, 39).
- Confuses syntax with diction (lines 12–13).
- Lacks development of literary technique in paragraph 4.
- Displays faulty diction and syntax.
- Does not develop an important part of the prompt—how Gabriel views himself.
- Incorporates faulty logic at times (lines 44–49).

This essay is a solid, middle-range paper. The writer has a facility with literary analysis. Even though there are flashes of real insight, they are not sustained throughout the essay. There is a strong opening paragraph which makes it clear to the reader what the topic of the paper is. The writer obviously grasps Gabriel's character and the needed details to support the character analysis. But the weakness in this paper is the writer's incomplete development of the relationship of literary techniques to character analysis.

Note: Both essays have concluding paragraphs that are repetitive and largely unnecessary. It is best to avoid this type of ending.

FINAL COMMENTS

How about sharing these essays with members of your class or study group and discussing possible responses?

Try a little reverse psychology. Now that you are thoroughly familiar with this passage, construct two or three alternate AP level prompts. (Walk a little in the examiner's shoes.) This will help you gain insight into the process of test-making. Perhaps, as extra practice, you would like to try one or two alternative questions as enrichment.

RAPID REVIEW

After you've absorbed the ideas in this chapter, the following points will provide you with a quick refresher when needed.

- Familiarize yourself with the types of prose questions (prompts).
- Highlight the prompt and understand all the required tasks.
- Time your essay carefully.
- Spend sufficient time "working the passage" before you begin writing.
- Mark up the passage.
- Create a strong opening paragraph.
- Refer often to the passage.
- Use concrete details and quotes to support your ideas.
- Always stay on topic.
- Avoid plot summary.
- Include transitions and echo words.
- Check the models and rubrics for guidance for self-evaluation.
- Practice—vary the question and your approach.
- Share ideas with others.

Chapter 5

The Poetry Essay

INTRODUCTION TO THE POETRY ESSAY

It's obvious to any reader that poetry is different from prose. And, writing about each is different also. This chapter will guide you through the expectations and processes associated with the AP Poetry section.

What is the purpose of the poetry essay?

The College Board wants to determine your facility in reading and interpreting a sustained piece of literature. You are required to understand the text and to analyze those techniques and devices the poet uses to achieve his or her purpose.

The AP Lit exam is designed to allow you to demonstrate your ease and fluency with terminology, interpretation, and analysis. The level of your writing should be a direct reflection of your critical thinking.

The AP Lit exam is looking for connections between analysis and interpretation. For example, when you find a metaphor, you should identify it and connect it to the poet's intended purpose or meaning. You shouldn't just list items as you locate them. You must connect them to your interpretation.

Tip: Before beginning to work with an actual poem, read the review of processes and terms in the Comprehensive Review section of this book. You should also have completed some of the activities in that section.

TYPES OF PROMPTS USED IN THE POETRY ESSAY

Not every poetry essay prompt is the same. Familiarizing yourself with the various types is critical. This familiarity will both increase your confidence and provide you with a format for poetry analysis.

What kinds of questions are asked in the poetry essay?

 Let's look at a few of the types of questions that have been asked in the poetry essay on the AP Literature exam in the past:

- How does the language of the poem reflect the speaker's perceptions, and how does that language determine the reader's perception?
- How does the poet reveal character? (i.e., diction, sound devices, imagery, allusion)
- Discuss the similarities and differences between two poems. Consider style and theme.
- Contrast the speakers' views toward a subject in two poems. Refer to form, tone, and imagery.
- Discuss how poetic elements, such as language, structure, imagery, and point of view convey meaning in a poem.
- Given two poems, discuss what elements make one better than the other.
- Relate the imagery, form, or theme of a particular section of a poem to another part of that same poem. Discuss changing attitude or perception of speaker or reader.
- Analyze a poem's extended metaphor and how it reveals the poet's or speaker's attitude.
- Discuss the way of life revealed in a poem. Refer to such poetic elements as tone, imagery, symbol, and verse form.
- Discuss the poet's changing reaction to the subject developed in the poem.
- Discuss how the form of the poem affects its meaning.

 You should be prepared to write an essay based on any of these kinds of prompts. Apply these questions to poems you read throughout the year. Practice anticipating questions. Keep a running list of the kinds of questions your teacher asks. Practice. Practice.

TIMING AND PLANNING THE POETRY ESSAY

Successful writing is directly related to both thought and structure, and you will need to consider the following concepts related to pre-writing.

How should I plan to spend my time writing the poetry essay?

Remember, timing is crucial. With this in mind, here's a workable strategy:

- 1–3 minutes reading and "working the prompt."
- 5 minutes reading and making marginal notes about the poem. Try to isolate two references that strike you. This may give you your opening and closing.
- 10 minutes preparing to write. (Choose one or two of the following methods that you feel comfortable with.)
  - Highlighting
  - Marginal mapping (see Chapter 4 for samples)
  - Key word/one word/line number outlining
  - Numerical clustering
- 20 minutes to write your essay, based on your preparation
- 3 minutes for proofreading

WORKING THE PROMPT

It is important to understand that the quality of your essay greatly depends upon you correctly addressing the prompt.

How should I go about reading the prompt?

As we did in the prose section, we will deconstruct a poetry essay prompt for you now. (This is the same question that is in the Diagnostic/Master exam earlier in this book.)

You should plan to spend 1–3 minutes carefully reading the question. This will give you time to really digest what the question is asking you to do.

Here's the prompt:

In "On the Subway," Sharon Olds brings two worlds into close proximity. Identify the contrasts that develop both portraits in the poem and discuss the insights the narrator comes to as a result of the experience. Refer to such literary techniques as poetic devices, tone, imagery, and organization.

Tip: In the margin, note what time you should be finished with this essay. For example, the test starts at 1 p.m. You write 1:40 in the margin. Time to move on.

Here are three reasons why you should do a 1–3 minute careful analysis of the prompt:

1. Once you know what is expected, you will read in a more directed manner.
2. Once you internalize the question, you will be sensitive to the details that will apply as you read the poem.
3. Once you know all the facets that need to be addressed, you will be able to write a complete essay that demonstrates adherence to the topic.

 Do this now. Highlight, circle, or underline the essential terms and elements in the prompt. Time yourself. How long did it take you?

Compare our highlighting of the prompt with yours.

In "<u>On the Subway</u>," <u>Sharon Olds</u> brings <u>two worlds into close proximity</u>. <u>Identify</u> the <u>contrasts that develop both portraits</u> in the poem and <u>discuss the insights the narrator comes to</u> as a result of the experience. Refer to such literary techniques as <u>tone</u>, <u>poetic devices</u>, <u>imagery</u>, and <u>organization.</u>

In this prompt, anything else you may have highlighted is extraneous.

Note: When the question uses the expression "such as," you are *not* required to use only those ideas presented; you are free to use your own selection of techniques and devices. Notice that the prompt requires more than one technique. One will not be enough. You *must* use more than one. If you fail to use more than one technique, no matter how well you present your answer, your essay will be incomplete.

Tip: See Chapter 9 to review terms, techniques, and poetic devices necessary for analysis.

Finally, read the poem. Depending on your style and comfort level, choose one of these approaches to your reading:

1. A. Read quickly to get the gist of the poem.
   B. Reread, using the highlighting and marginal notes approach.
2. A. Read slowly, as if speaking aloud. Let the structure of the poem help you with meaning. (See the terms *enjambment* and *caesura* in the glossary at the back of this book.)
   B. Reread to confirm that you understand the full impact of the poem. Do your highlighting and make marginal notes.

Note: In both approaches, you *must* highlight and make marginal notes. There is no way to avoid this. Ignore what you don't immediately understand. It may become clear to you after reading the poem. Practice.

Practice. Concentrate on those parts of the poem that apply to what you highlighted in the prompt.

There are many ways to read and interpret any poetry. You have to choose your own approach and which specifics to include for support. <u>Don't be rattled if there is leftover material.</u>

We've reproduced the poem for you below so that you can practice both the reading and the process of deconstructing the text. Use highlighting, arrows, circles, underlining, notes, numbers, and whatever you need to make the connections clear to you.

Do this now. Spend between 8–10 minutes working the material. *Do not skip this step.* It is time well spent and is a key to the high score essay.

On the Subway
by Sharon Olds

"When I read poetry out loud, it's easier for me to understand it."
-Jennifer L.
–AP student

The boy and I face each other
His feet are huge, in black sneakers
laced with white in a complex pattern like a
set of intentional scars. We are stuck on
opposite sides of the car, a couple of   5
molecules stuck in a rod of light
rapidly moving through darkness.
He has the casual cold look of a mugger,
alert under hooded lids. He is wearing
red, like the inside of the body   10
exposed. I am wearing dark fur, the
whole skin of an animal taken and
used. I look at his raw face,
he looks at my fur coat, and I don't
know if I am in his power—   15
he could take my coat so easily, my
briefcase, my life—
or if he is in my power, the way I am
living off his life, eating the steak
he does not eat, as if I am taking   20
the food from his mouth. And he is black
and I am white, and without meaning or
trying to I must profit from his darkness,
the way he absorbs the murderous beams of the
nation's heart, as black cotton   25
absorbs the heat of the sun and holds it. There is

no way to know how easy this
white skin makes my life, this
life he could take so easily and
break across his knee like a stick the way his   30
own back is being broken, the
rod of his soul that at birth was dark and
fluid and rich as the heart of a seedling
ready to thrust up into any available light

Now compare your reading notes with what we've done below. Yours may vary from ours, but the results of your note-taking should be similar in scope.

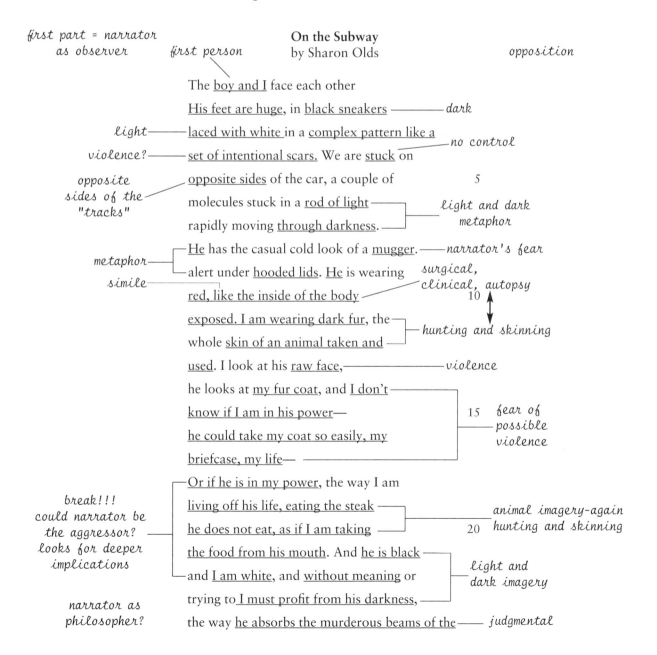

first part = narrator
as observer

first person

On the Subway
by Sharon Olds

opposition

The boy and I face each other

His feet are huge, in black sneakers ——— dark

light ——— laced with white in a complex pattern like a
no control
violence? ——— set of intentional scars. We are stuck on

opposite
sides of the
"tracks"

opposite sides of the car, a couple of   5

molecules stuck in a rod of light ———
light and dark
metaphor
rapidly moving through darkness. ———

metaphor ——— He has the casual cold look of a mugger. ——— narrator's fear
simile ——— alert under hooded lids. He is wearing   surgical,
clinical, autopsy
red, like the inside of the body ———   10

exposed. I am wearing dark fur, the ———
hunting and skinning
whole skin of an animal taken and ———

used. I look at his raw face, ——— violence

he looks at my fur coat, and I don't ———

know if I am in his power—   15   fear of
possible
he could take my coat so easily, my   violence

briefcase, my life— ———

break!!!
could narrator be
the aggressor?
looks for deeper
implications

Or if he is in my power, the way I am

living off his life, eating the steak ———
animal imagery-again
hunting and skinning
he does not eat, as if I am taking   20

the food from his mouth. And he is black ———

and I am white, and without meaning or ———
light and
dark imagery
trying to I must profit from his darkness, ———

narrator as
philosopher?

the way he absorbs the murderous beams of the —— judgmental

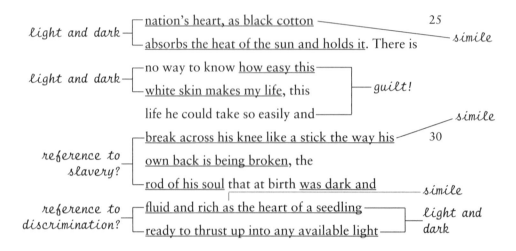

After you have marked the poem, review the prompt. When you look at your notes, certain categories will begin to pop out at you. These can be the basis for the development of the body of your essay. For example:

- Light and dark imagery
- Speaker's insights
- Contrast in status
- Metaphors

- Animal imagery
- Implied violence
- Shift in middle of poem
- Similes

 Notice that we have ignored notes that did not apply to the prompt.

Now choose the techniques that develop the contrasting portraits and reveal the narrator's perceptions.

In response to the prompt, we have decided that the techniques/devices we will analyze are:

- Imagery
- Poetic devices
- Organization

If you expand the above techniques/devices and the above categories into interpretive statements and support those statements with appropriate details that you've already isolated, you will be writing a defended essay.

WRITING THE OPENING PARAGRAPH

Your opening statement is the one that sets the tone of your essay and possibly raises the expectations of the reader. Spend time on your first paragraph to maximize your score.

Make certain that your topic is very clear. This reinforces the idea that you fully understand what is expected of you and what you will communicate to the reader. Generally, identify both the text and the poet in this first paragraph.

Highlight these points to see if you've done them. You may be surprised at what is actually there.

Do this now. Take 5 minutes to write your opening paragraph for the prompt on page 80. Write quickly, referring to your notes.

Let's check what you've written.

- Have you included the poet and title?
- Have you addressed the portraits, contrasts, and insights?
- Have you specifically mentioned the techniques you will refer to in your essay?

Here are three sample opening paragraphs that address each of the above criteria.

A

Sharon Olds in the poem, "On the Subway," presents a brief encounter between two people of different races which leads to several insights of one participant. This is accomplished through Olds's use of poetic devices, imagery, and imagination.

B

The observer and the observed. One has control over the other. In her poem, "On the Subway," Sharon Olds asks her readers to enter the mind of a white woman who observes a young, black man as they travel together, neither knowing the other. Using poetic devices, imagery, and organization, Olds takes the reader on a ride through the contrasts and images that spark the imagination of the white onlooker.

C

"And he is black and I am white" establishes the basic contrast and conflict in Sharon Olds's poem, "On the Subway." Through imagery, organization, and poetic devices, Olds creates two contrasting portraits. The narrator's confrontation becomes the reader's also as she reveals her troubling fears and insights through her images and comments concerning her encounter with the black youth.

These three introductory paragraphs identify the poet and the title and clearly indicate an understanding of the prompt. Now, let's note what is different about each.

Sample **A** is a straightforward, unadorned restatement of the prompt. It is correct, yet, lacks a writer's voice. (If you are unsure of how to proceed, this is the type of opening you may want to consider.) This type of opening paragraph will at least allow you to get into the essay with as little complexity as possible.

Sample **B** immediately reveals the writer's confidence and mature writing style. The prompt is addressed in a provocative and interesting manner, letting the reader know the tone of the essay.

Sample **C** incorporates a direct quotation from the poem which indicates the writer is comfortable with citation. The writer also links the reader with the poem and feels confident that his or her judgments about the encounter are supportable.

Note: There are many other types of opening paragraphs that could do the job as well. The paragraphs above are just a few samples.

Does your opening paragraph resemble any of these samples?

WRITING THE BODY OF THE POETRY ESSAY

When you write the body of your essay, take only 15–20 minutes. Time yourself and try your best to finish within that time frame.

Since this is practice, don't panic if you can't complete the essay within the allotted time. You will become more and more comfortable with the tasks presented to you as you gain experience with this type of question.

3 What should I include in the body of the poetry essay?

1. Obviously, this is where you present your interpretation and the points you wish to make that are related to the prompt.

2. Use specific references and details from the poem.

   - Don't always paraphrase the original; refer directly to it.
   - Place quotation marks around those words and phrases that you extract from the poem.

3. Use "connective tissue" in your essay to establish adherence to the question.

   - Use the repetition of key ideas from opening paragraph.
   - Try using "echo words" (i.e., synonyms such as insight can be inference/observation/perception; fear can be apprehension/insecurity).
   - Create transitions from one paragraph to the next.

 To understand the process, carefully read the following sample paragraphs. Each develops one of the categories and techniques/devices asked for in the prompt. Notice the specific references and the "connective tissue." Also, notice that details that do not apply to the prompt have been ignored.

A
This paragraph develops **poetic devices.**

"Black sneakers laced with white in a complex pattern like a set of intentional scars" is the jarring simile Olds uses to establish the relationship between the woman and the "boy" on the subway. Immediately, the poetic device implies the bondage and pain of the oppressed minority and the deliberate complexity of race relations. This idea of interwoven lives is further developed by the metaphor that links both as "molecules stuck in a rod of light." The youth, however, is compared to a reptile with "hooded lids," and all the fear and repulsion associated with this creature is transferred to the boy who is hiding his true intentions with such a look. The woman follows her fearful insights with still another extreme simile—worrying about "this life he could take so easily and break across his knee like a stick." Still, she proves the complexity of her thoughts by creating a sympathetic metaphor to ponder "the rod of his soul—the heart of a seedling" yearning to grow into the light.

B
This paragraph develops **imagery**.

The images in the poem are predominantly drawn from the contrast between light and dark. "Black sneakers," "white laces," "rod of light rapidly moving through darkness" are all images that immediately establish the contrast that is at the heart of the meaning of the poem. This juxtaposition becomes reality in lines 20–22 when we learn that "he is black and I am white." The problem is how the "white" profits from his "darkness." [line 23] What should be light, "the beams of the nation's heart," is murderous, and he "as black cotton," absorbs this heat. This angry contrast leads the speaker to her insight about her life in lines 26–28. Empathizing with the black youth, the narrator moves beyond her prejudices and finds promise in the last three lines which see the dark being born into the light.

C
This paragraph develops **organization**.

The organization of "On the Subway" is rather linear. Olds narrator proceeds from a frightened observer to a philosophical questioner to finally a mature, sympathetic forecaster of the promise of the young, black man. The first thirteen lines provide the interior monologue of a woman who sits across from a young, black male and looks him over from head to toe. In line 10 she begins to move deeply into the hidden person across from her, with this "introspection" ending in lines 14–16 with her questioning who actually has power over whom. Line 18 presents a true shift from personal observation to an almost societal conscience which is sympathetic to the plight of all blacks in America as seen in lines 21–26. Bringing the reader back to the opening section of the poem, the speaker intimates at the promise of the young man with "the rod of his soul . . . rich as the heart of a seedling/ready to thrust up into any available light." [lines 32–34]

Tip: Refer to our list of recommended poets at the back of this book. Look for poems similar in length and complexity to those we've provided and apply a variety of prompts. You can try these alone, with a study group, or with your class.

Note: Look at the last sentence of Sample **B** on imagery: "Empathizing with the black youth, the narrator moves beyond her prejudices and finds promise in the last three lines which see the dark being born into the light."

This final sentence would be fine as the conclusion to the essay. A conclusion does not have to be a paragraph. It can be the writer's final remark, observation, or reference and may be only a sentence or two.

Do this now. Write the body of your essay. Time yourself. Allow 15–20 minutes to complete this task.

> Tip: Again, sharing your writing with members of your class or study group will allow you to gain experience and to find a comfort zone with requirements and possibilities.

SAMPLE STUDENT ESSAYS

Following are two actual student essays followed by a rubric and comments on each.

Student Essay A

The three sections of "On the Subway" by Sharon Olds express the complicated relationship between Caucasians and African-Americans. In the first section the author presents an exposition that contrasts a white person with a black (lines 1-13). In the second, the speaker begins to develop the apparent disparities so that inter-relationships emerge (lines 13-20). In the third, the narrator gains insight into how this scene is representative of American culture at large (lines 20-34).

The imagery Olds uses in the first section emphasizes the difference between the white woman who is the narrator and the observer and the black boy, who is the observed, as they ride the subway. The shoes he is wearing are black "laced with white" (line 3). The speaker describes the white zigzags as "intentional scars" (line 4). The scars allude to the discrimination against the black man by white society. The adjective "intentional" denotes that whites purposely harm blacks. The image contrasts whites with blacks: whites are powerful; blacks are subservient. Similarly, the two characters are described as being "stuck on opposite sides" of the subway car; they are separated permanently from each other (lines 4-5). The description of the clothing is a third contrasting element. Here, the black man is "exposed," while the speaker is covered in fur (line 11). This image reinforces the opposition between the white woman and the black boy.

The second section sees a shift in tone. Where the first section is composed of finite physical descriptions, the second is more philosophical and indicates the speaker's apprehension. She is uncertain and writes that "I don't/ know if I am in his power . . . or if he is in my power" (lines 14-15, 18). Such a statement is important because it illustrates that the boundaries between whites and blacks are not as clear-cut as they may seem. Perhaps the speaker begins to realize that the image of the subservient black and the powerful white presented in the first section of the poem is incorrect. The repetition of the word "life" is another way the interconnection between the two characters is developed. The narrator cannot decide whether her wealth usurps the power of the black man or whether his potential aggression usurps her power. (lines 17, 19). 25

The tone, again, shifts in the third segment. Here, it is clear that the speaker is trying to gain an understanding of the relationship between the white world and that of the black boy. At first, she realizes that they are different because "he is black and I am white" (lines 21-22). The image of the "black cotton" alludes to slavery, once again referring to the scars, or distinctions, imposed by the white society. Yet, at the end of this section, the differences between the two people are strangely reconciled. This is accomplished using the technique of repetition. Instead of repeating a word as in the second section, an image is repeated. Lines 29-31 state that the black man could hurt the white woman; he could "break [her] across his knee the way his own back is being broken." In other words, both whites and blacks can hurt; both races can be injured by either repression or aggression, and so they are connected through their pain and unrealized dreams. 30 35 40

Student Essay B

In the poem "On the Subway" by Sharon Olds, she contrasts the worlds of an affluent white person and a poor black person. The two people have many opposing characteristics, and the author uses literary techniques such as tone, poetic devices, and imagery to portray these differences. The narrator is the white woman, and she realizes how people get "stuck" in places of society based on their skin color. The word "stuck" is repeated twice to stress this idea. 5

The major difference between the two people is obviously their skin color. This one difference causes many aspects of each person's life to be unlike the other's. The white woman is above the black man in the eyes of much of society. The narrator states that "without meaning or trying to I must profit from his darkness." This is basically saying that the black man is living in a white man's world, where his skin color alone has given him a predisposition in the eyes of many. This idea is further supported when the speaker thinks "There is no way to know how easy this white skin makes my life." Olds uses the following simile to show the black man's situation: ". . . he absorbs the murderous beams of the nation's heart, as black cotton absorbs the heat of the sun and holds it." 10 15

Another contrast that is in the poem is the rawness of the black man versus the sheltered and refined look of the white woman. Olds uses a simile to describe the red that the black youth is wearing: "Like the inside of the body exposed." The white

woman is the outside of the animal wearing a fur coat. The black man is the inside   20
of the body, the true animal, while the white woman is not; she is simply wearing
the outer covering of an animal.

As a result of this experience, the narrator realizes that there is a balance of
power and control between her and the young man. She realizes that at times, and
in certain situations, she rules, while in others the black man does. Her life, her   25
"easier" life, can be taken away by the black youth. Who has the power on the train?
The big, strong, raw black man or the weaker, but richer, white woman? Society has
given the white woman a false sense of superiority and security. She is protected by
wealth, her job, and her possessions, but when alone on the subway with this
black man, she feels fear. She is confronted by her own vulnerability. The black   30
youth who is being broken by society can break the white woman who is society.

Overall, this poem effectively contrasts the two people and exposes a fallacy of
society. The black man must live in eternal darkness because he is never allowed
to "thrust up into any available light."

5 RATING THE STUDENT ESSAYS

*"Even though
I hate doing it,
my writing really
improves when
I spend the time
revising what
I've written."*
   -Mike T.
   –AP student

Let's take a look at a set of rubrics for the poetry essay.

A 9 essay has all the qualities of an 8 essay, and the writing style is especially <u>impressive</u>, as is the interpretation and/or discussion of the specifics related to the prompt and poem.

An 8 essay will <u>effectively</u> and <u>cohesively</u> address the prompt. It will cite appropriate devices called for in the question. And, it will do so using appropriate evidence from the poem. The essay will indicate the writer's ability to interpret the poem and/or poet's attitude toward the subject in a clear and mature style.

A 7 essay has all the properties of a 6, only with <u>more complete</u>, <u>well-developed</u> interpretation and/or discussion or a more mature writing style.

A 6 essay <u>adequately</u> addresses the prompt. The interpretation and/or discussion is on target and makes use of appropriate specifics from the test. But these elements are less fully developed than scores in the 7, 8, or 9 range. The writer's ideas are expressed with clarity, but the writing may have a few errors in syntax and/or diction.

A 5 essay demonstrates that the writer <u>understands the prompt</u>. The interpretation/discussion is generally understandable but is limited or uneven. The writer's ideas are expressed clearly with a few errors in syntax or diction.

A 4 essay is <u>not an adequate response</u> to the prompt. The writer's interpretation/discussion of the text indicates a misunderstanding, an oversimplification, or a misrepresentation of the given poem. The writer may use evidence that is not appropriate or not sufficient to support the interpretation/discussion.

A 3 essay is a lower 4 because it is <u>even less effective</u> in addressing the prompt. It is also less mature in its syntax and organization.

A **2 essay** indicates <u>little success in speaking to the prompt</u>. The writer may misread the question, only summarize the poem, never develop the required interpretation/discussion, or simply ignore the prompt and write about another topic altogether. The writing may also lack organization and control of language and syntax. (*Note*: No matter how good a summary is, it will never rate more than a 2.)

A **1 essay** is a lower 2 because it is <u>even more simplistic</u>, <u>disorganized</u>, <u>or lacking in control of language and syntax</u>.

Tip: The essay is really a first draft. The readers know this and approach each essay with this in mind.

Student Essay A

This is a high range essay (9–8) for the following reasons:

- A sophisticated, indirect indication of the task of the prompt and organization.
- Tightly constructed and thorough discussion of the contrasts and opposition in the poem.
- Effective analysis of imagery (lines 1–13, 15–17).
- Effective and coherent discussion of tone.
- Understanding of the subtleties of tone (lines 19–21).
- Strong support for assertions and interpretations (lines 22–29).
- Effective analysis of literary techniques (lines 11, 33–34, 36–38).

This high-ranking essay is subtle, concise, and on target. There is nothing that takes away from the writer's focus. Each paragraph grows out of the previous one, and the reader always knows where the author is taking him or her. The syntax, diction, and organization are mature and confident.

Student Essay B

This is a middle-range essay (7–6–5) for the following reasons:

- Clearly identifies the task, the poem, and poet.
- States the techniques that will be discussed in the essay.
- Lacks a transition to the body of the essay (lines 6–7).
- Provides an adequate discussion of the insights of the speaker (lines 23–25).
- Cites appropriate specifics to support the thesis of the essay (lines 14–16).
- Uses standard style, diction, and structure, but does not reflect a sophisticated or mature writer.
- Attempts a universal statement within a rather repetitive and summary-like conclusion (lines 31–34).

While adhering to the prompt, this midrange essay is an adequate first draft. It shows promise but comes dangerously close to paraphrasing lines.

The analysis is basic and obvious, depending on only one device, that of simile. The writer hints at the subtleties but misses the opportunity to respond to further complexities inherent in the poem.

Note: Both essays have concluding paragraphs which are repetitive and mostly unnecessary. It is best to avoid this type of ending.

How about sharing these samples with members of your class or study group and discussing possible responses.

> Tip: Try a little reverse psychology. Now that you are thoroughly familiar with this passage, construct two or three alternate AP level prompts. (Walk a little in the examiner's shoes.) This will help you gain insight into the process of test-making. Perhaps, as extra practice, you would like to try one or two of these alternative questions as enrichment.

RAPID REVIEW

Need a Quick Review? Spend a minute or two reading through . . . that'll do.

- Review terms and techniques in Chapter 8.

- Become familiar with types of poetry questions (prompts).

- Highlight the prompt to make certain you are aware of required tasks.

- Time your essay carefully.

- Read the poem a couple of times.

- Spend sufficient time "working the poem" before writing.

- Mark up the poem.

- Create a strong opening paragraph, including prompt information.

- Refer often to the poem for concrete details and quotes to support your ideas.

- Always stay on topic.

- Avoid simply paraphrasing.

- Include transitions and echo words.

- Practice—vary the prompt and your response.

- Consult the models and rubrics for self-evaluation.

- Share ideas with others.

Chapter 6

The Free-Response Essay

INTRODUCTION TO THE FREE-RESPONSE ESSAY

Nothing in life is free, but this essay does indicate that the end is near. So, hang in there. However, a cliché-clogged essay is *not* the indicator of the high-range essay. This chapter will provide the information and the practice you need to "Knock their socks off."

What is a free-response essay?

 The free-response essay is based on a provocative question that highlights specific insights applicable to a broad range of literary texts. The question provides for varied personal interpretations and multiple approaches. It allows students to truly create the specific substance of their own essay.

What is the purpose of the free-response essay?

The College Board wants to assess your ability to discuss a work of literature in a particular context. The illustrations you include in your essay will demonstrate your insights and critical thinking as well as your writing ability.

What makes this essay "free"?

Although the question is the same for all students, you have total freedom to choose the piece of literature to which you will refer. Once chosen, you have total freedom to select the specifics that will support your thesis. Unlike the other two essays, which have rubrics based on certain concrete interpretations and directions of the text, your free-response essay will be uniquely your own.

If this is total freedom of expression, how can I ever get less than a 9?

The test reader is expecting an essay that demonstrates a mature understanding and defense of the prompt. Your paper must be specific and well organized. It must also adhere to the topic. You will lose major credit for providing only plot summary. Your illustrations should be cogent and insightful rather than obvious or superficial. For a high score you must bring something specific and relevant to the page.

What are the pitfalls of the free-response essay?

It is our experience that the free-response question is a double-edged sword. Students can suffer from overconfidence because of the open nature of this essay. They depend on memory rather than on preparation and often go for the most obvious illustrations. They tend to ramble on in vague and unsupported generalities, and they frequently provide incorrect information. *The failure to plan and limit can undermine this essay.*

Students often have trouble choosing the appropriate work and lose valuable time pondering a variety of choices. It is important to be decisive and confident in your presentation.

What kinds of works may I refer to in this essay?

Generally, you are asked to choose a full-length work, almost always a novel or play. However, if the prompt says "choose a work," you may use a poem, short story, novella, or a work of nonfiction. Note: You may *never* use a film.

Must I use the list of works provided at the bottom of the prompt?

Absolutely not! Since this is a free-response essay, the choice of a literary work is up to you. You should choose a work that is appropriate to the prompt and one that is comfortable for you.

Must I use works read this year?

No, but why would you choose any work that could be a faded memory or unsuitable for AP level analysis? We always recommend using works that you studied in class and have read and discussed throughout the year. One exception occurs when you have written a literary term or research paper or a sustained critical analysis. In this situation, you may have real in-depth familiarity with a work that you could adapt to a free-response question. By all means, go for it!

How do I prepare for the free-response essay?

You need to tell yourself in September or October that you will be taking the exam next May. This will emphasize the point that throughout the year you will have to keep some type of record of the works you have read and some specific points you want to make about each of them. (In Chapter 7, we introduce several techniques and processes that will enable you to keep these records.)

By the time of the exam in May, you need to be thoroughly conversant with at least three to five full-length works from different genres, eras, and literary movements.

You also need to practice. Practice writing questions, practice choosing appropriate works, and practice writing responses to questions. Practice!

What criteria do the AP readers use to rate a free-response essay?

The readers are looking for literary insights and awareness of character, comprehension of theme, and the ability to transfer specific ideas and details to a universal concept. In addition, the readers are hoping to see a writer who reveals and understands the relationships among form, content, style, and structure and their effects on the meaning of the work. The essay should indicate the writer's ability to choose appropriate illustrations from a full-length work and to connect them in a thoughtful way. The sophisticated writer will refer to plot but not summarize. As always, the reader is looking for a well-organized essay written in a mature voice.

What happens if I use a work that the reader doesn't know?

This should not be a major concern to you. Throughout the year, your AP instructor has provided you with appropriate literary experiences suitable for addressing this prompt. In addition, be assured that any work we mention in this book will be appropriate. Be sure to consult our suggested reading list to increase your range of choices. Any other works by the same author would probably be on an appropriate AP level. For the most part, the AP prefers works from the literary canon because they exhibit breadth and complexity for literary scholarship. Don't fight these requirements. <u>You do yourself a disservice when you insist on trying to outwit or beat the system.</u>

Having said all this, if by chance you do choose an obscure work and present it well, the reader will respond accordingly.

TYPES OF FREE-RESPONSE PROMPTS

Here are some topics that could be the basis for a free-response prompt. We also include some suggested works for these.

"I really like hearing and reading how the other students do the same questions. It helps me evaluate my own ideas and essays."

–Adam S.
student

- The journey as a major force in a work. (*Gulliver's Travels, As I Lay Dying, The Stranger,* etc.)
- What happens to a dream deferred? (*Hedda Gabler, Desire Under the Elms,* etc.)
- Transformation (literal and/or figurative). (*Dr. Jekyll and Mr. Hyde, Black Like Me, Hamlet,* etc.)
- Descent into madness/hell. (*Medea, Heart of Darkness, Secret Sharer,* etc.)
- An ironic reversal in a character's beliefs or actions. (*Heart of Darkness, The Stranger, Oedipus,* etc.)
- Perception and reality—"What is, is not." (*Twelfth Night, Hamlet,* etc.)
- A child becomes a force to reveal _____. (*Jane Eyre, Huckleberry Finn, Lord of the Flies,* etc.)
- Ceremony or ritual plays an important role. (*The Stranger, Lord of the Flies, The Sun Also Rises, Suddenly Last Summer,* etc.)
- The role of the fool, comic character, or wise servant who reveals _____. (*King Lear, The Importance of Being Earnest, Tartuffe,* etc.)

Note: Fill in works you would use to respond to the above prompts.

_____

_____

_____

_____

_____

Here's another set of possible free-response prompts for development:

- How an opening scene or chapter establishes the character, conflict, or theme of a major literary work.
- How a minor character is used to develop a major character.
- How violence relates to character or theme.
- How time is a major factor.
- The ways in which an author changes the reader's attitude(s) toward a subject.
- The use of contrasting settings.
- Parent/child or sibling relationships and their significance.
- The analysis of a villain with regard to the meaning of the work.
- The use of an unrealistic character or element and its effect on the work.

- The relevance of a nonmodern work to the present day.
- The conflict between passion and responsibility.
- The conflict between character and society.

Note: To our knowledge, a free-response question has never been repeated. Therefore, we suggest:

1. Use the prompts cited above when you discuss works you read or when you write about those works throughout the year.
2. Generate a list of topics that would also be suitable for free-response prompts. Discuss, outline, or prepare sample essays utilizing these questions.

Tip: Anticipating prompts and responses is a productive way to prepare for this exam.

GENERAL RUBRICS FOR THE FREE-RESPONSE ESSAY

Let's take a look at the general rubrics for the free-response essay.

A 9 essay has all the qualities of an 8 essay, and the writing style is especially <u>impressive</u>, as is the relationship between the text and the subtext and the inclusion of supporting detail.

An 8 essay will <u>effectively</u> and <u>cohesively</u> address the prompt. It will refer to an appropriate work for the task and provide specific and relevant references from the text to illustrate and support the writer's thesis related to the journey indicated in the prompt and its relationship to character and theme. The essay will present the writer's ability to perceive the relationship between text and subtext in a clear and mature writing style.

A 7 essay has all the properties of a 6, only with <u>more well-developed</u> analysis/discussion of the relationship between development of character and how it relates to the journey or a more mature writing style.

A 6 essay <u>adequately</u> addresses the prompt. The analysis/discussion is on target and makes use of appropriate references from the chosen literary work to support the interrelationship between the character, his journey, and the work's theme. But these elements are less fully developed than they are in essays in the 7, 8, 9 range. The writer's ideas are expressed with clarity, but the writing may have a few errors in syntax and/or diction.

A 5 essay demonstrates that the writer <u>understands the prompt's requirements</u>. The analysis/discussion of the journey and how it relates to the character and the theme is generally understandable, but it is limited or uneven. The writer's ideas are expressed clearly with a few errors in syntax and/or diction.

A 4 essay is <u>not an adequate response to the prompt</u>. The writer's analysis/discussion of the journey and how it relates to character and theme indicates a misunderstanding, an oversimplification, or a misrepresentation of the chosen literary work. The writer may use evidence that is not appropriate or not sufficient to support his or her thesis.

A **3 essay** is a lower 4 because it is even <u>less effective</u> in addressing the journey and how it relates to character and theme. It is also less mature in its syntax and organization.

A **2 essay** indicates <u>little success in speaking to the prompt</u>. The writer may misread the question, choose an unacceptable literary work, only summarize the selection, never develop the required analysis, or simply ignore the prompt and write about another topic altogether. (*Note*: No matter how good a summary is, it will never rate more than a 2.)

A **1 essay** is a lower 2 because it is <u>even more simplistic,</u> <u>disorganized,</u> <u>off topic,</u> <u>and lacking in control of language.</u>

4 TIMING AND PLANNING THE FREE-RESPONSE ESSAY

This essay is the real challenge of the exam. Keep in mind that with the other two essay questions, half the job was done for you; the material was limited and provided for you. But now you are faced with the blank page that you must fill. Therefore, you *must* plan this essay carefully and completely. With this in mind, here's a workable strategy:

- 1–3 minutes working the prompt. (At this point, you might even chart the prompt.)
- 3–5 minutes choosing your work. (You should mentally run through two or three works that might be appropriate.) This is a crucial step for laying the foundation for your essay.
- 10 minutes for brainstorming, charting, mapping, outlining, and so on the specifics you plan to use in your essay. (Remember, a vague, general, unsupported essay will cost you points.)
- 20 minutes to write your essay based on your preparation.
- 3 minutes for proofreading.

WORKING THE PROMPT FROM THE DIAGNOSTIC/MASTER EXAM

Before you read the prompt, immediately cover the list of suggested works. There are several good reasons for this:

- It requires time to read the list.
- Chances are you will have read very few works on the list. If you are like many students, this could make you feel insecure and rattle your confidence.
- If you are familiar with a work or two, you may be predisposed to use the work to answer the question even if it is not necessarily your best choice. You may find yourself considering a work that you would not have considered if it were not listed, and you may find yourself taking precious time to fit that choice unsuccessfully to the prompt.

Here is the PROMPT:

Often in literature, a literal or figurative journey is a significant factor in the development of a character or the meaning of the work. Choose a full-length work and write a well-organized essay in which you discuss the literal and/or figurative nature of the journey and how it affects characterization and theme. You may choose from the list below or another full-length work of literary merit.

As I Lay Dying	*Tom Jones*
Jane Eyre	*Heart of Darkness*
The Odyssey	*Moby Dick*
Don Quixote	*The Sun Also Rises*
Candide	*The Grapes of Wrath*
A Streetcar Named Desire	*The Stranger*
A Passage to India	*Ulysses*
Gulliver's Travels	*Their Eyes Were Watching God*
No Exit	*Obasan*

Notating the Prompt

 We recommend that you chart or map the prompt. This is a simple visualization of your task. Before you look at our samples, you might want to try charting or mapping the prompt on your own.

Following is a sample chart:

Jane Eyre

	journey	effect on character	effect on theme
literal			
figurative			

Here is a sample map:

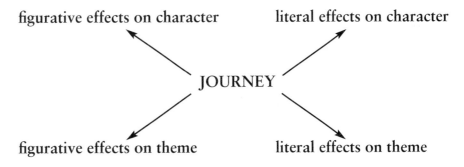

Following is a sample topic outline:

Journey

- Literal
  - character
  - theme
- Figurative
  - character
  - theme

When you provide the specifics, either mentally or by writing them down, you will ensure that you have addressed all parts of the prompt. It also will provide the basic structure of your essay.

Note: Although this may feel awkward and contrived at first, if you actually practice this technique, it will become automatic and help you to immediately get into the writing of your essay.

Now that you are familiar with the prompt, take a few moments to think about works that might be appropriate for this question. One or two will immediately pop into your mind. Mentally examine them for scenes or details that you might be able to use. *If you can't think of specifics, abandon this choice.*

If you wish, now take a look at the list of suggested works, because:

- You may find your choice there, and you will feel very validated.
- You may see a different work by the same author which may also boost your confidence.
- You might see another work or author you recognize you had not considered that could possibly spark a better response to the prompt.

This process should only take a minute or so.

Do this now. Spend 8–10 minutes working your choice to fit the requirements of the prompt. For example, prior to the exam, you will have prepared a cross section of works from various genres, time periods, and literary movements. Since these are works with depth, you will be able to take your basic scene or references and modify them to suit the task of the given prompt.

Using *Hamlet* as an example, you could have reviewed the graveyard scene prior to the exam. This scene would be appropriate to illustrate your thoughts on such varied prompts as:

- The use of humor—the gravedigger.
- The role of a minor character—Horatio.
- The concept of death as the great leveler—motif.
- Use of ritual—funeral.
- The impact of a character *not* seen in the work—Yorick.
- The use of coincidence or irony in the work—Ophelia's grave.
- The use of setting to develop theme or character—"To be or not to be."

You get the point. Obviously, you could not answer a question about the effectiveness of a work's conclusion by using this scene, which is exactly why you prepare *several* different literary examples.

Note: We know that Shakespeare is so universal that any work could be used to answer almost any free-response question. Therefore, we urge you to prepare at least one Shakespearean play as a "safe" work.

There is another reason to spend several minutes planning your essay. Frequently, your first responses and examples are the obvious and common ones. This is not to say that you could not write an adequate essay using these. But if they came to you this quickly, they probably also came to many thousands of other students taking the exam. It is usually more challenging and rewarding to find a unique focus for your essay. For example: choosing the gravedigger's scene in *Hamlet* rather than the "To be or not to be" scene may reveal a more creative thinker.

Sometimes, as you are planning, you realize that your work will answer only part of the prompt and that it would be better to switch to another work. If you have prepared well prior to the test, you will be able to do this without taking up much time. Sometimes it's better to abandon your initial choice in favor of the second and more productive one. This is why you have not yet begun to write.

DEVELOPING THE OPENING PARAGRAPH

Now you are ready to write. Remember, your opening paragraph is the one that raises the expectations of the reader and sets the tone of your essay. Spend time on your first paragraph to maximize your score.

Make certain that your topic is very clear to the reader. This reinforces the idea that you fully understand what is expected of you and what you will communicate to the reader. Generally, identify both the text and the author in this first paragraph.

Do this now. Take 5 minutes and write your opening paragraph for this prompt. Write quickly, referring to your notes.

Let's check what you've written:

Actually highlight these to see if you've done it. You may be surprised at what is actually there.

- Have you included the author and title?
- Have you addressed the literal and figurative journeys?
- Have you addressed characterization and theme?

Here are three sample opening paragraphs that address each of the above criteria.

A

"There was no possibility of taking a walk that day" says young Jane in Chapter One of Charlotte Bronte's novel, *Jane Eyre.* Little did she know that her very existence would evolve from her personal odyssey as she journeyed from Gateshead to Lowood to Thornfield and beyond;

from child to adolescent to woman. This literal and figurative journey enables Bronte to develop both the character and the theme of her work.

B

Up the hill, down the street, across the road from cafe to cafe, the characters in Ernest Hemingway's novel, *The Sun Also Rises,* wander interminably. Hemingway employs this aimless journey to reveal the lost nature of his characters and his theme of the search for meaning and direction in their post World War I existence.

C

In *Heart of Darkness* by Joseph Conrad a literal journey from England to Africa becomes a nightmare of realization and epiphany for the main character, Marlowe. Conrad develops his themes through Marlowe's observations and experiences on his figurative journey from innocence to corruption, idealism to cynicism, and optimism to despair.

Note: These three introductory paragraphs identify the author and the title and clearly indicate an understanding of the prompt. Let's note what is different about each.

Sample **A** begins with an appropriate, direct quotation. It clearly delineates the two types of journeys and their relationship to the character. The writer indicates an understanding of the difference between literal and figurative interpretation.

Sample **B** has a clear writer's voice. The writer is not afraid to be judgmental. The tone of the essay is apparent and sustained.

Sample **C** alludes to the content of the body of the essay and touches on vague generalities. However, the maturity of the vocabulary and thought indicate the writer's understanding of Conrad's complex themes and their relationship to the prompt.

Note: There are many other types of opening paragraphs that could also do the job. The paragraphs above are just a few samples. Does your opening paragraph resemble any of these samples? When you write the body of your essay, take only 15–20 minutes. Time yourself and try your best to finish within that time frame.

DEVELOPING THE BODY OF THE ESSAY

 Time to pump some mental iron and to firm up and tone those flabby ideas and turn them into examples of intellectual fitness.

What should I include in the body of the free-response essay?

 1. Obviously, this is where you present your interpretation and the points you wish to make that are related to the prompt.

2. Use specific references and details from the chosen work.

- Incorporate direct quotations when possible.
- Place quotation marks around those words or phrases taken directly from the work.

3. Use connective tissue in your essay to establish adherence to the question.

- Use the repetition of key ideas in the prompt and in your opening paragraph.
- Try using "echo words" (i.e., synonyms such as journey/wanderings/travels or figurative/symbolic/metaphoric).
- Use transitions from one paragraph to the next.

To understand the process, carefully read the following sample paragraphs. Each illustrates an aspect of the prompt. Notice the specific references and the connective tissue.

A

At Gateshead, despite its material comforts, Jane was an orphaned outcast who felt "like a discord." She was, like Cinderella, abused by her cousins and aunt and nurtured only by Bessie, a servant. Jane's immaturity and rebellious nature cause her to be jealous and vengeful which culminates in a violent confrontation with her repulsive cousin, John. Her subsequent eviction from Gateshead forces her to embark on a journey that will affect her forever. The stark privations of Lowood humble Jane and open her to the true riches of friendship with Helen Burns. It is here she learns the academic, religious, and social skills that will enable her to move on to her destiny at Thornfield.

B

Throughout the novel Jake escorts the reader on the journeys that become the only purpose the group exhibits. The trip to San Fermin for the fiesta is also a journey to hell, away from civilization and morality. The fiesta "explodes" and for seven days any behavior is acceptable, for there is no accountability during this time. No one "pays the bill," yet. Brett is worshiped as a pagan idol; garlic is strung around her neck, and men drink to her powers. She is compared to Circe, and, indeed, she turns her companions into swine as they fight over her. This trip to the fiesta reinforces the lack of spirituality and direction that is a theme of the novel.

C

Referring to the map of the Congo, Marlowe states that "the snake had charmed me." This primal description prepares us for the inevitable journey up the river that will change the very core of his character. The snake implies temptation, and Marlowe is seduced by the mysteries of Africa and his desire to meet Kurtz in the interior. He is too naive and pure to anticipate the abominations that await him at the inner station. Like a descent into hell, the journey progresses. The encounters with Fresleven, the workers without rivets, the pilgrims shooting into the jungle, all foreshadow Marlowe's changing understanding of the absurdity of life and the flawed nature of man. Only when he is totally aware of "the horror, the horror" can he journey back to "another dark place of the universe," London, to see the Intended and to corrupt his own values for her sake.

Let's examine these three body paragraphs.

Sample **A** is about *Jane Eyre*. It addresses one aspect of the prompt—Jane's character at the beginning of the journey and continues with the first major change in her life. The writer demonstrates familiarity with the novel through concrete details and quotations. Theme is implied and leads the reader to anticipate further development in the rest of the body of the essay.

Sample **B** refers to *The Sun Also Rises*. This paragraph uses a single incident to develop the discussion of the journey as it affects character and theme. The writer includes very specific details of the San Fermin fiesta to support comments about Brett and Jake. The integration of these details is presented in a cohesive, mature style.

Sample **C** delves into *Heart of Darkness*. This paragraph is a philosophical approach, which assumes the reader is familiar with the novel. It focuses on theme and how the development of the character is used to illustrate that theme. The ending of the paragraph presents an insight that invites the reader to "stay tuned."

Do this now. Write the body of your essay. Time yourself. Allow 15–20 minutes to complete this task.

Tip: Again, sharing your writing with members of your class or study group will allow you to gain experience and provide you with a comfort zone regarding requirements and possibilities.

SAMPLE STUDENT ESSAYS

Here are two actual student essays which are followed by a rubric and comments on each essay.

Student Essay A

The journey taken by Edna in Kate Chopin's The Awakening exemplifies the journey that is a very common feature in many works of literature. This journey is not a commonplace journey; it is one that brings about development and change in the story's main character. In The Awakening, the spiritual journey that Edna takes changes the way she thinks, acts, and lives. The ramifications of her journey change her life.

5

The story takes place in New Orleans around the turn of the century. The women of society were treated as possessions, either of their fathers or their husbands, or even of their religion. The story's protagonist, Edna, is introduced as the respectable wife. She is a good mother and is faithful to her husband. The family vacations for the summer in Grand Isle. While there, Edna befriends Robert who every summer devotes himself to being an attendant to one of the married women, Edna being his current choice. While there, she undergoes a series of "awakenings" which begin her journey. One such push was Edna's learning to swim. Although she was previously afraid of the water and of swimming, one day she tried, and is successful. Her newfound ability signifies the steps she is taking towards no longer being a possession. It is one of the first signs that Edna is ready to break free and to be her own person. The water gives her a sense of freedom, and she relishes this sensation.

Edna's growing love for Robert alerts her of the journey upon which she has unknowingly embarked. After Robert leaves, giving very short notice, she misses him tremendously. She realizes that she is in love with him but has no such love for her husband, Leonce. While Robert gives into her every whim, Leonce only cares about Edna as if she were his possession. He does not consider her feelings and emotions, only his own. He leaves the family often to go into the city for work, sending candy and chocolates to Edna and her children in order to compensate for his absence. He constantly neglects Edna's emotional needs, and as a result, intensifies the strength of her journey. However, Leonce is not the only person who sees Edna merely as a possession. Even Robert, who is in love with her, feels that Edna belongs to Leonce. Because he knows that she cannot be his, Robert refuses to let their relationship progress any further than it has, and the only way for him to achieve this is to go away and cut off contact with Edna.

When the family returns to their home in New Orleans, Edna is not content with her life and begins to neglect performing some of her expected activities and duties, such as entertaining the wives of her husband's clients. Edna's refusal to accompany her husband on a business trip is the pinnacle of her journey. Leonce is shocked and appalled by her noncompliance, but he feels that she is going through a phase and will soon come to her senses.

While her husband is gone, Edna's children are sent to live with their grandmother. During this time, Edna is free and independent. She meets a variety of new people who she begins to spend time with. One of these people is Alcee Arobin, who becomes her lover. This relationship is important in Edna's journey because it represents a further rift from her previous life as a possession. More and more, Edna becomes her own person. Moreover, although he tries to make her his own possession as well, Edna refuses to let Alcee have the upper hand in their relationship. She refuses to let anyone control her life ever again. She even goes so far as to close up her house and rent a much smaller place to dwell in. Edna's actions come as a shock to many people, especially her husband, but she is really just trying to assert her individuality. However, no one understands what she is going through. In fact, many people, including her husband, blame her behavior on mental illness. Edna realizes that she cannot continue to live in this manner. 50

At the novel's conclusion, Edna decides to commit suicide. She swims into the ocean and drowns herself. It is fitting that she chooses the ocean, the place where she feels she has the most freedom, to end the journey. Edna decides that she would rather not live at all than to live a life where she cannot be her own person. 55

Student Essay B

It is easy to interpret the novel, <u>Things Fall Apart</u>, as a denouncement of white colonization, or simply as a detailed portrayal of African culture. But that would be all too banal; it has already been said and done by many authors. What makes this novel distinctive is the development and depiction of Okonkwo's journey through life and how his journey effects the novel's themes. 5

Given Okonkwo's rugged personality, he encounters many conflicts on his journey to self-awareness. Okonkwo clashes with his father, his wives, his children, his village, and perhaps every other character, but his greatest struggle is with himself. It seems as if Okonkwo's enemy is his father's flaws, but in reality, Okonkwo's hidden enemy is his fear of his father's reflection upon himself. Okonkwo spends his 10 whole life on a journey away from the values of his father, so much up to the point where he ruins his life as well as the lives of those around him. His tragic flaw is his obsessive aversion to his father's laid back character. Okonkwo is so engulfed by his life's mission to become a rejection of his father's character, that he fails to see Unoka's positive traits such as tenderness, wisdom, and a passion for life, which 15 Okonkwo lacks.

Even though Okonkwo is the protagonist in this book, he is also the antagonist; clearly, he is on a trip to disaster. He has not journeyed inside himself to understand what makes him act the way he does. He is extremely rash and explosive and does not think twice about throwing a fatal punch. He foolishly thinks that his aggressive- 20 ness is the only way for a man to act; it is this misconception that ultimately ruins him. Unfortunately for Okonkwo, he never realizes his flaw, and in the end, it is as if he cannot flee his father's reflection, for just like his father, he dies with shame and disgrace.

He had the ambition; he had the intelligence; he had the passion; but he had 25 all of these for the wrong reasons. Perhaps <u>Things Fall Apart</u> portrays Okonkwo's lack of development rather than his development through time. From his early youth he forms this strong aversion to weakness and ineptitude, and this controls all his actions throughout his life. In actuality, the fact that he is totally ruled by this fear of ineptitude underscores how internally weak Okonkwo is. In the end, when he 30 realizes that there is no possible way to triumph, that he cannot control people with his violent actions, and that he cannot control his fate, what does he do? He gives up and commits the most cowardly act of suicide.

⟨5⟩ RATING THE STUDENT ESSAYS

"Peer review groups unite the class as they begin to form a writing community that is open to ideas, criticism, and revision."

—Sandi F.
-AP teacher

Let's take a look at ranking comments about each of these essays. Student Essay A is a border-line high-range essay for several reasons:

- It addresses all aspects of the prompt.
- It is highly detailed (lines 13–14, 25–26, 34–35).
- It demonstrates strong topic adherence (lines 5–6, 14–15, 20, 36–37, 50–51).
- There is strong integration of specifics to support the thesis (lines 16–17, 29–32, 42–43).
- There is perceptive character analysis (lines 33–36, 49–51).
- There is clear linear development of the essay (lines 9, 13–14, 33, 39, 48).
- The essay is frequently repetitive and needs echo words.
- There are some syntax and diction errors.

This is an example of a strong midrange essay which could make the jump into the high-range area because of its organization, use of detail, and its insights. It's obvious that the writer thoroughly understands the work and presents various specifics to support the thesis. The diction and syntax are, at times, not as mature as would be found on more sophisticated essays.

Student Essay B is a basic midrange essay for the following reasons:

- It does begin to address the basic tasks of the prompt.
- It identifies character and theme.
- It refers to the character's journeys but does not really develop any of them (paragraphs 2–3).
- There are many generalizations which need more specific support (lines 10–16, 25–27).
- The essay loses its clear connection to the prompt at times (paragraph 4).
- The diction and syntax, although adequate, lack a maturity seen in higher-level papers.

This lower, midrange essay demonstrates that the writer understands the prompt. It does contain several perceptive insights which are unevenly developed. This is obviously a first draft in need of further revision. The essay would have benefited from more thorough preparation of the work prior to the exam. As it stands, it relies too heavily on generalizations.

FINAL COMMENTS

Warning! Although the free-response essay may appear to be the easiest and most accessible on the exam, it is fraught with danger. The worst danger is relying on vague references and general statements that are not supported by specific details or lines. In addition, you have to develop the organizational pattern of the essay and control its progression. All too often the essays read like capsule summaries of the plots.

Your lifesaver in this essay situation is preparation. We say this again because it bears repeating:

- Review full-length works you've read during the year.
- Choose a minimum of five works you've connected with.
- Classify the five works to ensure a broad spectrum of types, literary movements, and themes.
- Isolate several *pivotal* scenes, moments, or episodes from each of the five works and examine the suitability of those scenes for a variety of questions.
- Isolate quotations and details from these pivotal scenes.
- If necessary, reread only the pivotal scenes before you take the exam.

RAPID REVIEW

- Remember the pitfalls of the free-response essay: vagueness and plot summary.

- Choose AP level full-length novels or plays that you thoroughly recall and understand.

- Generally use this year's material.

- Familiarize yourself with sample free-response prompts.

- Anticipate free-response prompts.

- Develop specific review materials for several full-length works.

- Practice applying your knowledge to a variety of prompts.

- Highlight the prompt to make certain you are addressing the requirements of the question.

- Do not waste time looking at the suggested works. Choose from your own memory bank.

- Plan the essay thoroughly before you begin writing.

- Briefly chart your response. Fill in with concrete details and quotes, if possible.

- Write a clear opening paragraph that reflects the question's requirements.

- Stay on topic.

- *Avoid plot summary.*

- Include transitions and echo words

- Review our models and rubrics for self-evaluation,

- Share your ideas with others.

PART III

COMPREHENSIVE REVIEW: DEVELOPING THE KNOWLEDGE, SKILLS, AND STRATEGIES

INTRODUCTION TO REVIEW SECTION

Why a review section? Why not just provide a series of practice exams?

Since the AP Lit exam is the culminating, evaluative tool for your high school English career, it would be wonderful if it could be truly representative of all that you have learned. But, it is only a 3-hour test. Therefore, it must of necessity be general, and it must be wide ranging enough to provide equity and opportunity for every student who takes the exam. What the test makers assume about the students who take the AP Lit exam is a common background of terminology and skills.

The following two chapters are not a replacement for your serious in-class study and practice. Instead, they provide a resource for terminology and skills when you need clarification or explanation. We want the information to enhance your analytical skills and to present you with direction you might not have considered.

Chapter 7

Prose Review

INTRODUCTION TO PROSE

Our desire to know ourselves and others, to explore the unknown mysteries of existence, to make sense out of chaos, and to connect with our own kind are all primary reasons for engaging in the process of literary analysis.

The benefits to self and society that result from this interaction include a sense of wonder at the glory of humanity's imagination, a sense of excitement at the prospect of intellectual challenge, and a sense of connection with the universe.

You have already engaged in these lofty experiences. This section will provide a brief review of terms and processes associated with the study of literature. Included are some suggested activities for you to try which will help you prepare for the exam.

What is prose?

As you know, prose is the written equivalent of the spoken language. It is written in words, phrases, sentences, paragraphs, and chapters. It utilizes punctuation, grammar, and vocabulary to develop its message. Prose is made up of fiction and nonfiction. For the AP Lit exam, you are required to be well read in the areas of:

- Fiction, which includes:
  - Novels
  - Short stories

- Nonfiction writing, which includes:
  - Essays
  - Autobiographies
  - Speeches
  - Journals
  - Articles

Note: A brief word about drama. Since this section is a review of prose designed to prepare you for the AP Lit exam, it is not feasible to address every literary distinction and definition. Therefore, we wish to stress the following:

- Specific terminology can be found in the glossary at the back of this book.
- All the techniques examined for prose can be used to analyze drama as well.
- The overlapping nature of the analytical skills makes them suitable for prose, poetry, and drama.

FIVE ASPECTS OF EVERY NARRATIVE

There is a certain degree of universality regarding definitions of terms when analyzing literature. For clarity and understanding you should be aware of the following terms.

Plot

The plot is a series of episodes in a *narrative* carried out by the *characters*. Here are the primary terms related to plot. You should be familiar with all of them. Obviously each work manipulates these concepts in its own unique way.

- *Initial Incident*: the event that puts the story in gear.
- *Rising action*: the series of complications in the narrative.
- The *climax*: the highest point of interest, action, or tension. More subtly, it is a turning point in the protagonist's behavior or thoughts.
- *Falling action*: the series of events occurring after the climax.
- *Denouement*: the resolution that ties up the loose ends of the plot.

These form the skeleton of a discussion about plot. But there are also other elements that add to your comprehension.

- *Foreshadowing*: hints at future events.
- *Flashbacks*: cut or piece a prior scene into the present situation.
- *In medias res*: literally, to be in the middle. This is a device that places the reader immediately into the action.

- *Subplot*: secondary plot that explores ideas which are different from the main story line.
- *Parallel plot*: a secondary story line that mimics the main plot.

Setting

Traditionally, setting is the time and place of a work, but it is also so much more. Setting is not accidental. It is a vital part of the narrative, and it can serve many functions. You should consider setting in light of the following:

- *General*: to underscore the universality of the work ("The Open Boat")
- *Specific*: to create a definitive ambiance that impacts on the work's possibilities (*Gone with the Wind*)
- *Character or foil*: in relation to the protagonist (*The Perfect Storm*)
- *Limiting factor*: to allow the plot, character, and theme to develop (*Lord of the Flies*)
- To *reveal style* (*The Secret Sharer*)
- To *reveal character* (*Hedda Gabler*)
- To *reveal theme* (*Heart of Darkness*)

Character

Character development can be both simple and complex. The author has a variety of methods from which to choose. Here's a mnemonic device that may help you analyze character: Use the word *STAR*. S—what the character *says*; T—what the character *thinks*; A—how the character *acts* and interacts and; R—how the character *reacts*.

Traditionally, characters carry out the plot and it is around the characters that the plot revolves and the theme is developed. There can be many types of characters in a given work:

- *Protagonist*: the main character who is the central focus of the story. For example, Hamlet is the eponymous protagonist.
- *Antagonist*: the opposing force. It does not always have to be a person. For example, the sea or the fish in *The Old Man and the Sea*.
- *Major*: the character or characters who play a significant role in the work.
- *Minor*: the characters who are utilized for a specific purpose, such as moving the plot along or contrasting with a major character.
- *Dynamic*: refers to characters who undergo major changes, such as Jane Eyre.
- *Static*: generally refers to characters who remain the same throughout the story. For instance, Brutus in *Julius Caesar* always considers himself to be an "honorable man."
- *Stereotype*: a character who is used to represent a class or a group.

- *Foil*: a character who provides the opportunity for comparison and contrast. For example, in Shakespeare's *Julius Caesar*, Brutus and Cassius are foils for each other.

CHARACTER AS HERO

Once again, you may encounter many variations on the concept of hero:

- Aristotelian tragic hero:

  - Of noble birth; larger than life
  - Basically good
  - Exhibits a fatal flaw
  - Makes error in judgment
  - Possesses hubris (excessive arrogance or pride) which causes the error in judgment
  - Brings about his own downfall
  - Has a moment of realization, an epiphany
  - Lives and suffers
  - Examples: Creon in *Antigone*, Oedipus in *Oedipus*, Jason in *Medea*

- Classical hero: a variation on the tragic hero:

  - Examples: Macbeth in *Macbeth*, Lear in *King Lear*, Hamlet in *Hamlet*

- Romantic hero:

  - Larger than life
  - Charismatic
  - Possesses an air of mystery
  - "Saves the day" or the heroine
  - Embodies freedom, adventure, and idealism
  - Often outside the law
  - Examples: Robin Hood, Ivanhoe, James Bond, Mr. Rochester in *Jane Eyre*

- Modern hero:

  - May be everyman
  - Has human weaknesses
  - Caught in the ironies of the human condition
  - Struggles for insight
  - Examples: Willy Loman in *Death of a Salesman,* Tom Joad in *Grapes of Wrath*

- Hemingway hero:

  - Brave
  - Endures
  - Maintains a sense of humor
  - Exhibits grace under pressure
  - Examples: Santiago in *The Old Man and the Sea,* Jake Barnes in *The Sun Also Rises,* Butch and Sundance in *Butch Cassidy and the Sundance Kid*

- Antihero: Protagonist is notably lacking in heroic qualities:

  - Examples: Meursault in *The Stranger,* Randall McMurphy in *One Flew Over the Cuckoo's Nest,* Homer Simpson of cartoon fame

Theme

Theme is the main idea, the moving force, what it's all about, the "why" behind the "what," the universal concept or comment, the big picture, the major insight, the raison d'etre. But theme is much more than a simple checklist. And, we cringe each time we hear, "What is the theme?" Remember, the enlightened, complex mind questions, ponders, responds. A literary work evolves and can be validly interpreted in so many ways that it would be a disservice to limit it to any single, exclusive theme.

Keeping an open mind, understand that the following is an overview of ways of assessing themes. All elements of a literary work point toward the development of the theme. Therefore, you will apply all that you have been learning and practicing in your search for a discernible, supportable theme.

Motif   In its most general sense, motif is the repetition of an image. It may be closely connected to symbol, or it may be a thematic restatement.

The following is a preparation process for discovering and analyzing the function of motif. You can try this with any work.

- Isolate some general motifs you've noticed in a work.
- Provide specific examples to illustrate the motif.
- Draw inferences from your observations.

These rough inferences may lead you to a better understanding of character and theme. The following is a sample worksheet that uses the above process to analyze motif in Tennessee Williams's *A Streetcar Named Desire.*

Motif in *A Streetcar Named Desire*

Motif	Example	Thematic Implications
Color	White woods (Blanche DuBois)	Red/white/blue = American theme
	Blue piano	Blue/grey—Civil War?
	Red pajamas—Stanley	Rape of Old South?
	Allan Grey	Destruction of a way of life
Music	The blues	Loss/sorrow
	"Only a Paper Moon" (if you believed in me)	betrayal
		Lack of reality—insanity
	Captive maiden	Control/Slavery

(continued)

Motif in *A Streetcar Named Desire* (*continued*)

Motif	Example	Thematic Implications
Animals	Blanche: fine feathered/wild cat trapped bird/tiger moth to light	ego/id duality self-destruction
	Stanley: rooster/pig ape goat/Capricorn	survival of the fittest Darwinism/primitivism Dionysian—rape

Here's another way to work through an idea about theme. Sometimes it's easier to input a theme and then prove it with support from a work. If you can defend an idea with several specifics, you probably have identified a theme. Let's look at Shakespeare's *Hamlet*:

Hamlet

Possible Theme	Evidence
What is, is not	1. Hamlet is not mad, only north-northwest. 2. Polonius is not Claudius in Gertrude's chamber. 3. Ophelia is not disinterested in Hamlet's overtures. 4. Rosencrantz and Guildenstern are not Hamlet's "friends."
Vengeance	1. Old Hamlet's charge to Hamlet to redress his murder. 2. Laertes's vow to avenge his father's death. 3. Fortinbras's victory to avenge his father.

Obviously, we have provided the organization in our samples, but these two techniques are solid, reliable processes. They will work on the exam, too, especially as you interrelate ideas for your essays or identify points that may be the topic of multiple-choice questions.

Tip: Keep a section in your notes where you enter important motifs and their implications from works you study. These concrete details will be invaluable when you write the free-response essay. Keep in mind that motif, imagery, symbol, and theme build on one another and are interrelated.

Point of View

Point of view is the method the author utilizes to tell the story. It is the vantage point from which the narrative is told. You've had practice with this in both reading and writing.

- *First person*: The narrator is the story's protagonist. (I went to the store.)
- *Third-person objective*: The narrator is an onlooker reporting the story. (She went to the store.)
- *Third-person omniscient*: The narrator reports the story and provides information unknown to the character(s). (She went to the store unaware that in 3 minutes she would meet her long-lost mother selling apples on the corner.)
- *Stream of consciousness*: This is a narrative technique that places the reader in the mind and thought processes of the narrator, no matter how random and spontaneous that may be (e.g., James Joyce's *Ulysses*).
- *Chorus*: Ancient Greek plays employed a chorus as a narrative device. The chorus, as needed, could be a character, an assembly, the playwright's voice, the audience, an omniscient forecaster.
- *Stage manager*: This technique utilizes a character who comments omnisciently (e.g., *Our Town*, *The Glass Menagerie*).
- *Interior monologue*: This technique reflects the inner thoughts of the character.

Note: In modern literature, authors often use multiple forms of narration. For example, in *As I Lay Dying* by William Faulkner every chapter has a different narrator.

TYPES OF NOVELS

There are many types of novels you will encounter during your study of English literature. Some novels exhibit several qualities. A few of the most common genres are:

- *Epistolary*: These novels utilize the convention of letter writing and are among the earliest novel forms (e.g., *Pamela*, *Dracula*, *The Color Purple*).
- *Picaresque*: This early, episodic novel form concentrates on the misadventures of a young rogue (e.g., *Huckleberry Finn*, *Don Quixote*, *Tom Jones*, *Candide*).
- *Autobiographical*: This readily identifiable type is always told in the first person and allows the reader to directly interact with the protagonist (e.g., *David Copperfield*, *Catcher in the Rye*).
- *Gothic*: This type of novel is concerned with the macabre, supernatural, and exotic (e.g., *Frankenstein*, *Interview with a Vampire*, *Dr. Jekyll and Mr. Hyde*).

- *Historical*: This form is grounded in a real context and relies heavily on setting and factual detail (e.g., *A Tale of Two Cities, War and Peace*).
- *Romantic*: This novel form is idealistic, imaginative, and adventuresome. The romantic hero is the cornerstone of the novel, which often includes exotic locales (e.g., *Wuthering Heights, Madame Bovary*).
- *Allegorical*: This type of novel is representative and symbolic. It operates on at least two levels. Its specifics correspond to another concept (e.g., *Animal Farm, Lord of the Flies*).

✓   Consider this. *Jane Eyre* has elements of all these types as do many other novels. List and loosely categorize some of the major novels you've read.

_____

_____

_____

_____

_____

LITERARY TERMINOLOGY

Literary analysis assumes the working knowledge of a common vocabulary.

The Kaleidoscope of Literary Meaning

Literary meaning is developed and revealed through various devices and techniques. What follows is a brief listing of those terms and devices most often used in prose, poetry, and drama.

- *Allusion*: An allusion is a reference to another work, concept, or situation which generally enhances the meaning of the work that is citing it. There are many types of allusions, and they may be implicit or explicit, highly limited, or broadly developed. Often, modern readers may miss the context of a particular reference because they have a limited frame of reference. A few common categories of allusion follow:
  - *Mythological allusions*: These often cite specific characters. Common allusions might refer to the beauty of Aphrodite or the power of Zeus. "She followed like Niobe, all tears" (*Hamlet*). Sometimes the entire work may refer to a mythological event. The play *Desire Under the Elms* is a sustained allusion to the Phaedra legend.
  - *Biblical allusions*: These references may deal with circumstances as familiar as "the mark of Cain," "the fall from paradise," "the tribulations of Job," or "destruction by flood or fire." A character may have the "strength of Samson" or the "loyalty of Ruth."

- *Historical allusions*: These kinds of allusions might refer to major historical events, such as Napoleon meeting his Waterloo or Nixon dealing with Watergate.
- *Literary allusions*: Often works will refer to other well-known pieces. For example, *West Side Story* expects you to think of *Romeo and Juliet*. To describe a character as "quixotic" refers to Cervantes's great novel *Don Quixote*.
- *Political allusions*: These references would be sustained in works like *Gulliver's Travels* or *Alice in Wonderland*. They might also be used briefly. If a character were called the next Julius Caesar, we might sense that he would be betrayed in some manner. *The Crucible* is a historical allusion to the Salem witch trials and is also a statement about McCarthyism in the 1950s.
- *Contemporary allusions*: These are often lost when the current context is no longer in the public eye. For example, "valley girls" or "Beavis and Butthead" may not remain in vogue, and, therefore, references to them would lose their effectiveness.

- <u>Ambiguity</u>: This is the seemingly incongruous and contradictory interpretations of meaning in a work. James Joyce and William Faulkner utilize ambiguity often in their writing.
- <u>Allegory</u>: A work that operates on another level. The characters and events may be interpreted for both literal and symbolic meaning. For example, *Of Mice and Men* by Steinbeck is an indictment of the exploitation of the masses and a call to unionism as well as a story of doomed friendship. Other allegorical works include *The Old Man and the Sea* by Hemingway, "Shooting an Elephant" by Orwell, *Candide* by Voltaire, and *Pilgrim's Progress* by John Bunyan.
- <u>Parable</u>: A parable is an allegorical story that is intended to teach. It generally provides a moral lesson or illustrates a guiding principle. "The Nun's Tale" in *The Canterbury Tales* by Chaucer is a parable about vanity and pride.
- <u>Symbol</u>: This is an image that also represents something else. Some symbols appear to be extremely specific. In Hawthorne's *The Scarlet Letter* the scarlet letter is a symbol of Hester's impropriety. It can also represent Hester's pride, talent, responsibility, and shame. The reader should always be open to the broadest interpretation of the concept of symbol, whether about character, setting, situation, detail, or whatever. Another example of symbol is the splitting of the chestnut tree in *Jane Eyre*. Here Bronte symbolizes the breach in the relationship between Jane and Rochester. The white hat in *The Secret Sharer* by Conrad is a symbol of man's compassion and pity for his own kind.
- <u>Connotation</u>: This is the implication that is suggested by a word or phrase rather than the word or phrase's actual, literal meaning. For example, the use of "antique land" instead of "ancient land" brings a richer connotation to Shelley's "Ozymandias." The reader must be especially open to the varied levels of meaning in poetry.
- <u>Denotation</u>: The literal meaning of a word or phrase. If a reader is attempting to present a valid interpretation of a literary work, he or

she must pay attention to both the denotation and the connotation of the language.

- _Tone_: Tone is difficult to define but is relatively easy to assess. It is a subtle feeling that the author creates through diction. The following words are often used to describe tone. Notice that they are adjectives.

bitter	objective	idyllic
sardonic	naive	compassionate
sarcastic	joyous	reverent
ironic	spiritual	lugubrious
mocking	wistful	elegiac
scornful	nostalgic	gothic
satiric	humorous	macabre
vituperative	mock-serious	reflective
scathing	pedantic	maudlin
confidential	didactic	sentimental
factual	inspiring	patriotic
informal	remorseful	jingoistic
facetious	disdainful	detached
critical	laudatory	

- _Transition_: Do not be fooled into thinking that "transition" is an unimportant term. An author will give you a road map through his or her story's journey, and one of the best indicators of direction is the transition word or phrase. Transitions help to move the reader smoothly from one part of the text to another. Below is a list of the most effective commonly used transitions:

and	also	as a result	after
but	besides	for example	although
for	consequently	in addition	because
nor	furthermore	in the same way	once
or	however	on the contrary	since
so	likewise	on the other hand	until
yet	moreover	otherwise	unless
	nonetheless	unlike the former	while
	similarly		
	still		
	therefore		

PROSE ANALYSIS

A word about this section: There are many processes that will help you to understand prose, poetry, and drama.

These approaches may not all be suitable for every work, but they certainly are worth considering as methods for responding to subtleties that are in the work.

Name Analysis

Consider your name. Did your folks have a specific reason for choosing it? Does it have a family significance or a special cultural meaning? What would you choose for your name and why? Remember, names and identity are closely linked.

Authors often choose names that bring another dimension to a character or place. A good reader is sensitive to the implications of names. Here are a few interesting names and observations about each:

- Oedipus—swollen foot, seeker of truth
- Billy Budd—simple, melodic, young growth, ready to bloom
- Jane Eyre—Janus/beginning, air, err, heir, ere, eerie, ire
- Helen Burns—fever, fervor, mythological inspiration
- Mr. Mason—the Masons are a secret fraternity; he holds the secret
- Stella—star, light
- Kurtz—short, curt
- Willy Loman—low man

It's an Open and Closed Case

The first thing that catches your attention should be the title. By all means, consider it carefully. *David Copperfield* lets you know it will be a novel about character. *As I Lay Dying* involves plot and theme. *One Flew Over the Cuckoo's Nest* involves you immediately in symbol, character, and theme.

Authors place special emphasis on the first and last impressions they make on a reader. Their opening and closing lines of chapters or scenes are, therefore, usually very significant and should be closely examined. (This is much like an establishing shot in a movie that sets up the audience for future developments.)

Here's the opening line from Chapter 1 of *Jane Eyre*:

There was no possibility of taking a walk that day.

Here are some implications of this one line: no independence, locked in, no sense of curiosity, outside force preventing a journey, not ready to leave. Obviously, the character is not ready to experience the outside world or to embark on her journey.

Contrast that with the last line of Chapter 1:

Four hands were laid upon me and I was borne upstairs.

This line introduces a spiritual level to the novel. It also implies that a new Jane will emerge, and indeed she does.

Take a look at the last line of the novel:

We wended our way into the wood.

This lovely, alliterative line completes the journey. Jane and Edward have come full circle as they stroll their way together.

In a Shakespearean play, often a couplet at the end of a scene of act will neatly summarize or foreshadow events. For example:

> *And after this, let Caesar seat him sure*
> *For we will shake him, or worse days endure* (Julius Caesar)

Levels of Interpretation

Complex works of literature afford many avenues of interpretation. After you read a work, consider the following areas of exploration. We use Ibsen's *Hedda Gabler* as a model.

- *Literal level*: A young woman is frustrated in her life and eventually commits suicide.
- *Social level*: Ibsen explores the role of women in society and presents the despair connected with a male-dominated existence.
- *Psychological level*: The play traces a descent into madness and the motivations for aberrant human behavior.
- *Religious level*: The loss of a soul to temptation, the encounter with the devil, and the inspiration of godliness are all in the play.
- *Sexual level*: Gender issues, the Electra complex, phallic symbols, abortion, and homosexuality are all developed and explored through numerous love triangles.
- *Political level*: The play could be read as a treatise on socialism. It denigrates capitalism and pays homage to the ideas of Marx's *Communist Manifesto*. Obviously, you need to supply the evidence from the works to develop your interpretations in a concrete manner.

Practice looking beyond the literal presentation of the plays and novels you read. The following are richly suitable for such study:

Desire Under the Elms	Eugene O'Neill
Heart of Darkness	Joseph Conrad
Dubliners	James Joyce
The Grapes of Wrath	John Steinbeck
Les Miserables	Victor Hugo

FINAL COMMENTS

One of the most rewarding forms of preparation you can do involves developing a sensitivity to the words of a piece of literature.

Get a journal or set aside a section of your notebook for recording lines you respond to for their beauty, appeal, meaning, or relevance. For each work you read:

- Enter the lines.
- Identify the speaker and situation.

- Interpret, connect, comment, or reflect on your choice.
- Free-associate as well as relate the quotation to the original text.
- Make connections to other works you read.
- Project and expand on the lines

For each full-length work, record at least ten references. Write these quotations out and include the page numbers so you can easily find them if you need to. Try to take them from throughout the work. Here is what is going to happen. Soon, you will automatically identify and respond to significant lines and passages. It will become second nature for you to identify lines of import and meaning in a work as you read. You will also begin to remember lines from a work and to connect them to important details, episodes, and themes. You will be able to understand and analyze a character in light of his or her own language. In other words, you will be interpreting literature based on text.

RAPID REVIEW

- Every narrative is composed of plot, setting, character, theme, and point of view.

- Motifs develop characters and themes.

- Themes require specific illustrations to support them.

- There are many types of characters and heroes.

- There are many forms of narration.

- Novels may exhibit many characteristics.

- Meaning may be revealed via multiple approaches.

- Parables and allegories operate on symbolic levels. Connotations of words reveal the subtext of a work.

- Tone is a description of the attitude found in a piece of literature.

- Transitions aid movement and unity in a written work.

- Titles and names are important areas for analysis.

- First and last lines often carry great meaning in a work and demand careful attention.

- Works may be interpreted literally, socially, psychologically, sexually, politically, and so on.

- Quotations from works are an accurate way of understanding meaning and characterization. They also provide support for your interpretations.

Chapter 8

Poetry Review

INTRODUCTION TO POETRY

Poetry—the very word inspires fear and trembling, and well it should because it deals with the intensity of human emotion and the experiences of life itself. But there is no reason to fear that which elevates, elucidates, edifies, and inspires. Poetry is a gift of language, like speech and song, and with familiarity comes pleasure and knowledge and comfort.

However, it may still be intimidating to read poetry. After all, we've been speaking and reading prose our entire lives. This review assumes that by the time you reach an AP level literature course, you have some experience and facility with poetry. We provide you with definitions, examples, and practice with interpretation. Hopefully, you will provide the interest, diligence, and critical thinking necessary for a joyful and meaningful experience.

Remember our philosophy of firsts? First, we believe that you should read as much poetry as possible. Early in the year, pick up an anthology of poetry and read, read, read. Open to any page and read for pleasure and interest. Don't try to "study" the poems; just respond to them on an emotional level. Consider the following:

- Identify subjects that move you or engage you.
- Are there certain themes you respond to? Are there certain poets you like? List them and read more poetry by them.
- Are there certain types or styles of poems you enjoy? What do they seem to have in common?
- Are there images or lines you love? Keep a record of some of your favorites.

Make this a time to develop a personal taste for poetry. Use this random approach to experience a broad range of form and content. You should find that you are more comfortable with poetry simply because you have been discovering it at your own pace.

When you are comfortable and have honestly tried reading it for pleasure, it is time to approach it on a more analytical level.

THE STRUCTURE OF POETRY

What makes poetry different from prose?

 How do you know when you're working with poetry and not prose? Simple. Just look at it. It's shorter; it's condensed; it's written in a different physical form. The following might help you to visualize the basic differences:

Prose	Poetry
Words	Syllables
Phrases	Feet
Sentences	Lines
Paragraphs	Stanzas
Chapters	Cantos

It should not be news to you when we say that poetry sounds different from prose. It is more musical, and it often relies on sound to convey meaning. In addition, it can employ meter which provides rhythm. Did you know that poetry is from the ancient oral tradition of storytelling and song? Rhyme and meter made it easier for the bards to remember the story line. Try to imagine Homer in a dimly lit hall chanting the story of Odysseus.

As with prose, poetry also has its own jargon. Some of this lingo is specifically related to form and meter.

The Foot

The *foot* is the basic building block of poetry. It is composed of a pattern of syllables. These patterns create the meter of a poem. *Meter* is a pattern of beats or accents. We figure this pattern out by counting the stressed and unstressed syllables in a line. Unstressed syllables are indicated with a ˘ and stressed syllables are indicated with a ´.

There are five common patterns that are used repeatedly in poetry. They are:

- The iamb ˘ ´ (tŏ dáy) (bĕ cáuse)
- The trochee ´ ˘ (háp py̆) (líght ly̆)

- The anapest ‿ ‿ ´ (ŏb vĭ oús) (rĕ gŭ lár)
- The dactyl ´ ‿ ‿ (cíg ă rĕtte) (ín tĕr rŭpt)
- The spondee ´ ´ (dówn tówn) (slíp shód)

The Line

Unlike the prose sentence which is determined by subject, verb, and punctuation, the poetic line is measured by the number of feet it contains.

- 1 foot   monometer
- 2 feet   dimeter
- 3 feet   trimeter
- 4 feet   tetrameter
- 5 feet   pentameter
- 6 feet   hexameter
- 7 feet   heptameter
- 8 feet   octameter
- 9 feet   nonometer

Now answer the following. How many stressed syllables are in a line of:

Iambic pentameter   _____
Dactylic trimeter   _____
Anapestic dimeter   _____
Spondaic monometer   _____
Trochaic tetrameter   _____

Note: Answers can be found at the end of the definition of "meter" in the glossary of terms.

The Stanza

You should now understand that syllables form feet, feet form lines, and lines form stanzas. Stanzas also have names:

- 1 line   a line
- 2 lines   couplet
- 3 lines   tercet
- 4 lines   quatrain
- 5 lines   cinquain
- 6 lines   sestet
- 7 lines   septet
- 8 lines   octave

What is the total number that results from adding up all of the metric references in the following, make-believe poem?

- The poem is composed of 3 quatrains, 2 couplets and 1 sestet.
- Each quatrain is written in iambic tetrameter.
- The couplets are dactylic dimeter.
- The sestet is trochaic trimeter.

The total number is _____.

Note: You can find the answer at the end of the definition of "rhythm" in the glossary of terms.

You will never have to be this technical on the AP exam. However, you will probably find a question on meter, and technical terms may be included in the answers to the multiple-choice questions. In addition, sometimes in the poetry essay you may find opportunity to use your knowledge of scansion, or your analysis of the rhyme and meter of the poem, to develop your essay. This can be very effective if it is linked to interpretation.

Rhyme

One of the first processes you should become familiar with concerns the identification of a poem's rhyme scheme. This is easily accomplished by assigning consecutive letters of the alphabet to each new sound at the end of a line of poetry.

- A for the first
- B for the second
- C for the third
- D, E, and so forth

Try this with the opening stanza from "Peace" by George Herbert.

Sweet Peace, where dost thou dwell? I humbly crave,
*   Let me once know.*
I sought thee in a secret cave,
*   And asked if Peace were there.*
A hollow wind did seem to answer, "No,
*   Go seek elsewhere."*

You may restart the scheme with each new stanza or continue throughout the poem. Remember, the purpose is to identify and establish a pattern and to consider if the pattern helps to develop sound and/or meaning. Here's what the rhyme scheme looks like for the above selection: A B A C B C.

When you analyze the pattern, you can conclude that there is a very regular structure to this poem which is consistent throughout. Perhaps the content will also reflect a regular development. Certainly the rhyme enhances the sound of the poem and helps it flow. From now on we will refer to rhyme scheme when we encounter a new poem.

The rhymes we have illustrated are called *end rhymes* and are the most common. *Masculine rhyme* is the most frequently used end rhyme.

It occurs when the last stressed syllable of the rhyming words match exactly. ("The play's the thing/Wherein I'll catch the conscience of the king.") However, there are *internal rhymes* as well. These rhymes occur within the line and add to the music of the poem. An example of this is Poe's "The Raven." *Feminine rhyme* involves two consecutive syllables of the rhyming words, with the first syllable stressed. (The horses were prancing/ as the clowns were dancing.)

TYPES OF POETRY

Because of its personal nature poetry has evolved into many different forms, each with its own unique purpose and components. What follows is an examination of the most often encountered forms.

The Ballad

The ballad is one of the earliest poetic forms. It is a narrative which was originally spoken or sung and has often changed over time. It usually:

- Is simple.
- Employs dialogue, repetition, minor characterization.
- Is written in quatrains.
- Has a basic rhyme scheme, primarily A B C B.
- Has a refrain which adds to its songlike quality.
- Is composed of two lines of iambic tetrameter which alternates with two lines of iambic trimeter.

The subject matter of ballads varies considerably. Frequently, ballads deal with the events in the life of a folk hero, like Robin Hood. Sometimes they retell historical events. The supernatural, disasters, good and evil, love and loss are all topics found in traditional ballads.

The following is a typical folk ballad. Read this poem out loud. Listen to the music as you read. Get involved in the story. Imagine the scene. Try to capture the dialect or sound of the Scottish burr.

Bonny Barbara Allan
by Anonymous

It was in and about the Martinmas time,
  When the green leaves were falling,
That Sir John Graeme, in the West Country,
  Fell in love with Barbara Allan.

He sent his man down through the town,   5
  To the place where she was dwelling:
"O haste and come to my master dear,
  Gin ye be Barbara Allan."

O hooly, hooly rose she up,
  To the place where he was lying,   10
And when she drew the curtain by:
  "Young man I think you're dying."

"O it's I'm sick, and very, very sick,
  And 'tis a' for Barbara Allan."
O the better for me ye's never be,   15
  Though your heart's blood were a-spilling.

"O dinna ye mind, young man," said she,
  When ye was in the tavern a drinking,
That ye made the healths gae round and round,
  And slighted Barbara Allan?"   20

He turned his face unto the wall,
  And death was with him dealing:
"Adieu, adieu, my dear friends all,
  And be kind to Barbara Allan."

And slowly, slowly raise she up,   25
  And slowly, slowly left him,

And sighing said, she could not stay,
  Since death of life had reft him.

She had not gane a mile or twa,
  When she heard the dead-bell ringing,   30
And every jow that the dead bell geid,
  It cried, "Woe to Barbara Allan."

"O mother, mother, make my bed!
  O make it saft and narrow!
Since my love died for me to-day,   35
  "I'll die for him to-morrow."

After you've read the ballad, consider the following:

1. Check the rhyme scheme and stanza form. You should notice it is written in quatrains. The rhyme scheme is a little tricky here; it depends on pronunciation and is what is called a forced rhyme. If you soften the "g" sound in the word "falling," it more closely rhymes with "Allan." Try this throughout the ballad, recognizing that the spoken word can be altered and stretched to fit the intention of rhyme. If you do this, you should find each stanza is ABCB. This falls under the category of "poetic license."
2. Follow the plot of the narrative. Poor Barbara Allan, poor Sir John. They are a classic example of thwarted young lovers, a literary pattern as old as Antigone and Haemon or Romeo and Juliet. Love, unrequited love, and dying for love are all universal themes in literature.
3. Observe the use of repetition and how it unifies the poem by sound and structure. "Barbara Allan/Hooly, hooly/Adieu, adieu/Slowly, slowly/Mother, mother"
4. Notice that dialogue is incorporated into the poem for characterization and plot development.

> Tip: Don't be too inflexible when checking rhyme or meter.
> Remember, never sacrifice meaning for form. You're smart; you can
> make intellectual leaps.

Here are some wonderfully wicked and enjoyable ballads to read:

"Sir Patrick Spens"—the tragic end of a loyal sailor
"The Twa Corbies"—the irony of life and nature
"Edward"—a wicked, wicked, bloody tale
"Robin Hood"—still a great, grand adventure
"Lord Randall"—sex, lies, and death in ancient England
"Get Up and Bar the Door"—a humorous battle of the sexes
"La Belle Dame Sans Merci"—John Keats's fabulous tale of a
  demon lover

2 Have you read ballads? Traditional or modern? List them here. Jot down a few details or lines to remind you of important points. If you're musical, try singing one out loud.

_____

_____

_____

_____

_____

Remember that most poetry falls into one of two major categories. One is the narrative poem which tells a story. The second is the lyric poem which presents a personal impression.

The Lyric

Lyric poetry is highly personal and emotional. It can be as simple as a sensory impression or as elevated as an ode or elegy. Subjective and melodious, it is often reflective in tone.

The following is an example of a lyric:

A Red, Red Rose
by Robert Burns

O my luve's like a red, red rose,
That's newly sprung in June;
O my luve's like the melodie
That's sweetly played in tune.

As fair art thou, my bonnie lass,   5
So deep in luve am I;
And I will luve thee still, my dear,
Till a' the seas gang dry.

Till a' the seas gang dry, my dear,
And the rocks melt wi' the sun: 10
O I will luve thee still, my dear,
While the sands o' life shall run.

And fare the weel, my only luve,
And fare the weel awhile!
And I will come again, my luve,   15
Though it were ten thousand mile.

Now answer the following questions:

1. The stanza form is _____
2. The rhyme scheme is _____
3. The meter of line 6 is _____
4. The first stanza depends on similes. Find them. _____
5. Find assonance in stanza one. _____
6. Line 8 is an example of _____
7. Find alliteration in the poem _____
8. Did you recognize iambic trimeter? How about hyperbole? _____

The following are wonderful lyric poems. Try some.

> Edna St. Vincent Millay—"Childhood Is the Kingdom Where
>   Nobody Dies"
> Emily Dickinson—"Wild Nights, Wild Nights"
> Dylan Thomas—"Fern Hill"
> Matthew Arnold—"Dover Beach"
> Andrew Marvell—"To His Coy Mistress"

The Ode

The ode is a lyric poem that addresses subjects of elevated stature. One of the most beautiful odes in English literature is by Percy Bysshe Shelley.

Ode to the West Wind

O wild West Wind, thou breath of Autumn's being,
Thou, from whose unseen presence the leaves dead
Are driven, like ghosts from an enchanter fleeing,

Yellow, and black, and pale, and hectic red,
Pestilence-stricken multitudes: O thou,   5
Who chariotest to their dark wintry bed

The wingéd seeds, where they lie cold and low,
Each like a corpse within the grave, until
Thine azure sister of the Spring shall blow

Her clarion* o'er the dreaming earth, and fill   10
(Driving sweet buds like flocks to feed in air)
With living hues and odors plain and hill:

Wild Spirit, which art moving everywhere;
Destroyer and preserver; hear, oh, hear!

                    2

Thou on whose stream, mid the steep sky's commotion,   15
Loose clouds like earth's decaying leaves are shed,
Shook from the tangled boughs of Heaven and Ocean,

Angels of rain and lightning: there are spread
On the blue surface of thine aery surge,
Like the bright hair uplifted from the head   20

Of some fierce Maenad,† even from the dim verge
Of the horizon to the zenith's height,
The locks of the approaching storm. Thou dirge

*Melodious trumpet call
†Frenzied dancer

Of the dying year, to which this closing night
Will be the dome of a vast sepulcher,   25
Vaulted with all thy congregated might

Of vapors, from whose solid atmosphere
Black rain, and fire, and hail will burst: oh, hear!

3

Thou who didst waken from his summer dreams
The blue Mediterranean, where he lay,   30
Lulled by the coil of his crystalline streams

Beside a pumice isle in Baiae's * bay,
And saw in sleep old palaces and towers
Quivering within the wave's intenser day,

All overgrown with azure moss and flowers   35
So sweet, the sense faints picturing them! Thou
For whose path the Atlantic's level powers

Cleave themselves into chasms, while far below
The sea-blooms and the oozy woods which wear
The sapless foliage of the ocean, know   40

They voice, and suddenly grow gray with fear,
And tremble and despoil themselves: oh, hear!

4

If I were a dead leaf thou mightest bear;
If I were a swift cloud to fly with thee;
A wave to pant beneath thy power, and share   45

The impulse of thy strength, only less free
Than thou, O uncontrollable! If even
I were as in my boyhood, and could be

The comrade of thy wanderings over Heaven,
As then, when to outstrip thy skiey speed   50
Scarce seem a vision; I would ne'er have striven

As thus with thee in prayer in my sore need.
Oh, lift me as a wave, a leave, a cloud!
I fall upon the thorns of life! I bleed!

A heavy weight of hours has chained and bowed   55
One too like thee: tameless, and swift, and proud.

5

Make me thy lyre,‡ even as the forest is:
What if my leaves are falling like its own!
The tumult of thy mighty harmonies

*A village near Naples, Italy
‡small, harplike instrument

Will take from both a deep, autumnal tone,   60
Sweet though in sadness. Be thou, Spirit fierce,
My spirit! Be thou me, impetuous one!

Drive my dead thoughts over the universe
Like withered leaves to quicken a new birth!
And, by the incantation of this verse,   65

Scatter, as from an unextinguished hearth
Ashes and sparks, my words among mankind!
Be through my lips to unawakened earth

The trumpet of a prophecy! O Wind,
If Winter comes, can Spring be far behind?   70

3   As always, read the poem carefully. (Find a private place and read it out loud. You'll be carried away by the beauty of the sounds and imagery.) Now answer the following questions.

1. Look at the configuration of the poem. It is divided into five sections. Is it safe to assume each section will explore a separate idea?

_____

2. Count the lines in each section. How many? _____ Name the two stanza forms you encountered. _____

3. Check the rhyme scheme. Did you come up with A B A B C B C D C D E D E E? The first four tercets are written in a form called *terza rima*. Notice how this rhyme scheme interweaves the stanzas and creates unity throughout the poem. Did it cross your mind that each section might be a variation on the sonnet form? _____

4. Check the meter. You should notice that it is very irregular. (Freedom of form was a tenet of the Romantic Movement.)

5. Stanza one: Did you catch the *apostrophe*? The direct address to the wind places us in the poem's situation and provides the subject of the ode. Highlight the *alliteration* and trace the similes in line 3. _____

6. Stanza two: What are the "pestilence stricken multitudes"? In addition to leaves, could they be the races of man? _____

7. Stanza three: See how the enjambment pulls you into this line. Find the simile. _____ Alliteration can be seen in "azure," "sister," "Spring," "shall."

8. Stanza four: What images are presented? _____ Locate the simile. _____ Find the con-

trast between life and death. _____ Highlight the personification.

9. Find the essential paradox of the poem and life itself in the couplet.

We are not going to take you through the poem line by line. You may isolate those lines that speak to you. Here are a few of our favorites that are worth a second look:

- Lines 29–31
- Lines 35–42 for assonance
- Lines 53–54
- Lines 55–56
- Lines 57–70

You should be able to follow the development of ideas through the five sections. Were you aware of:

- The land imagery in section 1.
- The air imagery in section 2.
- The water imagery in section 3.
- The comparison of the poet to the wind in section 4.
- The appeal for the spirit of the wind to be the poet's spirit in section 5.

After you have read the poem, followed the organization, recognized the devices and images, you still have to interpret what you've read.

This ode has many possibilities. One interpretation linked it with the French Revolution and Shelley's understanding of the destructive regeneration associated with it. Another valid reading focuses on Shelley's loss of faith in the Romantic Movement. He asks for inspiration to breathe life into his work again. Try to propose other interpretations for this "Ode to the West Wind."

The Elegy

The elegy is a formal lyric poem written in honor of one who has died. "Elegiac" is the adjective which describes a work that laments any serious loss.

One of the most famous elegies is by Percy Bysshe Shelley. It was written to mourn the loss of John Keats. Here is the first stanza of "Adonais." It contains all the elements of an elegy.

Adonais*

I weep for Adonais—he is dead!
O, weep for Adonais! Though our tears
Thaw not the frost which binds so dear a head!
And thou, sad Hour, selected from all years
To mourn our loss, rouse thy obscure compeers,   *5*

And teach them thine own sorrow, say: "With me
Died Adonais; till the Future dares
Forget the Past, his fate and fame shall be
An echo and a light unto eternity!"

* An Elegy on the death of John Keats, author of
"Endymion," "Hyperion," etc.

Read this stanza several times. Try it aloud. Get carried away by the emotion. Respond to the imagery. Listen to the sounds; let the meter and rhyme guide you through. Consider the following:

1. Adonais, Shelley's name for Keats, is derived from Adonis. This is a mythological allusion to associate Keats with love and beauty. (The meter will tell you how to pronounce Adonais.)

2. Check the rhyme scheme. Did you come up with A B A B B C B C C? See how the last two lines are rhymed to set this idea apart.

3. Line 1 contains a major *caesura* in the form of a dash. This forces the reader to pause and consider the depth of emotion and the finality of the event. The words that follow are also set off by the caesura and emphasized by the exclamation point. Notice that the meter is not interrupted by the caesura. (˘ ´ ˘ ´ ˘ ´ ˘ ´ ˘ ´ is perfect iambic pentameter.) This line is a complete thought which is concluded by punctuation and is an example of an *end-stopped line*.

4. Line 2 utilizes repetition to intensify the sense of loss. Here the caesura is an exclamation point. Notice that the last three words of the line fulfill the meter of iambic pentameter but do not express a complete thought as did line 1. This is an example of *enjambment*.

5. Lines 2 and 3 contain *alliteration* ("Though," "tears," "Thaw," "the") and *consonance* ("not," "frost," continuing into line 4 with "thou").

6. Line 3 contains *imagery* and *metaphor*. What does the frost represent? _____

7. Line 4 contains an *apostrophe* which is a direct address to the sad Hour, which is personified. To what event does the "sad Hour" refer? _____

8. Lines 4, 5, and 6 incorporate *assonance*. The vowel sounds provide a painful tone through "ow" sounds ("thou," "hour," "our," "rouse," "sorrow").

9. Notice how the enjambment in lines 7–9 speeds the stanza to the final thought. This helps the pacing of the poem.

10. Choose images and lines you respond to. Reread the poem.

 Have you read any elegies? List them here. Jot down the poet, title, and any images and lines you like. Add your own thoughts about the poem.

_____

_____

_____

_____

_____

Following is a list of some of the most beautiful elegies in the English language. Make it a point to read several. You won't be sorry.

"Elegy for Jane" by Theodore Roethke—a teacher's lament for his student.
"Elegy in a Country Church Yard" by Thomas Gray—a reflective look at what might have been.
"When Lilacs Last in the Dooryard Bloomed" and "O Captain, My Captain" by Walt Whitman—tributes to Abraham Lincoln.
"In Memory of W. B. Yeats" by W. H. Auden—a poet's homage to a great writer.

The Dramatic Monologue

The dramatic monologue relates an episode in a speaker's life through a conversational format which reveals the character of the speaker.

Robert Browning is the acknowledged master of the dramatic monologue. The following is an example of both the dramatic monologue and Browning's skill as a poet.

Porphyria's Lover

The rain set early in tonight,
  The sullen wind was soon awake,
It tore the elm-tops down for spite,
  And did its worst to vex the lake:
I listened with heart fit to break.   5

When glided in Porphyria; straight
  She shut the cold out and the storm,
And kneeled and made the cheerless grate
  Blaze up, and all the cottage warm;
Which done, she rose, and from her form   10

Withdrew the dripping cloak and shawl,
　And laid her soiled gloves by, untied
Her hat and let the damp hair fall,
　And, last, she sat down by my side
　And called me. When no voice replied,　　15
She put my arm about her waist,
　And made her smooth white shoulder bare,
And all her yellow hair displaced,
　And, stooping, made my cheek lie there,
　And spread, o'er all, her yellow hair,　　20
Murmuring how she loved me – she
　Too weak, for all her heart's endeavor,
To set its struggling passion free
　From pride, and vainer ties desever,
　And give herself to me forever.　　25
But passion sometimes would prevail,
　Nor could tonight's gay feast restrain
A sudden thought of one so pale
　For love of her, and all in vain:
　So, she was come through wind and rain.　　30
Be sure I looked up at her eyes
　Happy and proud; at last I knew
Porphyria worshipped me: surprise
　Made my heart swell, and still it grew
　While I debated what to do.　　35

That moment she was mine, mine, fair,
　Perfectly pure and good: I found
A thing to do, and all her hair
　In one long yellow string I wound
　Three times her little throat around,　　40
And strangled her. No pain felt she;
　I am quite sure she felt no pain.
As a shut bud that holds a bee,
　I warily oped her lids: again
　Laughed the blue eyes without a stain.　　45
And I untightened next the tress
　About her neck; her cheek once more
Blushed bright beneath my burning kiss:
　I propped her head up as before,
　Only, this time my shoulder bore　　50
Her head, which droops upon it still:
　The smiling rosy little head,
So glad it has its utmost will,
　That all it scorned at once is fled,
　And I, its love, am gained instead!　　55
Porphyria's love: she guessed not how
　Her darling one wish would be heard.
And thus we sit together now,
　And all night long we have not stirred,
　And yet God has not said a word!　　60

 Read the poem aloud, or have someone read it to you. Try for a conversational tone.

1. Concentrate on following the storyline. (Were you surprised by the concluding events?) _____

2. Once you know the "story," look closely at the poem for all the clues concerning character and episode.

3. Automatically check for the relationship between form and content. Quickly scan for rhyme scheme and meter. You should notice a definite presence of rhyme in an unusual form A B A B B C D C D D E F E F F, etc. You should be able to recognize that the meter is iambic tetrameter. Rather than scan the entire poem, try lines throughout to see if a pattern exists.

4. *Lines 1–5:* What does the setting indicate or foreshadow? _____

　_____

　Lines 6–9: What diction and imagery is associated with Porphyria?

　_____

　Lines 10–12: Why are we told her gloves were soiled? _____

　_____

Lines 20–25: Try to understand what the narrator is telling you here. This reveals what is important to him. _____

Lines 30–37: Have you found the turning point? _____ Remember, literary analysis is like unraveling a mystery. Find motivational and psychological reasons for the narrator's behavior. _____

_____

Line 41: Notice how the caesura emphasizes the finality of the event. You are forced to confront the murder directly because of the starkness of the syntax. This is followed by the narrator's justification.
Line 43: Did you catch the simile? It's a little tricky to spot when "as" is the first word. _____

Line 55: What character trait is revealed by the narrator? _____

Lines 59–60: Notice how the rhyming couplet accentuates the final thought and sets it off from the previous lines. Interpret the last line. Did you see that the last two lines are end-stopped; whereas, the majority of the poem utilizes enjambment to create a conversational tone. _____

_____

5. Did you enjoy this poem? Did you feel as if you were being spoken to directly? _____

The AP often uses dramatic monologues because they can be very rich in narrative detail and characterization. This is a form you should become familiar with by reading several from different times and authors. Try one of these: Robert Browning—"My Last Duchess," "The Soliloquy of the Spanish Cloister," "Andrea Del Sarto"; Alfred Lord Tennyson—"Ulysses."

How many dramatic monologues have you read? List them here and add details and lines that were of interest and/or importance to you.

_____

_____

_____

_____

The Sonnet

The sonnet is the most popular fixed form in poetry. It is usually written in iambic pentameter and is always made up of 14 lines. There are two basic sonnet forms: the Italian or Petrarchan sonnet, named after Petrarch, the poet who created it, and the English or Shakespearean sonnet, named after the poet who perfected it. Each adheres to a strict rhyme scheme and stanza form.

The subject matter of sonnets varies greatly, from expressions of love to philosophical considerations, religious declarations, or political criticisms. The sonnet is highly polished, and the strictness of its form complements the complexity of its subject matter. As you know by now, we like to explore the relationship between form and function. The sonnet effectively integrates these two concepts.

Let's compare the two forms more closely. The <u>Italian sonnet</u> is divided into an octave and a sestet. The rhyme scheme is:

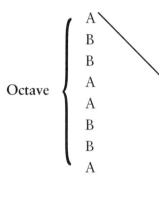

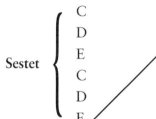

By observing the natural break between the octave and the sestet and noting how the rhyme connects the lines in each, you should see that this form would be suitable for organizing the poem in the following ways:

- General to specific
- Comparison and contrast
- Question and answer
- Cause and effect
- Before and after

The <u>Shakespearean sonnet</u> has a different rhyme scheme and stanza form:

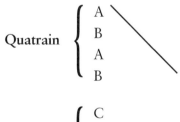

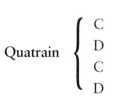

This form is comprised of three quatrains and a couplet. The rhyme scheme indicates the separate nature of each stanza. The Shakespearean sonnet's quatrains lend themselves to the following organizational patterns:

- Beginning, middle, end
- Thesis, example, example
- Past, present, future
- Morning, noon, night
- Birth, life, death

The couplet then serves to present:

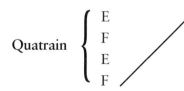

- A summary
- A conclusion
- A universal statement

Modern sonnets often vary rhyme and stanza form, but they will always have 14 lines.

For more practice with the sonnet, see Poems for Comparison and Contrast in this chapter. We recommend you read sonnets written by Shakespeare, Milton, Wordsworth, e e cummings, Edna St. Vincent Millay, and Keats.

The Villanelle

The villanelle is a fixed form in poetry. It has six stanzas: five tercets, and a final quatrain. It utilizes two refrains: The first and last lines of the first stanza alternate as the last line of the next four stanzas and, then, form a final couplet in the quatrain.

As an example, read: "Do Not Go Gentle Into That Good Night" by Dylan Thomas. Other villanelles that are worth a close reading include "The Art of Losing" by Elizabeth Bishop and "The Waking" by Theodore Roethke.

INTERPRETATION OF POETRY

Interpretation is not license for you to say just anything. Your comments/analysis/interpretation must be based on the given text.

How do I begin to interpret poetry?

To thoroughly understand a poem, you should be able to view it and read it from three different angles or viewpoints.

The first level is the *literal reading* of the poem. This is the discovery of what the poem is actually saying. For this, you only use the text:

• Vocabulary
• Structure
• Imagery
• Poetic devices

The *second level* builds on the first and draws conclusions from the connotation of the form and content and the interpretation of symbols. The *third level* refers to your own reading and interpretation of the poem. Here, you apply the processes of levels one and two, and you bring your own context or frame of reference to the poem. Your only restriction is that your interpretation is grounded in, and can be supported by, the text of the poem itself.

To illustrate this approach, let's analyze a very simple poem.

Where ships of purple gently toss
On seas of daffodil,
Fantastic sailors mingle
And then, the wharf is still.

1. Read it.
2. Respond. (You like it; you hate it. It leaves you cold. Whatever.)
3. Check rhyme and meter. We can see there is some rhyme, and it is iambic and predominantly trimeter. And the first and third lines are irregular. (If this does not prove to be critical to your interpretation of the poem, move on.)
4. Check the vocabulary and syntax. Are there any words you are not familiar with?
5. Look for poetic devices and imagery.
6. Highlight, circle, connect key images and words.
7. Begin to draw inferences from the adjectives, phrases, verbs.

Movement

- Toss
- Mingle   } **Progression**
- Still

Images

- Ships
- Seas   } **Literally nautical and on**
- Sailors   **a dock metaphysically?**
- Wharf

Syntax

- Ships of purple = purple ships (Where or when do you see purple ships?)
- Seas of daffodils = daffodil seas (When would seas be yellow?)
- Fantastic sailors = sailors of fantasy = clouds moving, birds flying (What might they be?)
- Wharf is still = place is quiet =?

Put it all together and see what you come up with. Did you see a sunset? Emily Dickenson, the poet, was writing about a sunset. Now to the real challenge. What is your interpretation?

_____

_____

_____

Some students have said that they saw a field of flowers, bees and butterflies, a coronation, a celebration, and a royal event. These are all valid interpretations. Remember, this is only a simple exercise to acquaint you with the approaches you can use to analyze complex poetry.

Poetry for Analysis

This section will walk you through the analysis of several poems, presenting the poetry and a series of directed questions for you to consider. For maximum benefit, work with a highlighter and refer often to the poem. *Always* read the entire poem before you begin the analysis.

The Snake
by D. H. Lawrence

A snake came to my water-trough
On a hot, hot day, and I in pyjamas for the heat
To drink there.

In the deep, strange-scented shade of the great dark carobtree
I came down the steps with my pitcher   5
And must wait, must stand and wait, for there he was at the trough
   before me.

He reached down from a fissure in the earth-wall in the gloom
And trailed his yellow-brown slackness soft-bellied down, over the
   edge of the stone trough,   10
And rested his throat upon the stone bottom,
And where the water had dripped from the tap, in a small clearness,
He sipped with his straight mouth,
Softly drank through his straight gums, into his slack long body,
Silently.   15

Someone was before me at my water trough,
And I, like a second comer, waiting.
He lifted his head from his drinking, as cattle do,
And looked at me vaguely, as drinking cattle do,
And flickered his two-forked tongue from his lips, and mused a   20
   moment,
And stooped and drank a little more,
Being earth-brown, earth-golden from the burning bowels of the earth
On the day of Sicilian July, with Etna smoking.

The voice of my education said to me   25
He must be killed,
For in Sicily the black, black snakes are innocent, the gold are
   venomous.

The voice in me said, If you were a man
You would take a stick and break him now, and finish him off.   30

But must I confess how I liked him,
How glad I was he had come like a guest in quiet, to drink at my
   water-trough
And depart peaceful, pacified, and thankless,
Into the burning bowels of this earth?   35

Was it cowardice, that I dared not kill him?
Was it perversity, that I longed to talk to him?

Was it humility, to feel so honoured?
I felt so honoured.

And yet those voices: 40
If you were not afraid, you would kill him!
And truly I was afraid, I was most afraid,
But even so, honoured still more
That he should seek my hospitality
From out the dark door of the secret earth.   45

He drank enough
And lifted his head, dreamily, as one who has drunken,
And flickered his tongue like a forked night on the air, so black,
Seeming to lick his lips,
And looked around like a god, unseeing, into the air,   50
And slowly turned his head,
And slowly, very slowly, as if thrice a dream,
Proceeded to draw his slow length curving round
And climb again the broken bank of my wall-face.

And as he put his head into that dreadful hole,   55
And as he slowly drew up, snake-easing his shoulders, and entered
    farther,
A sort of horror, a sort of protest against his withdrawing into that
    horrid black hole,
Deliberately going into blackness, and slowly drawing himself   60
    after,
Overcame me now his back was turned.

I looked round, I put down my pitcher,
I picked up a clumsy log
And threw it at the water-trough with a clatter.   65

I think it did not hit him,
But suddenly that part of him that was left behind convulsed in
    undignified haste,
Writhed like lightning, and was gone
Into the black hole, the earth-lipped fissure in the wall-front,   70
At which, in the intense still noon, I stared with fascination.

And immediately I regretted it.
I thought how paltry, how vulgar, what a mean act!
I despised myself and the voices of my accursed human education.

And I thought of the albatross,   75
And I wished he would come back, my snake.

For he seemed to me again like a king,
Like a king in exile, uncrowned in the underworld,
Now due to be crowned again.
And so, I missed my chance with one of the lords   80
Of life.
And I have something to expiate:
A pettiness.

3

1. The form of the poem indicates it is written in _____.

2. Since there is no regular rhyme scheme or length of lines or stanza form, we may conclude that this is *free verse*.

3. After reading the poem, you should be able to determine the situation, which is _____, and the speaker who is _____.

4. The first stanza establishes the conflict, which is _____ _____.

5. Find evidence of the developing conflict in lines 4–6. _____

6. Find examples of alliteration and assonance in lines 7–13. Notice how the sounds are appropriate for a snake rather than just random sounds.

7. Read line 12 aloud. Hear how slowly and "long" the sounds are, like the body of the snake itself.

8. Circle or highlight the imagery in lines 14–21. _____ Notice how the scene is intensifying.

9. Restate the speaker's position in lines 21–26.

10. In lines 27–36 identify the conflict and the thematic ideas of the poem. Highlight them.

11. Identify the opposition facing the speaker in lines 37–40. State it. _____

12. In lines 41–49 highlight the simile presented. Explore the nature of a snake and the connotation associated with one. _____

13. Interpret the setting as presented in lines 50–54. _____

14. The poem breaks at line 63. Highlight the change in the speaker at this point. Who is to blame for this action? _____

15. In line 67 there is a reference or allusion to the "Rime of the Ancient Mariner" by Coleridge, which is a poem in which a man learns

remorse and the meaning of life as the result of a cruel, spontaneous act. Is this a suitable comparison for this poem's circumstances? Why? _____

16. Identify the similes and metaphor in lines 69–72. _____

17. Elaborate on the final confession of the speaker. May we conclude that the poem is a modern dramatic monologue? _____

After you have considered these ideas, expand your own observations. Might the entire poem be a metaphor? Can it be symbolic of other pettinesses? Can you interpret this poem socially, religiously, politically, psychologically, sexually?

The following poem is particularly suitable for the interpretation of symbolism. Apply what you have learned and reviewed and respond to this sample.

The Sick Rose
by William Blake

O Rose, Thou Art Sick!
The Invisible Worm
That flies in the night
In the howling Storm,

Has found out thy bed
Of Crimson joy,
And his dark secret love
Does thy life destroy.

Try to interpret this poem:

1. Literally
2. Sexually
3. Philosophically
4. Religiously
5. Politically

Might this poem refer to:

1. Passion
2. Deceit
3. Betrayal
4. Corruption
5. Disease
6. Madness

Interesting, isn't it, how much can be found or felt in a few lines. Read other poems by Blake, such as "Songs of Innocence" and "Songs of Experience."

POEMS FOR COMPARISON AND CONTRAST

Sometimes the AP exam requires you to compare and contrast two poems or prose selections in the essay section. Do not panic. The selections will usually be short and the points of comparison/or contrast plentiful and accessible. This type of question can be interesting and provide you with a chance to really explore ideas.

Following are two poems suitable for this kind of analysis. Read each poem carefully. Take a minute to look at them and allow a few ideas to take shape in your mind. Then plan your approach logically. Remember, form and content are your guidelines.

She Walks in Beauty
by Lord Byron

She walks in Beauty, like the night
   Of cloudless climes and starry skies;
And all that's best of dark and bright
   Meet in her aspect and her eyes:
Thus mellowed to that tender light   5
   Which heaven to gaudy day denies.

One shade the more, one ray the less,
   Had half impaired the nameless grace
Which waves in every raven tress,
   Or softly lightens o'er her face;   10
Where thoughts serenely sweet express,
   How pure, how dear their dwelling-place.

And on that cheek, and o'er that brow,
   So soft, so calm, yet eloquent,
The smiles that win, the tints that glow,   15
   But tell of days in goodness spent,
A mind at peace with all below,
   A heart whose love is innocent!

Sonnet 130
by William Shakespeare

My mistress' eyes are nothing like the sun;
Coral is far more red than her lips' red;
If snow be white, why then her breasts are dun;
If hairs be wires, black wires grow on her head.
I have seen roses damasked red and white,   5

But no such roses see I in her cheeks;
And in some perfumes is there more delight
Than in the breath that from my mistress reeks.
I love to hear her speak, yet well I know
That music hath a far more pleasing sound;   10
I grant I never saw a goddess go:
My mistress, when she walks, treads on the ground.
And yet, by heaven, I think my love as rare
As any she belied with false compare.

 It is essential that you read each poem again, marking, highlighting, connecting, etc. those points you will develop. List or chart your findings before you begin to write your essay.

Common Elements

- Both have the same form—sonnet
- Both have the same topic—to a lover
- Both address and adore the beloved
- Both use similes: "She Walks"—"like the night"; "Sonnet 130"—"nothing like the sun"
- Both rely on nature imagery: "She Walks"—"starry skies"; "Sonnet 130"—"Coral, roses"
- Both deal with light or dark
- Both include references to lover's hair: "She Walks"—"raven tresses"; "Sonnet 130"—"black wires"
- Both appeal to the senses: perfume, roses, music, garlic stink
- Both use alliteration: "She Walks"—"cloudless climes"; "Sonnet 130"—"goddess go"

Differences

*"Practice. Practice.
Practice."*
   –Martha W.
   -AP teacher

- Form: "She Walks" has sestets; "Sonnet 130," 12 + 2 (couplet)
- Kind of love: "She Walks" serious; "Sonnet 130" critical and humorous
- Diction: "She Walks"—positive; "Sonnet 130"—negative
- Ending: "She Walks"—adoring; "Sonnet 130"—realistic
- Tone: "She Walks"—idyllic; "Sonnet 130"—realistic

To recap: If you are given two selections, consider the following:

- What is the form or structure of the poems?
- What is the situation or subject?
- How are the poetic devices used?
- What imagery is developed?
- What thematic statements are made?
- What is the tone of each poem?
- What is the organization or progression of each poem?
- What attitudes are revealed?
- What symbols are developed?

RAPID REVIEW

- Poetry has its own form.

- The foot, line, and stanza are the building blocks of poetry.

- Meter and rhyme are part of the sound of poetry.

- There are many types of rhyme forms.

- There are many types of poetic feet. They may be iambic, trochaic, anapestic, dactylic, or spondaic.

- There are several stanza forms.

- Narrative poetry tells stories.

- Ballads are simple narratives.

- Lyric poetry is subjective and emotional.

- Odes are formal lyrics that honor something or someone.

- Elegies are lyrics that mourn a loss.

- Dramatic monologues converse with the reader as they reveal events.

- The sonnet is a 14 line form of poetry.

- The villanelle is a fixed form that depends on refrains.

- Levels of interpretation depend on the literal and figurative meaning of poems.

- Symbols provide for many levels of interpretation.

- When comparing and contrasting poems, remember to consider speaker, subject, situation, devices, tone, and theme.

PART IV

DEVELOPING CONFIDENCE BY APPLYING SKILLS

Chapter 9

Practice Exam 1

" I need to honestly time myself on the practice exams, or else I don't really concentrate the way I should."

–Carol K.
-AP student

1. _____	14. _____	27. _____	40. _____
2. _____	15. _____	28. _____	41. _____
3. _____	16. _____	29. _____	42. _____
4. _____	17. _____	30. _____	43. _____
5. _____	18. _____	31. _____	44. _____
6. _____	19. _____	32. _____	45. _____
7. _____	20. _____	33. _____	46. _____
8. _____	21. _____	34. _____	47. _____
9. _____	22. _____	35. _____	48. _____
10. _____	23. _____	36. _____	49. _____
11. _____	24. _____	37. _____	50. _____
12. _____	25. _____	38. _____	51. _____
13. _____	26. _____	39. _____	

I ____ did ____ did not complete this part of the test in the allotted 1 hour.

Scoring Formula:

I had ____ correct answers. I had ____ incorrect answers. I left ____ blank.

_____ – _____ = _____

   number right   –   (number wrong × .25) = raw score

I have carefully reviewed the explanations of the answers, and I think I need to work on the following types of questions:

PRACTICE EXAM 1
ADVANCED PLACEMENT ENGLISH LITERATURE
Section I

Total time—1 hour

Carefully read the following passages and answer the questions that follow.

Questions 1–14 are based on the following passage.

Samuel Johnson on Pope, from *The Lives of the English Poets* (1779–1781)

The person of Pope is well known not to have been formed by the nicest model.
He has compared himself to a spider, and by another is described as protuberant behind
and before. He is said to have been beautiful in his infancy; but he was of a constitution
feeble and weak; and as bodies of a tender frame are easily distorted, his deformity was
probably in part the effect of his application. But his face was not displeasing, and his   5
eyes were animated and vivid.

By natural deformity, or accidental distortion, his vital functions were so much
disordered, that his life was a "long disease."

He sometimes condescended to be jocular with servants or inferiors; but by no
merriment, either of others or his own, was he ever seen excited to laughter.   10

Of his domestic character frugality was a part eminently remarkable. Having
determined not to be dependent, he determined not to be in want, and therefore wisely and
magnanimously rejected all temptations to expense unsuitable to his fortune.

The great topic of his ridicule is poverty; the crimes with which he reproaches his
antagonists are their debts and their want of a dinner. He seems to be of an opinion not   15
very uncommon in the world, that to want money is to want everything.

He professed to have learned his poetry from Dryden, whom he praised through his
whole life with unvaried liberality; and perhaps his character may receive some illustration,
if he be compared with his master.

Integrity of understanding and nicety of discernment were not allotted in a less   20
proportion to Dryden than to Pope. But Dryden never desired to apply all the judgment that
he had. He wrote merely for the people; and when he pleased others, he contented himself.
He never attempted to mend what he must have known to be faulty. He wrote with very
little consideration; and once it had passed the press, ejected it from his mind.

Pope was not content to satisfy; he desired to excel, and, therefore always endeavored   25
to do his best; he did not court the candour, but dared the judgment of his reader, and,
expecting no indulgence from others, he showed none to himself. He examined lines and words
with minute and punctilious observation, and retouched every part with diligence, till he had
nothing left to be forgiven.

Poetry was not the sole praise of either; for both excelled likewise in prose.   30
The style of Dryden is capricious and varied; that of Pope is cautious and uniform. Dryden
observes the motions of his own mind; Pope constrains his mind to his own rules of
composition. Dryden's page is a natural field, diversified by the exuberance of abundant
vegetation. Pope's is a velvet lawn, shaven by the scythe, and leveled by the roller.

If the flights of Dryden are higher, Pope continues longer on the wing. If of Dryden's   35
fire the blaze is brighter, of Pope's the heat is more regular and constant. Dryden is read with
frequent astonishment, and Pope with perpetual delight.

1. The passage is primarily a(n)

    A. character sketch of Pope
    B. discussion of poetic style
    C. criticism of Dryden
    D. model for future poets
    E. opportunity for the writer to show off his own skills

2. The passage discusses a contrast between all of the following *except*

    A. prose and poetry
    B. Pope and Dryden
    C. body and mind
    D. poverty and wealth
    E. body and soul

3. "If the flights . . ." (line 35) means

    A. Pope's writing will outlast Dryden's
    B. both Pope and Dryden are equal
    C. Pope is not idealistic
    D. Pope is more wordy
    E. Pope is not as bright as Dryden

4. The character of Pope is developed by all of the following *except*

    A. examples
    B. comparison
    C. contrast
    D. satire
    E. description

5. According to the passage, Pope and Dryden are

    A. rivals
    B. equally intelligent
    C. outdated
    D. equally physically attractive
    E. in debt

6. From the passage, the reader may infer that Pope

    A. was extravagant
    B. was a man of the people
    C. was jealous of Dryden
    D. had a desire to be popular
    E. had a bitter, satirical nature

7. The tone of the passage is

    A. informal and affectionate
    B. formal and objective
    C. condescending and paternalistic
    D. laudatory and reverent
    E. critical and negative

8. Lines 20–25 indicate that Dryden was what type of writer?

    A. one who labored over his thoughts
    B. one who wrote only for himself
    C. one who wrote only for the critics
    D. one who wrote to please Pope
    E. one who did not revise

9. Using the context of lines 27–29, "punctilious" means

    A. precise
    B. timely
    C. cursory
    D. scholarly
    E. philosophical

10. In the context of the passage, "Till he had nothing left to be forgiven" (lines 28–29) means

    A. Pope outraged his readers
    B. Pope suffered from writer's block
    C. Pope exhausted his subject matter
    D. Pope's prose was revised to perfection
    E. Pope cared about the opinions of his readers

11. "Shaven" and "leveled" in line 34 indicate that Pope's style of writing was

    A. natural
    B. richly ornamented
    C. highly controlled
    D. mechanical
    E. analytical

12. Based upon a close reading of the final paragraph of the passage, the reader could infer that the author

    A. looks on both writers equally
    B. prefers the work of Pope
    C. sees the two writers as inferior to his own writing style
    D. indicates no preference
    E. prefers the work of Dryden

13. Johnson's attitude toward the general public can be best described as

A. laudatory and respectful
B. flattering and fearful
C. critical and condescending
D. moralistic and concerned
E. pedantic and taunting

14. According to Johnson, the qualities of a great writer include all of the following *except*

A. "unvaried liberality"
B. "nicety of discernment"
C. "punctilious observation"
D. "excelling likewise in prose" and poetry
E. "integrity of understanding"

Questions 15–25 are based on the following poem.

The Writer
by Richard Wilbur

In her room at the prow of the house
Where light breaks, and the windows are tossed with linden,
My daughter is writing a story.

I pause in the stairwell, hearing
From her shut door a commotion of typewriter-keys   5
Like a chain hauled over a gunwale.

Young as she is, the stuff
Of her life is a great cargo, and some of it heavy:
I wish her a lucky passage.

But now it is she who pauses,   10
As if to reject my thought and its easy figure.
A stillness greatens, in which

The whole house seems to be thinking,
And then she is at it again with a bunched clamor
Of strokes, and again is silent.   15

I remember the dazed starling
Which was trapped in that very room, two years ago;
How we stole in, lifted a sash

And retreated, not to affright it;
And how for a helpless hour, through the crack in the door, 20
We watched this sleek, wild, dark

And iridescent creature
Batter against the brilliance, drop like a glove
To the hard floor, or the desk-top,

And wait then, humped and bloody,   25
For the wits to try it again; and how our spirits
Rose when, suddenly sure,

It lifted off from a chair-back,
Beating a smooth course for the right window
And clearing the sill of the world.   30

It is always a matter, my darling,
Of life or death, as I had forgotten. I wish
What I wished you before, but harder.

15. The last line of the poem "What I wished for you before, but harder" implies that

    A. the speaker loves his daughter more than at the beginning of the poem
    B. the speaker realizes the intensity of life's challenges
    C. the speaker cannot be as creative as she
    D. the speaker feels he has failed her
    E. the daughter will never be a successful writer

16. Which of the following is used to develop the poem?

    A. cause and effect
    B. argument
    C. general to specific examples
    D. definition
    E. parallel analogy

17. Line 13 is an example of

    A. allusion
    B. alliteration
    C. personification
    D. simile
    E. apostrophe

18. "A smooth course for the right window" in line 29 parallels line(s)

    A. 1
    B. 5–6
    C. 8
    D. 9
    E. 11

19. The poem breaks after line

    A. 3
    B. 6
    C. 8
    D. 15
    E. 27

20. The final stanza serves all the following purposes *except*

    A. to restate the theme
    B. to reemphasize the father's love for his daughter

    C. to solidify the daughter's character
    D. to connect the two major sections of the poem
    E. to allow the father to be more sympathetic

21. Stanzas 1–3 include all the following analogies *except*

    A. the house as a ship
    B. the daughter's room as a ship's cabin
    C. life's problems as a ship's cargo
    D. writing as a safe harbor
    E. life is a sea journey

22. The father's sensitivity is supported by line(s)

    A. 3
    B. 4
    C. 11
    D. 19
    E. 21–22

23. Contrasts developed in the poem include all the following *except*

    A. stillness and clamor
    B. house and cargo
    C. bird and daughter
    D. life and/or death
    E. light and dark

24. According to the poem, the daughter, as young as she is, has

    A. endured hardships
    B. published her writing
    C. fought for her independence
    D. saved a starling
    E. left home and returned

25. The poet alludes to all the following as part of the process of a creative life *except*

    A. "Batter against the brilliance"
    B. "Drop like a glove to the hard floor"
    C. "clearing the sill of the world"
    D. "the wits to try it again"
    E. "Beating a smooth course for the right window"

Questions 26–38 are based on the following passage.

Jane Eyre
by Charlotte Bronte

Miss Temple got up, took her hand and . . . returned to her own seat: as she resumed it, I heard her sigh low. She was pensive a few minutes, then rousing herself, she said cheerfully:—

"But you two are my visitors to-night; I must treat you as such." She rang her bell.

"Barbara," she said to the servant who answered it, "I have not yet had tea; bring the tray, and place cups for these two young ladies." 5

And a tray was soon brought. How pretty, to my eyes, did the china and bright teapot look, placed on the little round table near the fire! How fragrant was the steam of the beverage, and the scent of the toast! of which, however, I, to my dismay (for I was beginning to be hungry), discerned only a very small portion: Miss Temple discerned it too:— 10

"Barbara," said she, "can you not bring a little more bread and butter? There is not enough for three."

Barbara went out: she returned soon:—

"Madam, Mrs. Harden says she has sent up the usual quantity." 15

Mrs. Harden, be it observed, was the housekeeper: a woman after Mr. Brocklehurst's own heart, made up of equal parts of whalebone and iron.

"Oh, very well!" returned Miss Temple; "we must make it do, Barbara, I suppose." And as the girl withdrew, she added, smiling, "Fortunately, I have it in my power to supply deficiencies for this once." 20

Having invited Helen and me to approach the table, and placed before each of us a cup of tea with one delicious but thin morsel of toast; she got up, unlocked a drawer, and taking from it a parcel wrapped in paper, disclosed presently to our eyes a good-sized seed-cake.

"I meant to give each of you some of this to take with you," said she; "but as there is so little toast, you must have it now," and she proceeded to cut slices with a generous hand. 25

We feasted that evening as on nectar and ambrosia; and not the least delight of the entertainment was the smile of gratification with which our hostess regarded us, as we satisfied our famished appetites on the delicate fare she liberally supplied. Tea over and the tray removed, she again summoned us to the fire; we sat one on each side of her, and now a conversation followed between her and Helen, which it was indeed a privilege to be admitted to hear. 30

Miss Temple had always something of serenity in her air, of state in her mien, of refined propriety in her language, which precluded deviation into the ardent, the excited, the eager: something which chastened the pleasure of those who looked on her and listened to her, by a controlling sense of awe; and such was my feeling now: but as to Helen Burns, I was struck with wonder. 35

The refreshing meal, the brilliant fire, the presence and kindness of her beloved instructress, or, perhaps, more than all these, something in her own unique mind, had roused her powers within her. They woke, they kindled: first, they glowed in the bright tint of her cheek, which till this hour I had never seen but pale and bloodless; then they shone in the liquid lustre of her eyes, which had suddenly acquired a beauty more singular than that of Miss Temple's—a beauty neither of fine colour nor long eyelash, nor pencilled brow, but of meaning, of movement, of radiance. Then her soul sat on her lips, and language flowed, from what source I cannot tell: has a girl of fourteen a heart large enough, vigorous enough to hold the swelling spring of pure, full, fervid eloquence? Such was the characteristic of Helen's discourse on that, to me, memorable evening; her spirit seemed 40 45

hastening to live within a very brief span as much as many live during a protracted
existence.   50

They conversed of things I had never heard of! Of nations and times past; of
countries far away: of secrets of nature discovered or guessed at: they spoke of books: how
many they had read! What stores of knowledge they possessed! They seemed so
familiar with French names and French authors: but my amazement reached its climax
when Miss Temple asked Helen if she sometimes snatched a moment to recall the Latin her   55
father had taught her, and taking a book from a shelf, bade her read and construe a page of
"Virgil"; and Helen obeyed, my organ of Veneration expanding at every sounding line.
She had scarcely finished ere the bell announced bedtime: no delay could be admitted;
Miss Temple embraced us both, saying, as she drew us to her heart:—

"God bless you, my children!"   60

Well has Solomon said—"Better is a dinner of herbs where love is, than a stalled ox
and hatred therewith."

26. From the passage, it can be concluded
that Mrs. Harden is

A. in love with Mr. Brocklehurst
B. generous with the girls
C. a confidante of Miss Temple's
D. strong-willed and inflexible
E. Miss Temple's superior

27. Religious imagery in this passage is
developed by all the following
except

A. Miss Temple's name
B. feasting on nectar and ambrosia
C. the taking of tea and toast
D. Miss Temple's benediction
E. being summoned to sit by the fire

28. The "smile of gratification with which
our hostess regarded us" (line 29) indicates that Miss Temple derives pleasure
from

A. having power over the girls
B. being a role model for the girls
C. keeping secrets
D. outsmarting the girls
E. providing for the girls

29. For the speaker, the most nourishing
part of the evening was

A. the seed cake
B. the tea and toast
C. the company of an adult

D. the conversation
E. the brilliant fire

30. The speaker is amazed by

A. Miss Temple's beauty
B. the breadth of Helen's knowledge
C. Miss Temple's generosity
D. her own knowledge
E. her envy of the attention Helen
receives

31. ". . . Her spirit seemed hastening to live
within a very brief span as much as
many live during a protracted existence"
(lines 48–49) is an example of

A. circular reasoning
B. satire
C. foreshadowing
D. denouement
E. digression

32. The reader can infer from lines 45–47
("Then her soul sat on her lips . . .
eloquence") that

A. Helen has traveled the world
B. Helen likes to show off intellectually
C. Miss Temple has been tutoring
Helen
D. the speaker is afraid of Helen
E. Helen is an instrument of divine
inspiration

33. The last line of the passage may be best
interpreted to mean

A. It is better to be rich than poor
B. Everything in moderation
C. The greatest of all riches is love
D. Denial of riches leads to love
F. Riches lead to hatred

34. The pronoun "they" in lines 41–42 refers to

A. her powers
B. her unique mind
C. the meal and the fire
D. Helen and Miss Temple
E. Helen's eyes

35. The tone developed in the passage is best described as

A. amused indifference
B. subdued admiration
C. pedantic
D. reverent wonder
E. remorseful

36. The reader may infer all the following *except that*

A. the evening has transformed Helen
B. the speaker is observant of and sensitive to human nature

C. the evening is in contrast to their daily lives
D. Miss Temple will save the two children
E. love of learning is important to the speaker

37. The description of Miss Temple in lines 34–38 reveals her to be a woman of

A. religious fervor
B. restraint and reservation
C. passionate beliefs
D. submissive inclinations
E. dominating sensibilities

38. Based on the passage, all the following can be inferred about Jane's character *except that* she is

A. cognizant of her limitations
B. a great observer
C. of an inquisitive nature
D. highly impressionable
E. religious

Questions 39–51 are based on the following poem.

The Pulley
by George Herbert

When God at first made man,
Having a glass of blessings stand by,
Let us, said He, pour on him all we can.
Let the world's riches, which dispersed lie,
Contract into a span.   5

So Strength first made a way,
Then Beauty flowed, then Wisdom, Honor, Pleasure.
When almost all was out, God made a stay,
Perceiving that alone of all his treasure
Rest in the bottom lay.   10

For if I should, said He,
Bestow this jewel also on my creature,
He would adore my gifts instead of me,

And rest in Nature, not the God of Nature:
So both should losers be.   15

Yet let him keep the rest,
But keep them with repining restlessness.
Let him be rich and weary, that at least
If goodness lead him not, yet weariness
May toss him to my breast.   20

(Note: Poem reprinted in its original form.)

39. The "pulley" of the title refers to

    A. the balance between God and nature
    B. the conflict between beauty and riches
    C. the conflict between blessings and curses
    D. God's method of controlling mankind
    E. the conflict between winners and losers

40. In line 9, "alone of all his treasure" refers to

    A. wisdom
    B. honor
    C. pleasure
    D. strength
    E. rest

41. According to the first stanza, God is

    A. totally generous
    B. suspicious of humankind
    C. drunk with power
    D. planning to test humanity
    E. forgiving of human weakness

42. In line 16, "Yet let him keep the rest" refers to

    A. all the gifts, except "rest"
    B. the Sabbath
    C. nature
    D. a glass of blessings
    E. "this jewel"

43. God will control humans by keeping them

    A. away from evil
    B. poor
    C. alone
    D. weak
    E. fatigued

44. The pun in this poem depends upon the reading of which word?

    A. pour
    B. alone
    C. rest
    D. losers
    E. least

45. The dominant imagery concerns

    A. wealth
    B. goodness
    C. God
    D. nature
    E. contracts

46. In line 12, "this jewel" refers to

    A. wisdom
    B. my creature
    C. glass of blessings
    D. rest
    E. nature

47. The first and last lines of each stanza are written in

    A. iambic pentameter
    B. iambic trimeter
    C. trochaic trimeter
    D. spondaic tetrameter
    E. dactylic trimeter

48. The conflict of the poem is best expressed in line

    A. 3
    B. 8
    C. 13
    D. 15
    E. 17

49. For George Herbert, the God of all mankind is

    A. all-forgiving and generous
    B. disappointed and jealous
    C. judgmental and punitive
    D. regretful and plaintive
    E. speculative and manipulative

50. The organization of the first two stanzas depends upon

    A. contrast and comparison
    B. paradox
    C. chronological order
    D. specific to general
    E. description

51. We can infer that the speaker is

    A. heretical
    B. nonmaterialistic
    C. scientific
    D. skeptical
    E. materialistic

End of Section I

Section II

Total time–2 hours

Question 1

(Suggested time 40 minutes. This questions counts as one-third of the total score for Section II.)

In a well-organized essay discuss how Alice Walker conveys the meaning of "The Flowers" and how she prepares the reader for the ending of this short story. Consider at least two elements of the writer's craft such as imagery, symbol, setting, narrative pace, diction, and style.

The Flowers
by Alice Walker

It seemed to Myop as she skipped lightly from her house to pigpen to smokehouse that the days had never been as beautiful as these. The air held a keenness that made her nose twitch. The harvesting of the corn and cotton, peanuts and squash, made each day a golden surprise that caused excited little tremors to run up her jaws.

Myop carried a short, knobby stick. She struck out at random at chickens she liked, and worked out the beat of a song on the fence around the pigpen. She felt light and good in the warm sun. She was ten, and nothing existed for her but her song, the stick clutched in her dark brown hand, and the tat-de-ta-ta-ta of accompaniment. 5

Turning her back on the rusty boards of her family's sharecropper cabin, Myop walked along the fence till it ran into the stream made by the spring. Around the spring, where the family got drinking water, silver ferns and wildflowers grew. Along the shallow banks pigs rooted. Myop watched the tiny white bubbles disrupt the thin black scale of soil and the water that silently rose and slid away down the stream. 10

She had explored the woods behind the house many times. Often, in late autumn, her mother took her to gather nuts among the fallen leaves. Today she made her own path, bouncing this way and that way, vaguely keeping an eye out for snakes. She found, in addition to various common but pretty ferns and leaves, an armful of strange blue flowers with velvety ridges and a sweetsuds bush full of the brown, fragrant buds. 15

By twelve o'clock, her arms laden with sprigs of her findings, she was a mile or more from home. She had often been as far before, but the strangeness of the land made it not as pleasant as her usual haunts. It seemed gloomy in the little cove in which she found herself. The air was damp, the silence close and deep. 20

Myop began to circle back to the house, back to the peacefulness of the morning.

It was then she stepped smack into his eyes. Her heel became lodged in the broken ridge between brow and nose, and she reached down quickly, unafraid, to free herself. It was only when she saw his naked grin that she gave a little yelp of surprise. He had been a tall man. From feet to neck covered a long space. His head lay beside him. When she pushed back the leaves and layers of earth and debris Myop saw that he'd had large white teeth, all of them cracked or broken, long fingers, and very big bones. All his clothes had rotted away except some threads of blue denim from his overalls. The buckles of the overalls had turned green. 25 30

Myop gazed around the spot with interest. Very near where she'd stepped into the head was a wild pink rose. As she picked it to add to her bundle she noticed a raised mound, a ring, around the rose's root. It was the rotted remains of a noose, a bit of shredding plow-line, now blending benignly into the soil. Around the overhanging limb of a great spreading oak clung another piece, frayed, rotted, bleached, and frazzled—barely there—but spinning restlessly in the breeze. Myop laid down her flowers. 35

And the summer was over.

Question 2

(Suggested time 40 minutes. This questions counts as one-third
of the total score for Section II.)

In a well-organized essay discuss the distinguishing differences between the connotations of the two main words in the title of the poem "The Naked and the Nude" as they are developed in this poem by Robert Graves. Refer to such literary techniques as tone, style, poetic devices, structure, and imagery.

The Naked and the Nude
by Robert Graves

For me, the naked and the nude
(By lexicographers construed
As synonyms that should express
The same deficiency of dress
Or shelter) stand as wide apart   5
As love from lies, or truth from art.

Lovers without reproach will gaze
On bodies naked and ablaze;
The Hippocratic eye will see
In nakedness, anatomy;   10
And naked shines the Goddess when
She mounts her lion among men.

The nude are bold; the nude are sly
To hold each treasonable eye.
While draping by a showman's trick   15
Their dishabille in rhetoric,
They grin a mock-religious grin
Of scorn at those of naked skin.

The naked, therefore, who compete
Against the nude may know defeat;   20
Yet when they both together tread
The briary pastures of the dead,
By Gorgons with long whips pursued,
How naked go the sometime nude!

Question 3

(Suggested time 40 minutes. This question counts as one-third
of the total score for Section II.)

From your study of full-length works, choose one in which a character or group intentionally dissembles in order to advance a specific agenda. Be sure to discuss the nature of the deceit or misrepresentation and how it contributes to the development of that character or the meaning of the work. You may choose a work from the list below or another novel or play of literary merit.

The Stranger
Oedipus
Jane Eyre
Desire Under the Elms
Heart of Darkness
The Secret Sharer
Beloved
A Streetcar Named Desire
Major Barbara

Hamlet
Twelfth Night
King Lear
The Great Gatsby
The Importance of Being Earnest
Hedda Gabler
A Doll's House
Catch-22

End of Section II

ANSWERS TO MULTIPLE-CHOICE QUESTIONS

Answer Key

1. A	14. A	27. E	40. E
2. E	15. B	28. E	41. A
3. A	16. E	29. D	42. A
4. D	17. C	30. B	43. E
5. B	18. D	31. C	44. C
6. E	19. D	32. E	45. A
7. B	20. C	33. C	46. D
8. E	21. D	34. A	47. B
9. A	22. D	35. D	48. C
10. D	23. B	36. D	49. E
11. C	24. A	37. B	50. C
12. B	25. B	38. E	51. B
13. C	26. D	39. D	

5 Explanation of the Answers to the Multiple-Choice Questions

1. **A.** Although references to poetic style and to Dryden are contained in the passage, they are included to illuminate the character of Pope.

2. **E.** There are no references to body and soul in the passage. We do find references to the prose and poetry of both Pope and Dryden. We are told of Pope's monetary concerns, and we can infer the contrast between Pope's broken body and healthy mind.

3. **A.** This is a fairly straightforward interpretation of a figurative line. The idea of "long on the wing" naturally leads the reader to think of endurance.

4. **D.** A careful reading of this passage will allow you to locate each of the devices, except satire.

5. **B.** Line 20 clearly states that the two men were equally gifted.

6. **E.** Lines 9–10 tell the reader that Pope's humor was condescending. Lines 14–15 allude to his use of ridicule, and the reader may infer that these characteristics were carried over into Pope's writing.

7. **B.** The author never interjects his own feelings, and the diction and syntax remain on a scholarly, elevated level.

8. **E.** Carefully read lines 23–24 and you will see a direct correlation between those lines and choice E.

9. **A.** This is strictly a vocabulary question. You should be able to use the context clues of "minute" and "diligent" to lead you to choose A.

10. **D.** If you go to lines 24–28, you will see that Pope demanded perfection of himself and his writing. This characteristic is further extended with the clause in line 29.

11. **C.** Both words indicate a practiced, continuous, and extreme control of the work at hand. Even the "velvet of the lawn" indicates a tightness, a smoothness, and a richness of form and content.

12. **B.** If it were a contest, Pope would be declared the winner by Johnson. A close reading of both the structure and content of the paragraph leads the reader to Pope. When discussing Dryden and Pope, it is Pope who has the last word. This allows Pope to linger in the reader's mind. "Frequent" with Dryden and "perpetual" with Pope is another indication of Samuel Johnson's preference.

13. **C.** In lines 15–16, Johnson expresses his critical observations and judgments. He dismisses the people with the adverb "merely" in line 22.

14. **A.** A close examination of the text finds Johnson tolerant of differences in style but constant with regard to the qualities of the great writer. "Unvaried liberality" in line 18 refers only to Pope's respect for Dryden and not to the process of writing.

15. **B.** The entire poem hinges on the speaker's epiphany about life and creativity which occurs in the last stanza. It is this realization that points to choice B. Choice A is silly and should be eliminated immediately. There is no discussion of the daughter's talent which eliminates choice E. Although C and D sound plausible and may even be insights raised by the reader, once again there is no concrete evidence in the poem to support these choices.

16. **E.** The careful reader should recognize that the poem introduces a new idea in lines 16–30, and he or she should question the reason for this. It is obvious that the episode of the starling is meant to parallel the intensity of the creative process the daughter is experiencing.

17. **C.** The house is personified as "thinking." This is a question that is really a freebie if you've done your preparation. The answer depends on your knowledge of simple terms and your ability to identify examples of them in a work.

18. **D.** A question of this type demands that you actually refer to the passage. (You might try highlighting or underlining to emphasize line 29 and the various choices. This will prevent you from losing your place or focus.) Use the process of elimination until you find an "echo" word or phrase. In line 9, "passage" parallels "course" and points to choice D. It is a good idea to follow the choices in order for clarity and continuity because each rereading may give you help with another question.

19. **D.** Question 2 may help you with this answer. Skim the poem from line 1 until you strike a new idea—the dazed bird. The answer has to be D. A, B, and C all describe the daughter and are on topic, while line 27 refers to the previous idea, in this case, the starling introduced earlier.

20. **C.** The perceptive reader will understand that the stanza is not about the daughter at all; whereas, each of the other ideas is valid and can be supported in the context of the stanza.

21. **D.** The use of nautical terms dominates the first section of the poem, establishing the concept of life as a sea journey or passage. The words, "prow" (line 1), "gunwale" (line 6), and "heavy cargo" (line 8), all support choices A, B, C, and E. The only image *not* stated concerns writing as a safe harbor.

22. **D.** This is essentially a reading question and one you should find easy to answer. Start with the first choice and work your way through each of the others. Highlight or underline lines and look for concrete evidence and eliminate unsupported choices. Line 19 indicates the sensitivity shown by the father's consideration for the trapped bird.

23. **B.** This type of question is more complicated than the others because there are many steps involved in finding the answer. Don't just rely on memory. Actually circle or highlight the contrasts as you skim the poem. You may have a quick flash. If so, look immediately to prove it. If you can't, you have your answer. In this case, B. To illustrate the process, here are the images that prove that the other choices are contained in the poem.

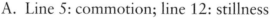

  A. Line 5: commotion; line 12: stillness
  C. Lines 22–23: the implied analogy of child and bird
  D. Line 32: life and death
  E. Line 2: light breaks; line 21: dark

24. **A.** This simple reading question is a giveaway. Stanza three tells the reader that "the stuff of her life is a great cargo, and some of it heavy." You should be able to interpret the metaphor as life's difficulties.

25. **B.** All the choices, with the exception of B, reflect the need to persist in order to achieve a goal—freedom and creation. Only B is grounded to the hard floor.

26. **D.** The answer is obvious if you carefully read lines 15–17. A heart made up of whalebones and iron is synonymous with strong-willed and inflexible.

27. **E.** Temple, feasting, food of the gods, and benediction can all imply religious connotations. Tea and toast can be a direct allusion to taking communion. Being asked to "come sit by the fire" is simply a request, nothing more.

28. **E.** "Gratification" involves thankfulness. And, in this case, Miss Temple is pleased that she is able to give the girls some special foods during their visit.

29. **D.** This is a metaphorical construction. With it, Jane lets the reader know that having the opportunity to be part of engaging and exciting conversation was like food for her mind and soul.

30. **B.** Lines 39–59 of this excerpt are devoted to Helen's mind, knowledge, and eloquence.

31. **C.** This is one of those questions that assumes the student is familiar with the definitions of specific terms. "Seemed hastening" is almost a literal flag waving in front of the reader's eyes signaling that something will happen in the future.

32. **E.** Helen's "soul sitting on her lips," her "secret sources of language," and her "purity and radiance" all relate to the realm of the divine.

33. **C.** Herbs are simple and of small quantity. An ox, on the other hand, is overwhelmingly large and overabundant. Love is better than hate. This analogy is straightforward and obvious.

34. **A.** This is the frequently used antecedent question. All you have to do is substitute each of the choices for the word "they," and it will be obvious that your only viable choice is "her powers."

35. **D.** If you read the passage carefully, Jane's wonder and deference are apparent. Look at lines 39–50 to see her sense of awe. Look at line 39. It clearly states Jane's wonder at Helen.

36. **D.** There is nothing in this passage that indicates either of the two girls needs to be saved.

37. **B.** "Serenity," "state in her mien," "refined propriety" in lines 34–35 are synonymous with one who is restrained. The remainder of the lines illustrates and supports this characterization.

38. **E.** Although there is considerable religious diction and imagery in the passage, none of it directly relates to Jane's character and her being a religious person.

39. **D.** A pulley is a device used to bring something to a particular destination. In this case, man to God.

40. **E.** If you recast lines 9 and 10 into a sentence, you can easily see that "treasure" is the antecedent of "Rest." This is an example of poetic inversion.

41. **A.** Lines 3 and 4 are the indicators. Look carefully at what God is doing—giving all the world's riches away.

42. **A.** Use the process of substitution to help you find the answer. If you place each of the choices in place of "Rest," you will see that the only appropriate choice is A.

43. **E.** Lines 17 and 18 clearly indicate that God intends for man to be without rest.

44. **C.** The pun depends on your knowing that a play on words and their meanings is essential to the understanding of this poem. Choice C refers to both renewal and the remains of the blessings.

45. **A.** Each stanza presents an image to support choice A. "Riches" (line 4), "treasure" (line 9), "jewel" (line 12), and "rich" (line 18) sustain the concept of wealth.

46. **D.** This is another question that benefits from using the process of substitution to locate an antecedent. This procedure will lead you to lines 9 and 10 and choice D.

47. **B.** You should notice immediately that the first and last lines of each stanza are shorter than the other lines. It is a good idea to briefly check to see if the form is iambic (˘ ´) because the iambic foot is the most common one in the English language. (See Chapter 8.) Count the number of iambs, and you will come up with three (tri). (*Note*: If meter presents a problem to you, this may be a question you should choose to skip.)

48. **C.** God is wary of man's potential goodness and loyalty and devises another method of ensuring mankind's adoration and reliance on Him.

49. **E.** A, B, C, and D are all partially supported in the poem. But, only E has *both* characteristics evident in the poem's context.

50. **C.** The words "when," "first," "then," and "when" are all indicative of the chronological pattern of the first two stanzas.

51. **B.** The text of the poem, especially in the choice of blessings the speaker presents, indicates that he is interested in the world of the spirit rather than the world of material possessions and investigations. The diction proves he considers these nonmaterial concepts to be the real "riches," "treasure," "jewel," and "gifts."

RATING THE ESSAY SECTION

2 Rubrics for "The Flowers" by Alice Walker

High-range scores (8, 9):

- Indicates complete understanding and support of the prompt.
- Uses appropriate literary techniques to illustrate how Walker prepares the reader for the ending of the story.
- Thoroughly explores the contrasts inherent in the story.
- Fully presents Myop's character.
- Recognizes the underlying theme related to prejudice and innocence.

- Responds insightfully to image, diction, and setting.
- Presents suitable and unique interpretations of the text.
- Demonstrates a mature, sophisticated writing style.

Midrange scores (5, 6, 7):

- Refers accurately to the prompt.
- Utilizes appropriate devices in the analysis of Walker's preparation for the surprise ending.
- Adequately supports the thesis.
- Uses obvious references and details.
- May miss the subtleties of the story.
- Inferences are based on an acceptable reading of the text.
- Demonstrates writing that is adequate to convey the writer's intent.
- May exhibit a few errors in syntax and/or diction

Sample Student Essays

Student Essay A

". . . the days had never been as beautiful as these . . . each day a golden surprise." Surprise is the element Alice Walker presents in her story "The Flowers." It is at the heart of the meaning of this story which is driven forward by imagery, setting, and diction.

In the beginning of the story, Walker utilizes diction that creates an atmosphere of euphoric childhood innocence. Myop, the main character, "skipped lightly." Walker describes the harvests, which evince "excited little tremors" in Myop as she anticipates the new day.

This jocund diction continues into the second paragraph. Specifically, Myop feels "light and good" in the heat of the warm sun. In addition, ten year old Myop creates her own world in which nothing exists "but her song." In line 8, the use of onomatopaeia, "tat-de'ta'ta'ta" reinforces the idea of a happy, carefree youth.

Paragraph three, however, marks a small yet significant shift in the passage. Walker begins the paragraph with "Turning her back on the rusty boards of her family's sharecropper cabin, Myop . . ." Myop's world is not behind her, but moves forward to the familiar woods.

As the story progresses, there is a significant shift in paragraphs four and five. Walker begins to prepare the reader for her profound conclusion. While Myop has often explored the woods behind the house with her mother, today she sets out alone and "made her own path." As she walks through the woods, she cautiously keeps an eye out for snakes. The solitude of her journey, and the possibility of danger, builds suspense and prepares the reader for the dark surprise of the ending.

The diction of paragraphs four and five also contributes to the sudden shift in the passage. While the diction in the beginning was blithe, describing "beautiful," the language in paragraph five is negative, foreshadowing the conclusion. Specifically, Myop is disoriented by the, "strangeness of the land." It was "not as pleasant" as her usual expeditions. Furthermore, words such as "gloomy" and "damp" reiterate the dark setting and prepare the reader for the grotesque conclusion of the story.

Paragraph six, which is only one sentence long, marks a brief transition into the ending of the passage. Myop wants to return to her house, to the "peacefulness of the morning." But, while she was able to turn her back on the reality of her poverty, she will not be able to ignore the next truth that hits her.

"Stepping smack into his eyes," Myop encounters death, but is unafraid as she "frees herself." She is filled with innocent curiosity and gazes "around the spot with interest." Ironically, as she picks her "wild pink rose," a symbol of beauty, she spots the noose and has her epiphany.

The transition in image, setting, and diction all propel Walker's theme—the coming of age. In the last paragraph Myop picks up the flowers and places her bouquet in front of the lynched man. It is as if she is at a funeral, as if she has sobered from her carefree state to one of realization. For, in the last line, the images of the beginning are finally crushed. Myop can no longer return to the world of flower-gathering or sun-lit skipping. For Myop, the "summer is over."

This is a high-ranking essay for the following reasons:

- Indicates complete understanding of the prompt (lines 3–4).
- Cites appropriate details to support the thesis:
  - Imagery (lines 15, 25–30, 36)
  - Diction (lines 5–6, 10, 30)
  - Setting (lines 1, 15–16)
- Thoroughly explores contrasts (lines 12, 16–17, 45).
- Presents unique insights into the underlying theme (lines 16–17, 22–23, 41–43).
- Adheres well to topic, exhibits transitions, and connective tissue.
- Has a definite, clear progression of thought and a strong writer's voice.

This high-ranking essay presents a solid, mature, and insightful discussion and analysis of Myop's "epiphany" and how Walker prepares the reader for it.

Student Essay B

In the short story "The Flowers" by Alice Walker, the author conveys the meaning of the story and prepares the reader for the ending by using various literary techniques. Some of these are symbol, narrative pace, and style.

The narrative pace starts out as slow and relaxed as Myop explores the land around her family's sharecropper cabin. Every little detail is described creating an image of the blissful summer day. Myop's exuberance is portrayed through diction such as "skipped lightly," "she felt light and good," "bouncing," and "she was singing." Her innocence is shown by the way she is able to block out everything but her happiness and her song. The colors used in the beginning of the story further form the image that is being set up because they are earthy yet shiny colors such as "golden," "silver," and "dark brown." 5

The fifth paragraph is a transition of narrative pace. The diction and tone change from peaceful and relaxed to tense and dark. Diction such as "strangeness" and "gloomy" take over. When describing the new atmosphere, Walker uses syntax like "the air was damp, the silence close and deep." 15

From here, the story continues to darken and reaches a climax when Myop steps on a dead man's face. She then discovers his body—in parts and decaying. Walker's use of colors suddenly changes too. Now, "blue," "green," and "wild pink" are used. Although these colors can be seen as positive, in this story, they represent "rotting." Myop finds the noose as she picks up a flower. Such irony. 20

The last paragraph/sentence is brief and compact. It simply reads, "And the summer was over." The summer can be seen as a symbol of Myop's innocence. With the end of her summer, when she lays down her flowers, her innocence is gone forever. She can no longer exist "for nothing but her song." She had seen death in the midst of her paradise. 25

This is a midrange essay (5, 6, 7) for the following reasons:

- Makes adequate, expedient presentation of the details in developing the thesis.
- Illustrates an understanding of the selected literary devices used in the story, but does not fully link or expand them with regard to the thesis (lines 14–15, 9–10).
- Has unsupported interpretation in lines 18–19.
- In many places, the syntax resembles a list because ideas are not fully developed (lines 16–20).

This midrange essay addresses the prompt and provides details to support the thesis. While the writer obviously understood both the story and the author's process, the subtleties are not fully explored and the syntax lacks fluidity.

◀2 Rubrics for "The Naked and the Nude" by Robert Graves

High-range scores (8, 9):

- Indicates complete understanding of the requirements for discussing the differences in connotation between "naked" and "nude."

- Recognizes and identifies the many differences between the two words.
- Utilizes appropriate literary techniques to present a coherent distinction between the two words.
- Responds to the irony in the final stanza.
- Perceives Graves's tone and preference for one of the words.
- Interprets allusions, images, symbols, etc.
- Uses smooth transitions and clear connective tissue.
- Demonstrates a mature writing style.

Midrange scores (5, 6, 7):

- Refers accurately to the thesis involving the contrast in meanings between two words.
- Adequately supports the thesis with appropriate details.
- Is less adept at interpreting the poem.
- May not be sensitive to the complex allusions and images or vocabulary.
- Demonstrates writing that is adequate to convey the writer's intent.

Sample Student Essays

Student Essay A

Many people tend to use the words "naked" and "nude" interchangeably. Yet Robert Graves objects to this misconception in his poem "The Naked and the Nude." Although both words mean "without clothes," Graves interprets them differently with regard to their connotations. He points out that "naked" refers to the body itself, whereas, "nude" refers to a personality or state of mind. Through 5 his use of various allusions and imagery, Graves contrasts the two synonyms.

Graves dedicates one stanza apiece to explain his perception of each word. When describing the "naked," Graves uses several classical allusions. He points out that "the Hippocratic eye will see in nakedness, anatomy." Likewise, "naked shines the Goddess when she mounts her lion among men." It's clear that 10 nakedness only refers to the naked body. However, Graves uses allusions to deception and trickery to explain his concept of the nude. He says, "the nude are bold, the nude are sly . . . they grin a mock religious grin of scorn at those of naked skin." The concept of nude seems to be more of a cunning state of mind—"being naked with attitude." 15

The poet uses these details to create a certain imagery that clearly explains this discrepancy. His use of classical allusions creates images of peace, beauty, and spirituality which imply the inherent beauty of the human body on a physical level. Yet, the imagery created by the second set of details does not deal with the physical body. Graves explains that the nude have a cunning state of mind, "while draping 20 by a showman's trick their dishabille in rhetoric."

The contrast described in the poem, body versus mind, is reinforced when Graves tells us that the naked are physical bodies that are admired by "Lovers without reproach" and men of medicine. The nude, however, are more than that; they "are sly" and "hold each treasonable eye." The writer concludes that the naked, therefore, who compete against the nude may know defeat because the nude are more complex and cynical.

Graves's final stanza transfers the vulnerability of the naked to the nude. "When treading the briary patches of the dead," the nude will not have artifice to protect them from the Gorgons' whips—they will be the naked as well as the nude.

This is a high-ranking essay for the following reasons:

- Shows complete understanding of the prompt.
- Immediately presents an accurate distinction between "naked" and "nude" (lines 4–5).
- Utilizes allusion and imagery correctly and links examples to meaning (lines 8–11, 12–15, 17–18).
- Reinforces the contrast throughout the essay (lines 16, 22, 29–30).
- Indicates perceptive, subtle analysis (lines 20–21, 29).
- Is well organized.
- Demonstrates mature writing style.

This high-ranking essay is indicative of a confident writer and thinker. The paper is well focused, and it exhibits the writer's facility with literary terminology and analysis.

Student Essay B

The poem "The Naked and the Nude" written by Robert Graves explicitly shows how connotations can change the meaning of a thought or statement through images and other poetic devices. Those who are "naked" and those who are "nude" are not, according to the poem, in the same state of undress.

The speaker of the poem describes the differences between the naked and the nude using a variety of images and descriptions. He feels that one who is naked is hiding nothing while one who is nude is a picture of deception and art. The images of "Lovers without reproach who gaze on bodies naked and ablaze" depicts the honesty and truth that is given with love. Also the "Hippocratic eye will see in nakedness, anatomy." When this "eye" sees a naked person it is seeing what is really there and not what could be held in the deception of a person who is nude.

Although the naked are personified as "love" and "truth," when they "compete against the nude they may know defeat." This statement shows how those that are naked can sometimes be deceived and beaten by those who are artful liars. However, when it comes to the life after death, those who have been nude will also be naked, meaning that no matter what they were in life, when they die there will be no hiding behind the art of the body. Also, the facade that was built in life to hide from the truth will not work when it comes to the end.

Tone is another device that is used to convey the different connotations of naked and nude. When those who are naked are being discussed, the tone is not only 20 positive, it presents an image of those who are happy with their position in life. For example, nakedness is linked with words such as "love," "truth," "shines," and "Goddess." However, when the speaker directs his attention on the nude, the tone is just the opposite. Nude is associated with "scorn," "showman," and "mock-religious." The speaker's tone in the descriptions of the two states of undress presents a clear 25 difference in the connotations of the two words in the title of the poem.

The style and structure of the poem also contribute to conveying the two different connotations of naked and nude. The simple rhyme scheme shows how simplistic those that are naked can be as opposed to the deception and intricacies of those who are nude. The four stanza's each have a theme that it conveys. The first stanza 30 exhibits the differences between the naked and the nude. The second stanza has the theme of the freedom of the naked, while the third shows the deception of the nude. The fourth and final stanza reinforces the theme that everyone will be naked after death.

This is a midrange essay for the following reasons:

- Accurately addresses the prompt.
- Understands deception and artifice (lines 6–7).
- Refers to suitable textual material to support the thesis (lines 8–9, 22–24).
- Demonstrates an ability to handle literary analysis (19–25, 27–29).
- Stays on topic.
- Has several awkward sentences and punctuation and agreement errors (lines 10–11, 30).
- Uses transitions and connective tissue.

It's obvious that the writer of this mid-range essay understands both the prompt and process of literary analysis. The second half of the paper is not as strong as the first. Perhaps, this writer was feeling the time pressure.

2 Rubrics for the Free-Response Essay

High-range scores (8, 9):

- Effectively and coherently addresses the intentional dissembling of a character or group.
- Effectively and coherently analyzes how the dissembling contributes to character development.
- Effectively and coherently discusses how the dissembling contributes to the meaning of the work.

- Chooses an appropriate novel or play.
- Uses references insightfully to support and illustrate the dissembling.
- Thoroughly discusses the character's nature and its relation to the theme.
- Strongly adheres to topic.
- Substantiates development of the thesis.
- Exhibits mature writing style.

Midrange scores (5, 6, 7):

- Identifies the intentional dissembling of a character or group.
- Chooses an acceptable novel or play.
- Adequately addresses the prompt with respect to intentional dissembling and how it contributes to both character development and meaning.
- Uses obvious references to support the prompt.
- Discussion of the character's nature and its relation to the theme is less developed.
- Adheres to topic, but may have lapses in coherence.
- Discussion of the theme is less developed.
- Writing style is acceptable but may show lapses in syntax and/or diction.

Sample Student Essays

Student Essay A

"To thine own self be true," advises Polonius in Shakespeare's <u>Hamlet</u>. Too bad he doesn't follow his own counsel when he continually dissembles to advance his own position in Claudius's court. This deceitfulness is the cause of the destruction of the lives of his children, himself, and ultimately the kingdom. His seemingly minor deceits reinforce the theme of betrayal and deception in the play. 5

Our first impression of Polonius is a positive one when we see him supporting Laertes's desire to return to his studies in Paris. However, his fatherly advice, "to not be false to any man" is ironic because he has already hired Reynaldo to spy on his son. He tells Reynaldo to use a "bait of falsehood" to see if Laertes's friends will be faithful 10 and true. Polonius plans for this to include starting rumors and even malicious lies. Later in the play, Shakespeare has Rosencrantz and Guildenstern play out a parallel scene with Hamlet.

As with his son, Polonius seems to be genuinely concerned with the well-being of his daughter Ophelia. He tells her to reject the "love" letters and tokens from Hamlet 15 because he fears Hamlet only wants to take advantage of her and will not and cannot marry her. But soon we see the other side of this paternal schemer when Polonius willingly uses his daughter's emotional connections to Hamlet for his own purpose of furthering his service to Claudius. Hoping to prove that Hamlet's madness is caused

by love sickness, he permits himself to advance his own agenda even though he has to 20
know that it will cause pain and distress for both Ophelia and Hamlet.

Inevitably, Polonius's dissembling leads to his own destruction. Ever the
deceitful sycophant, he suggests to Claudius that he hide behind the arras in Gertrude's
chamber in order to spy on both her and Hamlet. While eavesdropping, he cries out
when he believes that Hamlet is attacking the Queen. Believing the voice to be that of 25
Claudius, Hamlet thrusts his sword through the curtain, fatally wounding Polonius.
Here, the irony lies in his death resulting from an attempt to protect Gertrude.

It is this act that is the catalyst for the subsequent tragic events: Ophelia's
madness and death, Laertes's desire for revenge, and Hamlet's fleeing Denmark. The
final tragedies of the play—the deaths of Ophelia, Laertes, Gertrude, Claudius, and 30
Hamlet—are all the results of further dissembling which is foreshadowed by
Polonius's deceit.

Although Polonius dies in Act III, he sets the foundation for the theme of deceit
and murder throughout the remainder of the drama. Truly, something was rotten in
the state of Denmark, and it was Polonius. 35

This is a high-range essay for the following reasons:

- Demonstrates a clear and focused understanding of the prompt and its demands.
- Exhibits solid evidence of the writer's knowledge of the chosen work.
- Demonstrates the ability to garner insights from the work.
- Uses appropriate illustrations and details (lines 8–9, paragraphs 3 and 4).
- Uses strong connective tissue.
- Demonstrates thorough development of ideas that are linked to the meaning of the work (lines 3–6, 11–13, 19–21).
- Strongly adheres to topic and organization.
- Uses mature vocabulary and syntax (lines 22–23, 28).

This high-range essay is strong because of its clear voice and strong organization. The introductory paragraph establishes the premise, which is fully supported in the body paragraphs. Rather than a summary, the concluding paragraph makes an insightful final comment connecting the topic and student interpretation.

Student Essay B

Often, in literature, there is a gap between the appearance of a situation
and the meaning of the truth behind it. In Shakespeare's Hamlet, the protagonist
assumes the antic disposition as a means of investigating the veracity of the
ghost's admonition, "The serpent that did sting thy father's life, now wears his
crown." In addition to contributing to the psychological development of Hamlet's 5
character, this deceit augments many of the important themes in the play. In a

work whose main topic is the search for truth, Hamlet's misrepresentation acts as a warning to sift through the surface appearance of things to discover purpose in this world.

Throughout the play, nothing is really as it seems. Hamlet's feigned 10 madness is perhaps the most egregious example of this pattern. The melancholy Dane becomes a different man behind the mask of insanity. He is free to taunt Polonius regarding his lack of intelligence, or to scold his mother for her sexual improprieties, or to chastise Ophelia for her attempt to trick him. He is free to express himself without the fear of being held responsible for his insolence. This 15 is a psychological coping method for Hamlet to deal with the trauma of a father's death and a mother's betrayal. Hamlet represses his anger and is paralyzed by it. The course of the play is a struggle for Hamlet to overcome his repression and to deal with the problems before him. Pretending to be mad is symbolic of this inner struggle and Hamlet's shield from the world. 20

Many of the major themes in Hamlet are also embodied in Hamlet's misrepresentation. The pervading irony in the play is that the "madman" is really thinking rationally. He sees what others do not and recognizes that his father was killed at Claudius's hands. Hamlet is a man who can and does make plans to seek the truth, and he carries these plans out. Another major theme is that of appearance 25 versus reality. Connected to and with Hamlet's situation is a king who is a murderer, a mystery involving a ghost, a play within a play, a royal request which will turn into an invasion of Denmark, spying for proof of madness, fatherly advice to his children, and friends who are enemies. Each of these separately and all of them together enhance this theme of the play. 30

Hamlet is a search for truth. Through the protagonist's discovery of self and the revelation of Claudius's guilt, he embodies everyman's striving for understanding. Dissembling as a madman, Hamlet is able to work toward his goal of gaining authentic knowledge of past events and future battles.

This is a solid midrange essay (5, 6, 7) for the following reasons:

- Writer has an obvious voice that engages the reader.
- Uses strong vocabulary.
- Decisively identifies theme and character.
- References are appropriate.
- Uses parallel structure well.
- Indicates cause and effect with supporting details.
- Uses inferences rather than plot.
- Good use of connective tissue.

Here is a paper that shows great promise and strength in the first half, but it loses continuity and lacks development in the second half. It seems that the writer has run out of time and is anxious to complete the essay. This student is a real thinker, but is trapped by time constraints.

Chapter 10

Practice Exam 2

5 **Answer Sheet for Multiple-Choice Questions**

1. _____	15. _____	29. _____	43. _____
2. _____	16. _____	30. _____	44. _____
3. _____	17. _____	31. _____	45. _____
4. _____	18. _____	32. _____	46. _____
5. _____	19. _____	33. _____	47. _____
6. _____	20. _____	34. _____	48. _____
7. _____	21. _____	35. _____	49. _____
8. _____	22. _____	36. _____	50. _____
9. _____	23. _____	37. _____	51. _____
10. _____	24. _____	38. _____	52. _____
11. _____	25. _____	39. _____	53. _____
12. _____	26. _____	40. _____	
13. _____	27. _____	41. _____	
14. _____	28. _____	42. _____	

I _____ did _____ did not complete this part of the test in the allotted 1 hour.

Scoring Formula:

I had _____ correct answers. I had _____ incorrect answers. I left _____ blank.

$$\underline{\hspace{3cm}} - \underline{\hspace{4cm}} = \underline{\hspace{2cm}}$$
number right   −   (number wrong × .25)   =   raw score

I have carefully reviewed the explanations of the answers, and I think I need to work on the following types of questions:

PRACTICE EXAM 2
ADVANCED PLACEMENT ENGLISH LITERATURE

Section I

Total time–1 hour

Carefully read the following passages and answer the questions that follow.

Questions 1–10 are based on the following poem.

The End of the World
by Archibald MacLeish

Quite unexpectedly, as Vasserot
The armless ambidextrian was lighting
A match between his great and second toe,
And Ralph the lion was engaged in biting
The neck of Madame Sossman while the drum   5
Pointed, and Teeny was about to cough
In waltz-time swinging Jocko by the thumb—
Quite unexpectedly the top blew off:

And, there, there overhead, there, there, hung over
Those thousands of white faces, those dazed eyes,   10
There in the starless dark, the poise, the hover,
There with vast wings across the cancelled skies,
There in the sudden blackness the black pall
Of nothing, nothing, nothing—nothing at all.

1. "The End of the World" is an example of a(n)

   A. ballad
   B. elegy
   C. sonnet
   D. villanelle
   E. lyric

2. The line that best indicates the theme of the poem is

   A. 8
   B. 9
   C. 11
   D. 14
   E. 10

3. "The armless ambidextrian" in line 2 is an example of

   A. personification
   B. consonance
   C. simile

   D. hyperbole
   E. oxymoron

4. The organization of the poem moves from

   A. a general statement supported by specific details
   B. highly specific event to a universal conclusion
   C. a comparison to a contrast
   D. past to present
   E. a definition to an example

5. The effect of the second stanza is primarily developed through

   A. metaphor
   B. allusion
   C. repetition
   D. satire
   E. rhyme

6. The concepts expressed in the poem are most in keeping with

   A. romanticism

B. naturalism
C. realism
D. classicism
E. existentialism

7. For emphasis, line 14 utilizes

A. caesura
B. apostrophe
C. spondees
D. symbol
E. internal rhyme

8. In line 12, "Vast wings across the cancelled skies" implies

A. judgment day
B. the coming of night
C. the promise of redemption

D. the angel of death
E. the power of nature

9. The irony of this poem depends upon

A. Ralph biting Madame Sossman
B. the use of the circus as a dominant conceit
C. color imagery
D. the rhyme scheme
E. the audience

10. The meter of line 7 is

A. iambic tetrameter
B. blank verse
C. iambic pentameter
D. anapestic pentameter
E. spondaic trimeter

Questions 11–23 are based on the following passage.

The Solitude of Self
by Elizabeth Cady Stanton

The point I wish plainly to bring before you on this occasion is the individuality of each human soul; the right of individual conscience and judgment; our republican idea, the individual citizenship. In discussing the right of woman we are to consider, first, what belongs to her as an individual in a world of her own, the arbiter of her own destiny, an imaginary Robinson Crusoe, with her woman Friday, on a solitary island. Her rights under such circumstances are to use all her faculties for her own safety and happiness.   5

Secondly, if we consider her as a citizen, as a member of a great nation, she must have the same rights as all members, according to the fundamental principles of our government.

The strongest reason for giving woman all the opportunities for higher education,   10
for the full development of her faculties, her forces of mind and body; for giving her the most enlarged freedom of thought and action; a complete emancipation from all forms of bondage, of custom, dependence, superstition; from all the crippling influences of fear—is the solitude and personal responsibility of her own individual life. The strongest reason why we ask for woman a voice in the government under which she lives; in the religion   15
she is asked to believe; a quality in social life, where she is the chief factor; a place in the trades and professions, where she may earn her bread, is because of her birth right to self-sovereignty; because, as an individual, she must rely on herself. No matter how much women prefer to lean, to be protected and supported, nor how much men desire to have them do so, they must make the voyage of life alone, and for safety in an emergency, they   20
must know something of the laws of navigation. To guide our own craft, we must be captain, pilot, engineer, with chart and compass to stand at the wheel; to watch the winds and waves, and know when to take in the sail, and to read the signs in the firmament over all. It matters not whether the solitary voyager is a man or woman; nature, having endowed them equally, leaves them to their own skill and judgment in the hour of danger, and, if not   25
equal to the occasion, alike they perish.

We come into the world alone, unlike all who have gone before us, we leave it alone, under circumstances peculiar to ourselves. No mortal ever has been, no mortal ever will be just like the soul just launched on the sea of life. No one has ever found two blades of ribbon

grass alike, and no one will ever find two human beings alike. Seeing, then, that what must   30
be the infinite diversity of human character, we can appreciate the loss to a nation when any
class of the people is uneducated and unrepresented in the government.

We ask for the complete development of every individual, first, for his own benefit and
happiness. In fitting out an army, we give each soldier his own knapsack, arms, powder,
blanket, and utensils. We provide alike for all their individual necessities; then each man bears   35
his own burden. We ask complete individual development for the general good. The great
lesson that nature seems to teach us is self-dependence, self-protection, self-support.

Amid the greatest triumphs and darkest tragedies of life, we walk alone. On the divine
heights of human attainment, we stand alone. Alone we starve or steal . . . Seeing, then, that life
must ever be a march and a battle, that each soldier must be equipped for his own protection,   40
it is the height of cruelty to rob the individual of a single natural right.

Whatever may be said of man's protecting power in ordinary conditions, amid all the
terrible disasters by land and sea, in the supreme moments of danger, alone woman must ever
meet the horrors of the situation. In that solemn solitude of self that links us with the
immeasurable and the eternal, each soul lives alone forever . . .   45

And yet, there is a solitude which each and every one of us has always carried with
him, more inaccessible than the ice cold mountains, more profound than the midnight sea; our
inner being which we call ourself.

Such is individual life. Who, I ask you, can take, dare take on himself the rights, the
duties, the responsibilities of another human soul?   50

11. The attitude of the author toward the
education of women is

A. denigrating
B. ambivalent
C. imperious
D. indifferent
E. imperative

12. In the passage, the author uses each of
the following *except*

A. metaphor
B. complex sentence structure
C. satire
D. allusion
E. parallel structure

13. For the author, the primary purpose of
the education of women is

A. self-sufficiency
B. control of others
C. to be equal with men
D. to meet the demand of society
E. to teach others

14. Paragraph three is developed using all
the following *except*

A. ironic contrast
B. examples
C. cause and effect
D. extended metaphor
E. parallel structure

15. The concept that all people have
diversity in common is an example of

A. paradox
B. cause and effect
C. analogy
D. understatement
E. parody

16. The "laws of navigation" (line 21) refer to

A. military laws
B. celestial navigation
C. laws of nature
D. tools needed for survival
E. God's commandments

17. "Our own craft" (line 21) is a
metaphor for our

A. soul
B. skills
C. bodies

D. navy

E. place in government

18. The twentieth century civil rights movement could most easily embrace which of the following paragraphs?

    A. 1
    B. 3
    C. 4
    D. 6
    E. 7

19. According to the passage, man and woman are alike in all the following ways *except*

    A. Nature made them equal.
    B. They are both solitary voyagers.
    C. If unprepared, both will die.
    D. Each has an inner being.
    E. They are interdependent.

20. Paragraph 7 contains examples of

    A. allusion
    B. hyperbole
    C. rhetorical questions
    D. simile
    E. apostrophe

21. In exhorting the public to work for equal rights for women, the author stresses

    A. the military needs of the nation
    B. the physical strength of women
    C. women's conflict with the universe
    D. the eternal nature of the soul
    E. the individuality and solitude of each person

22. The last sentence of the passage is an example of

    A. oxymoron
    B. irony
    C. rhetorical question
    D. a question dependent upon a logical fallacy
    E. paradox

23. Which of the following lines is not a thematic statement of the passage?

    A. 1–3 ("The point . . . citizenship")
    B. 5–6 ("Her . . . happiness")
    C. 30–32 ("Seeing . . . government")
    D. 34–35 ("In . . . utensils")
    E. 49–50 ("Such is . . . soul")

Questions 24–38 are based on the following poem.

Love Poem
by John Frederick Nims

My clumsiest dear, whose hands shipwreck vases,
At whose quick touch all glasses chip and ring,
Whose palms are bulls in china, burs in linen,
And have no cunning with any soft thing

Except all ill-at-ease fidgeting people: 5
The refugee uncertain at the door
You make at home; deftly you steady
The drunk clambering on his undulant floor.

Unpredictable dear, the taxi drivers' terror,
Shrinking from far headlights pale as a dime   10
Yet leaping before red apoplectic streetcars—
Misfit in any space. And never on time.

A wrench in clocks and the solar system. Only
With words and people and love you move at ease.
In traffic of wit expertly manoeuvre   15
And keep us, all devotion, at your knees.

Forgetting your coffee spreading on our flannel,
Your lipstick grinning on our coat,
So gayly in love's unbreakable heaven
Our souls on glory of spilt bourbon float.   20

Be with me, darling, early and late. Smash glasses—
I will study wry music for your sake.
For should your hands drop white and empty
All the toys of the world would break.

24. As used in the second stanza, "undulant" most closely means

A. polished
B. inebriated
C. wavy
D. dirty
E. cluttered

25. With reference to the title, the irony lies in the

A. reversal of the speaker's thoughts
B. absence of the beloved
C. kindness of the lover
D. enumeration of the lover's weaknesses
E. wit of the lover

26. The image of "hands drop white and empty" (line 23) implies the

A. breaking of vases
B. death of the lover
C. lover's clumsy nature
D. spilt bourbon
E. smashed glasses

27. The word "only" in line 13 serves to

A. introduce a contrasting thought
B. indicate isolation
C. make the rhyme effective
D. indicate cause and effect
E. indicate passage of time

28. According to the poem, the lover is all the following *except*

A. clever
B. clumsy
C. playful
D. selfish
E. gracious

29. "Be with me, darling" (line 21) is an example of

A. hyperbole
B. personification
C. allusion
D. invective
E. apostrophe

30. The poem is essentially a

A. caricature
B. satire
C. narrative
D. character study
E. parable

31. Lines 5 and 6 illustrate an example of

A. enjambment
B. oxymoron
C. jargon
D. connotation
E. ambiguity

32. The tone of the poem is

A. effusive
B. elegiac
C. benevolent
D. didactic
E. adoring

33. The speaker's attitude toward his love is

    A. critical
    B. embarrassed
    C. enthralled
    D. impatient
    F. ill-at-ease

34. "Toys of the world" in the last line of the poem may be best understood as a metaphor for

    A. life's pleasures
    B. youthful infatuations
    C. shattered dreams
    D. material objects
    E. lovers of the world

35. "A wrench in clocks and the solar system" (line 13) can be best interpreted to mean

    A. the speaker is uncomfortable
    B. star-crossed lovers
    C. being obsessive about time
    D. the inability to face the future

    E. being out of synch with established conventions

36. The poem is written in

    A. iambic pentameter
    B. free verse
    C. quatrains
    D. blank verse
    E. epigrams

37. Line 3 includes an example of

    A. metaphor
    B. synecdoche
    C. metonymy
    D. simile
    E. onomatopoeia

38. Line 20 employs

    A. internal rhyme
    B. cacophony
    C. apostrophe
    D. literary conceit
    E. assonance

Questions 39–53 are based on the following passage.

Excerpt from *As I Lay Dying*, "Addie,"
by William Faulkner

In the afternoon when school was out and the last one had left with his little dirty snuffling nose, instead of going home I would go down the hill to the spring where I could be quiet and hate them. It would be quiet there then, with the water bubbling up and away and the sun slanting quiet in the trees and the quiet smelling of damp and rotting leaves and new earth, especially in the   5
early spring, for it was worst then.

I could just remember how my father used to say that the reason for living was to get ready to stay dead for a long time. And when I would have to look at them day after day, each with his and her secret and selfish thought, and blood strange to each other blood and strange to mine, and think that this seemed to be the   10
only way I could get ready to stay dead, I would hate my father for having planted me. I would look forward to the times when they faulted, so I could whip them. When the switch fell I could feel it upon my flesh; when it welted and ridged it was my blood that ran, and I would think with each blow of the switch: Now you are aware of me! Now I am something in your secret and selfish life, who have marked   15
your blood with my own for ever and ever.

And so I took Anse. I saw him pass the school house three or four times before I learned that he was driving four miles out of his way to do it. I noticed then how he was beginning to hump—a tall man and young—so that he looked already like a tall bird hunched in the cold weather, on the wagon seat.   20

In the early spring it was worst. Sometimes I thought that I could not bear it, lying in bed at night, with the wild geese going north and their honking coming faint and high and wild out of the wild darkness, and during the day it would seem as though I couldn't wait for the last one to go so I could go down to the spring. And so when I looked up that day and saw Anse standing there in his Sunday clothes, turning his hat   25
round and round in his hands, I said:

"If you've got any womenfolks, why in the world dont they make you get your hair cut?"

"I aint got none," he said. Then he said suddenly, driving his eyes at me like two hounds in a strange yard: "That's what I come to see you about."   30

"And make you hold your shoulders up," I said. "You haven't got any? But you've got a house. They tell me you've got a house and a good farm. And you live there alone, doing for yourself, do you?" He just looked at me, turning the hat in his hands. "A new house," I said. "Are you going to get married?"

And he said again, holding his eyes to mine: "That's what I come to see you   35
about."

Later he told me, "I aint got no people. So that wont be no worry to you. I dont reckon you can say the same."

"No. I have people. In Jefferson."

His face fell a little. "Well, I got a little property. I'm forehanded; I got a   40
good honest name. I know how town folks are, but maybe when they talk to me . . . "

"They might listen," I said. "But they'll be hard to talk to." He was watching my face. "They're in the cemetery."

"But your living kin," he said. "They'll be different."

"Will they?" I said. "I dont know. I never had any other kind."   45
So I took Anse.

39. The "geese" (line 22) are a symbolic representation of

   A. Addie's desire to be part of a family
   B. Addie's desire to be connected to nature
   C. Addie's desire to be free
   D. the children Addie teaches
   E. the people in Jefferson

40. In the first paragraph, the reader learns all the following *except*

   A. the point of view of the piece
   B. the speaker's tone
   C. the conflicts
   D. the setting
   E. the central event of the narration

41. In lines 29–44, the character of Anse is revealed by which of the following literary techniques?

   A. colloquial diction
   B. rhetorical questions
   C. a shift in tense
   D. omniscient point-of-view
   E. humor

42. Figurative language is found in lines

   A. 4 and 8
   B. 23 and 25–26
   C. 1 and 2
   D. 19–20 and 29–30
   E. 7–8 and 35

43. The concept of alienation is supported by all of the following *except*

   A. "each with his and her secret and selfish thought"
   B. "blood strange to each other blood and strange to mine"
   C. "when the switch fell I could feel it upon my flesh"

D. "they're in the cemetery"
E. "I aint got no people"

44. Addie marries because

A. she is in love with Anse
B. it was expected of women
C. she thinks he will take her north
D. Anse presents himself at that particular time
E. she wants children

45. The reader can infer that Addie's role in the marriage will be

A. supportive
B. controlling
C. submissive
D. grateful
E. erotic

46. The repetition of the phrase "so I took Anse" serves to

A. further develop the setting
B. establish an ironic situation
C. highlight the importance of the event
D. support Addie's ambivalence
E. establish a matter-of-fact explanation of the relationship

47. In line 21, "In early spring it was worst," "it" refers to Addie's

A. restless nature
B. longing for Anse
C. sadistic tendencies
D. students' behavior
E. desire to be married

48. Addie whips the children primarily because

A. they talk back to her
B. she hates her job
C. she believes corporal punishment will make the children learn better
D. she wants them to know she is there
E. she sees no other way to control them

49. Which of the following ideas are presented and supported in the passage?

I. The relationship between life and death
II. Isolation and alienation
III. Freedom and commitment
A. I only
B. II only
C. III only
D. I and III
E. I, II, and III

50. Addie's philosophy and behavior most likely come from

A. her religious beliefs
B. her father
C. her childhood experiences
D. her people in Jefferson
E. her education

51. Which of the following images are contrasted in the passage?

A. the hill . . . the spring (lines 2–3)
B. water bubbling up . . . sun slanting (line 4)
C. rotting leaves . . . new earth (line 5)
D. welted . . . ridged (line 13)
E. secret . . . selfish (line 15)

52. On an interpretive level, Addie associates quiet with all of the following except

A. hatred
B. innermost feelings
C. escape
D. nature
E. death

53. Symbolically, "early spring" may represent

A. bubbling water
B. the blood
C. "womenfolks"
D. Addie's life force
E. secret and selfish lives

End of Section I

Section II

Total time—2 hours

Question 1

(Suggested time 40 minutes. This questions counts
as one-third of the total score for Section II.)

In the short story "Reginald's Choir Treat" Saki contrasts two philosophies of life.
In a well-organized essay, identify and discuss these two views and which of them the reader
can infer is preferred by the narrator. Develop your discussion referring to at least two
elements of the writer's craft such as irony, contrast, narration, dialogue, allusion, and tone.

Reginald's Choir Treat
by Saki

"Never," wrote Reginald to his most darling friend, "be a pioneer. It's the Early Christian
that gets the fattest lion."

Reginald, in his way, was a pioneer.

None of the rest of his family had anything approaching Titian hair or a sense of
humour, and they used primroses as a table decoration.   5

It follows that they never understood Reginald, who came down late to breakfast,
and nibbled toast, and said disrespectful things about the universe. The family ate porridge,
and believed in everything, even the weather forecast.

Therefore the family was relieved when the vicar's daughter undertook the reformation
of Reginald. Her name was Anabel; it was the vicar's one extravagance. Anabel was   10
accounted a beauty and intellectually gifted: she never played tennis, and was reputed to
have read Maeterlinck's "Life of a Bee." If you abstain from tennis and read Maeterlinck in
a small country village, you are of necessity intellectual. Also she had been twice to Fecamp
to pick up a good French accent from the Americans staying there; consequently she had a
knowledge of the world which might be considered useful in dealings with a worldling.   15

Hence the congratulations in the family when Anabel undertook the reformation of
the wayward member.

Anabel commenced operations by asking her unsuspecting pupil to tea in the vicarage
garden; she believed in the healthy influence of natural surroundings, never having been in
Sicily, where things are different.   20

And like every woman who has ever preached repentance to unregenerate youth, she
dwelt on the sin of an empty life, which always seems so much more scandalous in the
country, where people rise early to see if a new strawberry has happened during the night.

Reginald recalled the lilies of the field, "which simply sat and looked beautiful, and
defied competition."   25

"But that is not an example for us to follow," gasped Anabel.

"Unfortunately, we can't afford to. You don't know what a world of trouble I take in trying
to rival the lilies in their artistic simplicity."

"You are really indecently vain in your appearance. A good life is infinitely preferable
to good looks."   30

"You agree with me that the two are incompatible. I always say beauty is only skin
deep."

Anabel began to realize that the battle is not always to the strong-minded. With the
immemorial resource of her sex, she abandoned the frontal attack and laid stress on her
unassisted labours in parish work, her mental loneliness, her discouragements—and at the   35
right moment she produced strawberries and cream. Reginald was obviously affected by the
latter, and when his preceptress suggested that he might begin the strenuous life by helping
her to supervise the annual outing of the bucolic infants who composed the local choir, his
eyes shone with the dangerous enthusiasm of a convert.

Reginald entered on the strenuous life alone, as far as Anabel was concerned. The   40
most virtuous women are not proof against damp grass, and Anabel kept to her bed with a
cold. Reginald called it a dispensation; it had been the dream of his life to stage-manage a
choir outing. With strategic insight, he led his shy, bullet-headed charges to the nearest
woodland stream and allowed them to bathe; then he seated himself on the discarded gar-
ments and discoursed on their immediate future, which, he decreed, was to embrace a   45
Bacchanalian procession through the village. Forethought had provided the occasion with
a supply of tin whistles, but the introduction of a he-goat from a neighbouring orchard was a
brilliant afterthought. Properly, Reginald explained, there should have been an outfit of
panther skins; as it was, those who had spotted handkerchiefs were allowed to wear them,
which they did with thankfulness. Reginald recognized the impossibility in the time at his   50
disposal, of teaching his shivering neophytes a chant in honour of Bacchus, so he started
them off with a more familiar, if less appropriate, temperance hymn. After all, he said, it
is the spirit of the thing that counts. Following the etiquette of dramatic authors on first
nights, he remained discreetly in the background while the procession, with extreme
diffidence and the goat, wound its way lugubriously towards the village. The singing had   55
died down long before the main street was reached, but the miserable wailing of pipes
brought the inhabitants to their doors. Reginald said he had seen something like it in pictures;
the villagers had seen nothing like it in their lives, and remarked as much freely.

Reginald's family never forgave him. They had no sense of humour.

Question 2

(Suggested time 40 minutes. This question counts
as one-third of the total score for Section II.)

In "The Tables Turned" by William Wordsworth and "To David, About His Education"
by Howard Nemerov, the poets reveal their attitudes toward education.
In a well-organized essay discuss their similarities and differences.
You may wish to consider style, tone, poetic devices, structure, and imagery.

The Tables Turned
by William Wordsworth

Up! up! my friend, and quit your books;
Or surely you'll grow double:
Up! up! my friend, and clear your looks;
Why all this toil and trouble?   4

The sun, above the mountain's head,
A freshening lustre mellow
Through all the long, green fields has spread,
His first sweet evening yellow.   8

Books! 'tis a dull and endless strife:
Come, hear the woodland linnet,
How sweet his music! on my life,
There's more of wisdom in it.   12

And hark! how blithe the throstle sings!
He, too, is no mean preacher:
Come forth into the light of things,
Let Nature be your teacher.   16

She has a world of ready wealth,
Our minds and hearts to bless,—
Spontaneous wisdom breathed by health,
Truth breathed by cheerfulness.   20

One impulse from a vernal wood
May teach you more of man,
Of moral evil and of good,
Than all the sages can.   24

Sweet is the lore which Nature brings;
Our meddling intellect
Misshapes the beauteous forms of things,—
We murder to dissect.   28

Enough of Science and of Art;
Close up those barren leaves;
Come forth, and bring with you a heart
That watches and receives.   32

To David, About His Education
by Howard Nemerov

The world is full of mostly invisible things,
And there is no way but putting the mind's eye,
Or its nose, in a book, to find them out,
Things like the square root of Everest
Or how many times Byron goes to Texas,   5
Or whether the law of the excluded middle
Applies west of the Rockies. For these
And the like reasons, you have to go to school
And study books and listen to what you are told,
And sometimes try to remember. Though I don't know   10
What you will do with the mean annual rainfall
On Plato's Republic, or the calorie content
Of the Diet of Worms, such things are said to be
Good for you, and you will have to learn them
In order to become one of the grown-ups   15
Who sees invisible things neither steadily nor whole,
But keeps gravely the grand confusion of the world
Under his hat, which is where it belongs,
And teaches small children to do this in their turn.

Question 3

(Suggested time 40 minutes. This question counts
as one-third of the total score for Section II.)

Frequently a work of literature will concern itself with a major transformation
in a character. This transformation could be actual or symbolic. Choose a full-length work
and write a well-organized essay in which you discuss the nature of the transformation
and its relationship to character and theme. You may choose from the list below
or another novel or play of literary merit.

Frankenstein   *Othello*
Hamlet   *I Know Why the Caged Bird Sings*
Metamorphosis   *Gulliver's Travels*
Native Son   *Sula*
Dr. Jekyll and Mr. Hyde   *The Importance of Being Earnest*
A Doll's House   *The Color Purple*
The Poisonwood Bible   *The Awakening*
Twelfth Night   *Things Fall Apart*
Invisible Man   *King Lear*
The Joy Luck Club   *The Stranger*
Madame Bovary   *The Scarlet Letter*
Pygmalion

End of Section II

ANSWERS TO MULTIPLE-CHOICE QUESTIONS

1 Answer Key

1. C	15. A	29. E	43. C
2. A	16. D	30. D	44. D
3. E	17. C	31. A	45. B
4. B	18. C	32. E	46. E
5. C	19. E	33. C	47. A
6. E	20. B	34. A	48. D
7. A	21. E	35. E	49. E
8. D	22. C	36. C	50. B
9. B	23. D	37. A	51. C
10. C	24. C	38. E	52. A
11. E	25. D	39. C	53. D
12. C	26. B	40. E	
13. A	27. A	41. A	
14. A	28. D	42. D	

Explanation of the Answers to the Multiple-Choice Questions

1. **C.** This is a simple question that addresses poetic form. The poem has two stanzas, one an octave, the other a sextet with a definite sonnet rhyme scheme. This is obviously a modern sonnet.

2. **A.** Use the title as a reference point and you will realize that this is the only point that can stand alone and express an idea synonymous with the title. The others all support what happens once this occurs.

3. **E.** This question can be attacked using the process of elimination. The student who knows poetic devices will quickly see that each of the other terms is not appropriate in the given situation.

4. **B.** The first stanza concerns itself with a specific circus. While it can be argued that the circus is a metaphor for the world, the organization is through concrete references. The second stanza expands to an ending which leaves no doubt that it encompasses all of existence.

5. **C.** Even though there is a definite rhyme scheme in this stanza, it does not emphasize the totality of the event. There are no metaphors, allusions, or instances of satire. The repetition of "There" and "nothing" stresses the enormity of the end of the world.

6. **E.** This question expects the student to have some familiarity with the major literary movements in Western literature. The emphasis on the concept of random nothingness (nada), or lack of meaning, is a cornerstone of existential thinking.

7. **A.** Caesura is an internal break within a line which requires the reader to pause and consider what follows. Look at the dash in this line.

8. **D.** "Vast wings across the cancelled skies" alludes to the angel of death because the implication is that all life is over. The other choices are associated with death but not as this specific poem is developed.

9. **B.** This choice associates life, light, innocence, and entertainment with the circus. To have its top blown off is unexpected and, therefore, ironic.

10. **C.** This question is one that requires your knowledge of meter. Iambic is ˘ /, and there are five of these feet in line 7.

11. **E.** This is one of those questions that assumes you have a working AP level vocabulary. You can immediately eliminate A and D because of their negative associations. "Ambivalent" relates to being undecided and "imperious" refers to a controlling attitude. Therefore, E is the appropriate choice since Stanton is stressing the need to ensure equal rights to women.

12. **C.** Metaphor can be spotted in paragraphs 3 and 5. Complex sentence structure is part of the author's style. Just look at the first sentence of paragraph 3. Allusions are part of paragraph 1, and parallel structure is incorporated into paragraphs 3 and 5. You will find no examples of satire in this passage.

13. **A.** The idea of self-sufficiency as the key to personal safety and happiness is stressed in almost every paragraph. Close reading reveals that none of the other choices is developed.

14. **A.** Ironic contrast is absent from the entire passage. You can locate examples of each of the other choices. Examples are found in paragraph 5. Cause and effect are part and parcel of paragraph 3; an extended metaphor is developed in paragraph 3, and parallel structure is used in paragraph 4.

15. **A.** "Diversity" and "common" are mutually exclusive terms. If you know the definition of paradox, this will lead you to paradox as the only appropriate choice.

16. **D.** The answer to this question depends on a clear understanding of the extended metaphor developed around sailing. A sailor needs to use the laws of navigation to safely sail the seas, just as a human being needs self-sufficiency to survive the world at large.

17. **C.** Following the structure of the extended sea/sailor metaphor, you should recognize that self-sufficiency refers to the "craft as body" being independent.

18. **C.** Paragraph 4 stresses the need for a strong nation to accept differences and to understand that any diminished class diminishes the entire country.

19. **E.** The focus of the entire passage is on the solitary nature of human beings and the need for self-sufficiency. Although men and women must interact, ultimately, each is responsible for himself or herself.

20. **B.** If you know the definition of hyperbole, you will recognize the examples in paragraph 7: "each and every one . . . ," "always . . . ," "more inaccessible than the ice cold mountains . . . ," and "more profound than the midnight sea."

21. **E.** The answer comes from a careful reading and understanding of the complete passage and its organization. The concept of equality and human rights was basic for Stanton as it is for anyone involved in civil rights.

22. **C.** Here, again, a working familiarity with literary terminology is required. Since Stanton asks a question that does not require a direct response, C is the appropriate choice.

23. **D.** These lines are part of the metaphor Stanton develops to support the other four choices cited.

24. **C.** You should use the context of lines 7–8 to help you. "Steady" implies a lack of movement and leads you to the best choice, "wavy," which implies motions.

25. **D.** The entire poem lists the beloved's faults, yet the speaker adores her for them. This contradiction is the essence of the ironic title. Choice A is close, but it refers to the situation of the entire poem, not just the title.

26. **B.** It is easy to jump to the conclusion that the lover has broken yet another object. However, A, C, D, and E all support that idea; therefore, they cancel one another out.

27. **A.** You are required to reread the lines prior to the word "only" in order to realize that it provides a contrast. B and C are readily eliminated with a glance, and D and E are not supported by the poem.

28. **D.** Pay careful attention to the word "except." Then use substitution to find the one quality she does not exhibit. The answer is supported in line 14 with "wit," line 1 with "clumsy," line 14 with "at ease," and line 19 with "gayly."

29. **E.** By definition, an apostrophe is an example of direct address.

30. **D.** Even though there is some exaggeration and humor, they are used to develop the character of the beloved, and a narrative requires elements of a story.

31. **A.** As you can see, it is imperative that you know terminology. (See Chapter 8.) To make sense, lines 4 and 5 must be read smoothly to the punctuation rather than to the end of the line.

32. **E.** The tone is revealed clearly in lines 16, 19, 23, and 24. The speaker adores his beloved.

33. **C.** This is a question that is almost too easy. Use your information from question 9 to help you recognize that all the other choices are negative.

34. **A.** As toys bring joy and delight, so, too, does the lover bring pleasure to the speaker's life. She holds toys and the speaker in her hands.

35. **E.** The clocks and solar system represent time and space. (See metonymy in Chapter 9.) "Wrench" indicates a breakdown of a system (e.g., "throwing a wrench into the system").

36. **C.** A straightforward, factual question. Again, you need to know your terms.

37. **A.** This is a poetic term and example question. The two metaphors are that palms are "bulls" and "burs in linen."

38. **E.** This is a subtle question which asks you to hear the sound of the line. All the open "O" sounds reinforce the idea of floating. None of the other given devices is present in this line.

39. **C.** One of the universal symbols of freedom is flight. To refer to "wild geese going north" is to reinforce Addie's desire to be free.

40. **E.** "I" indicates a first person narrator point of view. The phrases "little dirty snuffling nose," "the damp and rotting leaves," and "it was worst then" are indicative of conflict, setting, and tone. What is *not* mentioned in this first paragraph is a central event.

41. **A.** These lines are primarily composed of dialogue, so it is here that you should look for your answer. Vocabulary, similes, and syntax all point to colloquial (informal, conversational) diction.

42. **D.** The similes found in these two sets of lines are examples of figurative language. The other lines are factual and reportorial.

43. **C.** The concepts and images associated with alienation are found in phrases containing "secret," "blood strange," "cemetery," and "got no people." C, on the other hand, is cause and effect.

44. **D.** There is no evidence of any of the other choices in the passage. The very last line begins with the word "so." It is indicative of a matter-of-fact result of Anse being in the right place at the right time.

45. **B.** In this passage, Addie's conversation and interaction with Anse always places him in a subservient, uncomfortable position. See lines 27–28 and 31–33 to support the idea of her dominance.

46. **E.** Lines 17 and 46 indicate a straightforward cause and effect that just so happens to lead to Addie marrying Anse. Ambivalence, irony, setting, and highlighting an event are *not* references of the given phrase.

47. **A.** The "it" in this question is used the second time in the same way. See lines 4–6: The early spring, longing, potential, and desire to be free as wild geese lead to the conclusion that Addie has a restless nature.

48. **D.** Lines 1–15 give you the direct answer. ". . . and I would think with each blow of the switch: Now you are aware of me!"

49. **E.** A careful reading of the passage will lead you through Addie's experiences and thoughts about living and dying, about being alone,

about being in a relationship, and about being free. Therefore, you would correctly choose all three of the given possibilities.

50. **B.** The second paragraph gives you the correct answer. It directly refers to the father.

51. **C.** Contrast demands difference. The only appropriate choice, therefore, is "rotting leaves . . . new earth." Rotting and new are the contrast here.

52. **A.** Paragraphs 1, 2, and 4 allow the reader into Addie's psyche. The one characteristic *not* associated with her seeking quiet is hatred.

53. **D.** This is another universal symbol. The associations with spring, especially early spring, center around renewal, regeneration, hope, fertility, and the continuance of life.

RATING THE ESSAY SECTION

Rubrics for "Reginald's Choir Treat" by Saki

High-range scores (8, 9):

- Indicates complete understanding of the prompt.
- Identifies the two views of life presented in the story.
- Recognizes which view is preferred by the author.
- Effectively and coherently analyzes Saki's craft.
- Is cognizant of satire.
- Recognizes the humor in the allusions.
- Understands the irony and tone of the essay.
- Delineates Reginald's character.
- Cites appropriate textual references.
- Presents advanced insight.
- Strongly adheres to topic and uses connective tissue.
- Demonstrates an ability to manipulate language in a mature style.

Midrange scores (5, 6, 7):

- Refers accurately to the prompt.
- Presents the two philosophies.
- Refers accurately to Saki's craft.
- Infers the narrator's preference of lifestyle.
- Presents less developed discussion of the two views of life.
- Adequately links elements of the discussion.
- May miss the satire of the story.
- Concentrates on the obvious rather than on the inferences and implications.
- Organization is adequate.
- May exhibit a few errors in syntax and/or diction.

Sample Student Essays

Student Essay A

In the short story "Reginald's Choir Treat" Saki contrasts two philosophies of life. One is a daring, cynical, and whimsical approach to life, like Reginald's. The other is a conservative, intellectual, religious, reforming approach to life like Anabels's. The author's sarcastic tone with a hint of diffidence indicates that he agrees with Reginald's cause, but he pities the fact that few people can relate to or understand "pioneers." Saki contrasts and   5
shows the irony of both Anabel and Reginald's actions and perspectives about life to help the reader understand the two philosophies. However, even Anabel's philosophy shares some similarities to Reginald's and is more appealing to Saki's story than that of Reginald's family, which lives a modest, pedestrian, and uncompromising life, with no tolerance for the whims of Reginald.   10

Reginald does not fit in with his family's lifestyle. He questioned the universe and pleased himself with unconventional fantasies. Anabel is a gifted vicar's daughter who leads a charitable life and tries to be worldly at the same time. She attempts to make Reginald more religious and to coax him with her womanly charms but is unsuccessful. Saki ironically has her traveling to a French resort to pick up a good French accent from   15
the Americans living there. She also persuades Reginald to lead a more virtuous life like herself and then ironically leaves Reginald to complete one of her charitable obligations without her. In a dialogue between the two main characters, Saki uses conversation to contrast Reginald with Anabel's perspectives. She speaks against the "sin of an empty life," and Reginald recalls the artistic "simplicity of the lilies" that simply sit and look beautiful.   20
The greatest humorous irony of the story is Reginald turning religious charity work in the form of a choir outing into a whimsical pagan festival which is an allusion to the mythological Bacchus, the god of wine and pleasure. He shows his carefree and sarcastic approach to life by giving choirboys "tin whistles" and parading them through the streets with symbols of Bacchus. Another irony is that he has children honor Bacchus (god of wine) with a   25
temperance hymn familiar to them, and that the parade which was intended to be gay turns out to be a lugubrious procession with the "miserable wailing of pipes."

A sign that Saki sides with Reginald's unappreciated actions over those of Anabel, or especially those of his family, is in the story's conclusion. Reginald's family never forgives him, and Saki adds that they felt this way because "they had no sense of humour."   30
This makes it clear that the unfortunate and almost bitter ending is their flaw and not Reginald's because they should have appreciated the humor of the situation.

Saki shows that he shares some of Reginald's philosophy with his frequent use of irony and sarcasm. He shows that people who share Anabel's philosophy will not be able to reform those whimsical pioneers like Reginald. But, they should be amiable and attempt   35
to appreciate the sense of humor in the actions of those like Reginald. If not, they will be doomed to live an ill-humored, mundane life like that of Reginald's family.

This is a high-ranking essay for the following reasons:

- Contains a clear opening, which sets up the organization of the essay.
- Is direct and accurate.
- Establishes Saki's attitude.
- Introduces sarcasm and defends it (lines 3–5).
- Clarifies distinction between the two views and the characters (lines 5–10, 11–14).
- Contains strong textual references.
- Addresses the writer's craft.
- Juxtaposes the two characters and their opposing views (lines 18–20).
- Provides a perceptive interpretation of a grammatical detail (lines 29–31).
- Strongly adheres to topic.
- Uses echo words well.
- Draws appropriate conclusions based on the evidence presented (lines 34–37).
- Writes good transitions.
- Organization, syntax, and diction are adequate.

This is an essay that can be categorized as high. Its strong textual references and understanding of the subtleties allow it to be in the high range even though there are some lapses in syntax.

Student Essay B

Saki's short story "Reginald's Choir Treat" contrasts two different philosophies of life. Each philosophy is represented by different characters. Conformity is represented by Anabel and nonconformity is represented by Reginald. In this story, Anabel and Reginald's parents try to make Reginald conform to the rest of society. Yet, his choir treat demonstrates that their goal failed. Through his use of tone, dialogue, and contrast, Saki indirectly shows his support of Reginald's nonconformity.

Saki uses a sarcastic tone, particularly towards Anabel and the other conformists. The first line of the story has an adage from Reginald: "never be a pioneer. It's the Early Christian that gets the fattest lion." This saying sets the sarcastic tone for the rest of the story. Later on, in his description of Anabel, Saki notes that, "if you abstain from tennis and read Maeterlinck in a small country village, you are of necessity intellectual." Likewise, in his description of Reginald's family, Saki points out that the rest of his family . . . used "primroses as a table decoration." Saki is mocking all the conformists because of their desire to conform to society. He uses this sarcastic tone to demonstrate his partiality towards Reginald's free nature.

Saki also uses a contrast between Reginald and Anabel. The only direct description of Reginald is that "[He], in his way, is a pioneer." On the other hand, the author describes many details about Anabel. He calls Anabel, "the vicar's one extravagance."

Yet, in this case, Saki uses the pronoun "it" to refer to Anabel's fanciful name, demonstrating his distaste for her. He sarcastically relates that "Anabel was accounted 20 a beauty and intellectually gifted" because "she had been twice to Fecamp to pick up a good French accent from the Americans staying there." Saki presents the notion that many believe the conformists are better than the nonconformists and uses Anabel to refute that notion. Despite these accolades Saki has attributed to her, he mocks her and her philosophy.

Similarly, Saki uses dialogue to demonstrate his favoring nonconformity. The 25 conversation between Reginald and Anabel revolves around trying to convince Reginald to abandon his nonconformity. She tries to do so by insulting him. Anabel tells him that "[He is] really incessantly vain in [his] appearance." For a woman who is supposed to be smart and sweet, she does not display any of those qualities here. Her nasty nature towards Reginald in this dialogue further emphasizes Saki's distaste for her and 30 her philosophy.

Obviously, Saki views individual expression as important and nonthreatening. He recognizes that the best weapon to fight conformity is humor.

This is a midrange essay for the following reasons:

- Clearly sets up the prompt and the organization of the essay (lines 1–6).
- Establishes the characters of Reginald and Anabel.
- Recognizes and discusses sarcasm (lines 10–11).
- Presents dialogue as indicative of character (lines 25–30).
- Makes inferences and understands satire.
- Presents author's preference and defends it (lines 7, 13–15).
- Draws threads of essay together and synthesizes technique with interpretation (lines 32–33).

What does not allow this essay to be rated in the high range is its syntax and diction.

Rubrics for the Poetry Essay

High-range scores (8, 9):

- Effectively and coherently discusses each poet's attitude toward education.
- Effectively and coherently discusses the similarities and differences between the two poems.
- Indicates a fluency with poetic analysis.
- Identifies and analyzes appropriate references to support an interpretation.
- Exhibits strong topic adherence and connective tissue.
- Draws mature inferences.

- Responds to subtleties in both poems.
- Writer's syntax and diction demonstrate a mature style.

Midrange scores (5, 6, 7):

- Adequately addresses the prompt.
- Identifies and discusses the writers' techniques.
- Adequately discusses similarities and differences between the two poems.
- Presents an adequate discussion of each poet's attitude.
- Displays acceptable writing skills.
- May not be sensitive to inference and tone.
- Focuses on the obvious and may not recognize the subtleties in both poems.
- Writing may have a few errors in syntax and/or diction.

Student Essay A

"The Tables Turned" by William Wordsworth and "To David, About His Education" by Howard Nemerov promulgate two different views of education. While they both agree that being taught and learning are important and necessary, there is a disagreement about where the lessons should come from, the purpose and direction of education, and the value which education possesses. Not only are the ideas of each selection dissimilar, but the structure, tone, and imagery are as well, which facilitates each poet's argument.

"The Tables Turned" espouses learning through experience and living in nature. The speaker wants students to "quit their books" (1) and "Let Nature be your teacher" (16). He believes that there is a great deal more to be learned from experience than can ever be found in a book. The education suggested in this poem is a practical one. Learning about the environment and how the world works from experiencing it will allow a person to make his own conclusions and proceed as he sees fit. Wordsworth believes that his brand of education through nature will provide "spontaneous wisdom breathed by health/truth breathed by cheerfulness." (19-20) This education does not merely cultivate the mind, but also the soul and spirit.

On the other hand, "To David, About His Education" suggests that the important parts of life are learned through books. Where the Wordsworth poem calls books "dull and endless strife, (99) but putting the mind's eye/ or its nose, in a book" (2-3) to receive a proper education. Nemerov's poem suggests that studying from books is a more effective way to learn but cannot procure a benefit to the method. He merely states, "You will have to learn them/ in order to become one of the grown-ups," (14-15) not to become any kind of an enlightened, educated person. The images in the poem by Nemerov are of ridiculous facts and esoteric information, such as "the square root of Everest" (4) or the "calorie content of the Diet of Worms" (13).

The images are hyperbolic examples of the need for an education through books. Only this kind of an education will produce the answers to such questions.

In contrast, Wordsworth used natural images to explain the merit of education 30
through experience. He notes that there is more wisdom in the songs of birds than in the world's books.

The tone that Wordsworth uses is accusatory and somewhat didactic. In lines 17-18 he says that time is being wasted on books when nature has so much more to offer. He urges the student to "Let Nature be your teacher" (16). Yet, Nemerov uses 35
the tone of an all-knowing sage to suggest that there is a plethora of knowledge available in texts. The facts stated in his poem are obviously false, like "how many times Byron goes to Texas" (5), but their inclusion reinforces the tone of great wisdom and knowledge.

Likewise, the diction that Wordsworth uses, such as "intellect," "wisdom," and 40
"truth" convey a more complete education than words like "learn," "remember," or "find out" which appear in Nemerov's poem.

Although both poems advocate a form of education, the means to their ends are quite different.

This is a high-ranking essay for the following reasons:

- Contains a sophisticated and complex introduction to the task at hand (lines 1–8).
- Clearly and concisely identifies the attitude of both poets toward education and supports it with references to the text (lines 10–11, 23–25).
- Perceives implications arising from the poems (lines 12–13).
- Uses connective tissue well.
- Contrast discussed with support (lines 26–33, 30–33).
- Pulls together the similarities and differences with respect to imagery (lines 28–29), tone (lines 35–37), and diction (lines 40–42).

This spare essay falls into the high range because it is packed with appropriate detail and effective and coherent analyses and interpretation.

Student Essay B

William Wordsworth and Howard Nemerov disagree about how one should be educated. Their differences in style, structure, and most importantly, tone are quite obvious from the very opening line of each poem.

Although most people would tend to agree with Nemerov's viewpoint that a proper education is achieved through schooling, Wordsworth makes an interesting 5
opposition in his poem, "The Tables Turned," which questions the concept of an education through school, favoring a more "hands on" approach. By opening his poem with the exclamation "Up! Up!," he immediately attracts attention to the page. His instructions to quit studying, however, are quite ironic considering his allusion to

Shakespeare's <u>Macbeth</u>. While he attempts to prove that studying is worthless, he   10
is illustrating through his references that he is a learned man. Additionally,
Wordsworth glorifies Nature by pointing out the "freshening lustre" and "sweet music,"
which also makes studying seem dull and boring in comparison. The imagery
Wordsworth uses clearly illustrates his bias that nature is better than school. Nature is
always referred to as "light," and "sweet," whereas studies are thought of as "toil and   15
trouble," "a dull and endless strife," and "barren leaves." By continuing to use
exclamation points and "exciting" words including "hark" throughout the poem,
Wordsworth continues in his upbeat state when referring to Nature. In fact,
Wordsworth is so reverent toward nature that he personifies her. The most glaring
point illustrated in the poem comes in the last verse. Wordsworth basically sums up   20
his entire poem in those four lines, which exclaim that studying nature is a more
fulfilling education than constantly reading books of Science and Art.

   Throughout the poem "To David, About His Education," Nemerov illustrates
just as Wordsworth did through his reference to Shakespeare, that he is very educated.
At times, it seems as if Nemerov has a sarcastic, almost cynical approach toward   25
school, with his mocking of things taught in school, such as "the square root of Everest."
Yet, he realizes the underlying benefits of a proper education, as he points out that "such
things are said to be good for you." Nemerov uses a very unusual structure in this poem,
as he applies two or more academic subjects which may have nothing in common except
that they are both taught in school, and he is able to tie them together to make sense,   30
almost in joking manner. Statements such as "the law of the excluded middle applies
west of the Rockies" illustrate this method, as does the "calorie count of the Diet of
Worms." Although Diet of Worms has nothing to do with eating, Nemerov connects the
two almost as if his brain has been overloaded with useless information, similar to the
way a student might accidentally confuse the material of multiple subjects he is   35
studying. Nemerov fully understands the value of an education "in order to become
one of the grown-ups."

   Wordsworth and Nemerov have blatantly opposing opinions about the best method
of education. While Wordsworth illustrates through his poem that an education through
Nature is more valuable than spending hours reading books, Nemerov understands that   40
in order to be accepted by society, a knowledge of academic subjects is vital.

This is a midrange essay for the following reasons:

- Adequately illustrates a facility with analysis with respect to imagery (lines 13–16), tone (lines 18–19, 25–26, 31–32).
- Is clearly on topic with good use of connective tissue.
- Provides adequate evidence to defend interpretations (lines 31–36).

This is a strong midrange essay with clear analysis, topic adherence, and support. Details chosen are obvious, and the presentation has a few lapses in syntax and diction.

⬤ 2 Rubrics for the Free-Response Essay

High-range scores (8, 9):

- Effectively and coherently addresses the nature of the transformation.
- Effectively and coherently discusses the effects of the transformation on character and meaning.
- Insightful choice of details from an appropriate novel or play.
- Differentiates between actual and symbolic transformations.
- Focuses on the results of the transformation with regard to character and theme.
- Thoroughly discusses a specific character in context.
- Strongly adheres to topic.
- Demonstrates mature writing style.

Midrange scores (5, 6, 7):

- Adequately identifies and discusses the transformation.
- Adequately addresses the transformation's effect on the character and theme.
- Results of transformation are presented with less developed discussion and/or analysis.
- Relies on obvious details to support the prompt or discussion.
- Adequately adheres to topic and uses connective tissue.
- Demonstrates some errors in syntax and diction.

Sample Student Essays

Student Essay A

In the novel <u>The Color Purple</u> by Alice Walker, the heroine, Celie, grows and develops tremendously as an individual. Throughout the course of the story, Celie undergoes major spiritual and psychological transformations. In essence, Celie is reborn. The novel's themes of the power of faith, a united sisterhood, and rebirth are all emphasized by Celie's dramatic character evolution.

The novel begins with Celie writing a letter to God, telling him how her father has been raping her. Only fourteen years old, Celie is naive and still somewhat immature. She doesn't understand what her father is doing to her, and even more unfortunately, she doesn't have anyone to confide in. Thus, the reader senses Celie's immense isolation as she shares her confusion with, and only with, God.

Celie's life takes on a turn for the worse when she is sent to live with her arranged husband, Mr.−, who beats her and doesn't appreciate her. She does all of his work for him and his children, and again she has not a friend to turn to. However, when Mr.−'s son, Harpo, marries Sophia, Celie comes into contact with another woman. Celie doesn't really understand Sophia because she is a strong-willed, independent person who actually stands up to men. Thus, the reader senses the weakness in Celie's character when she advised Harpo to beat Sophia. Celie has been abused her whole life, and to her, being beaten is part of being a woman. She is totally numb to abuse; she even imagines herself to be a tree when being abused. This is her way to escape and void all feelings, to be indifferent to the pain.

Naturally, she is envious of Sophia's strength and character, and so she feels a beating would do Sophia good. When Sophia discovers that it was Celie who told Harpo to beat her, she is both furious and hurt. Sophia confronts Celie, and this a pivotal point in the novel. Celie realizes that she meant enough to Sophia for her to be upset, which means that Celie has actually affected another person. The two women quickly mend their relationship and begin a quilt to symbolize their friendship. This ties into the theme of sisterhood because now Celie has a friend, and the unity that the two share becomes an amazing force throughout the novel.

Celie's character undergoes the strongest transformation after meeting another "sister," Shug Avery. The circumstances under which Shug and Celie become friends are incredible, for Shug is Mr.-'s mistress. However, their unlikely bond is the main cause of Celie's rebirth. It was Shug who first expressed appreciation to Celie for helping her get better after a serious illness. No one had ever thanked Celie before, but Shug was so gratified for her care that she wrote a song for Celie. This small act of appreciation becomes the turning point in Celie's life. She now feels she is no longer as numb as a lifeless tree.

Shug's influence leads Celie to go from being a passive victim to becoming an assertive, vibrant, independent woman. Shug was the one who makes Mr.- stop beating Celie, as well as the one who found Celie's lost sister Nettie's letters which Mr.- had been hiding. Shug even inspires Celie to begin her own pants-making business, giving Celie total economic independence and creative freedom. Thus, the theme of rebirth is emphasized. Walker stresses how the human soul is an unbelievably powerful force, and how it contains the strength to emerge victorious despite adversity.

Shug Avery is also responsible for giving Celie a new spiritual outlook on life. She explains to Celie that God isn't necessarily an old, white-bearded man. Shug's view is that God is everything and is everywhere. The title becomes significant when Shug tells Celie that God becomes angry if you walk past the color purple in a field and don't notice it. This is a significant step in Celie's spiritual life because she now doesn't feel that God is a man who is indifferent and deaf to her prayers. She has renewed her belief, and the theme of the power of faith is reinforced, for Celie's faith has remained strong.

The Color Purple is a perfect example of a work of literature where the character undergoes a dramatic transformation. Celie changes from a numb, unassertive victim to being an aggressive, creative, vibrant, and independent woman. The unity of her female confidants and her unending faith allowed her to undergo such a deep transformation.

This essay is within the high-range parameters for the following reasons:

- Presents a clear, strong statement of the essay's purpose and indication of the organization of the essay.
- Presents clear appropriate information.
- Incorporates connected meaning with every point made.
- Thoroughly presents Celie's character.
- Provides pivotal moments and details to illustrate the prompt.
- Strongly adheres to topic.
- Uses good connective tissue.
- Organization allows presentation to build chronologically and from the merely physical to the metaphysical.
- Indicates both a perceptive reading of the novel and an understanding of some of its complexities.
- Demonstrates mature manipulation of language.

This is a solid high-range essay which clearly indicates a reader who not only "got" the novel but also "got" the tasks demanded of the prompt.

Student Essay B

Set in the malevolent, shadowy era of the Cold War, Ian McEwan's The Innocent centers on a fervent young Brit working for a covert anti-Soviet intelligence agency. His youthful good nature, manners, and naiveté are what make Leonard Marnham "the innocent." The new threat constantly slithering around the corner is the dreaded red snake of Communism, ensnaring and asphyxiating the world with its wicked omnipotence. Leonard travails scrupulously and surreptitiously for its willful opposition and relies on his innocence throughout his occupation and life. When suddenly thrust into a spiral of new and exciting, but vaguely frightening experiences exploring the life he never lived, something immense in Leonard changes. This flagrant transformation is momentous and permanent.

The most vital characterization of the protagonist is his underlying innocence, which is repeatedly and implicitly emphasized throughout the novel. The reader and revolving characters are drawn into Leonard's ingenuousness until he chooses to walk a path unknown to him which results in his surrendering his innocence. This transformation begins when Leonard becomes enraptured by the discovery of his own sexuality. He is an innocent in the purest sense of the word. Maria, his young, German lover, uncorks a surge of forceful new sensations and emotions in Leonard. This unleashing of unbridled passion allows him to give in to urges that ultimately push him over the edge. His exploration of sexuality brings new found masculinity and confidence. Leonard officially enters manhood and undergoes a tremendous transformation of temperament. His behavior is increasingly unrestrained. At a crucial turning point, 25 Leonard willfully imposes himself on Maria, ignoring all cries of distress of his lover. It is then that the reader becomes fully aware of Leonard's grave potential to give rein to his basest nature.

Following this traumatic incident with Maria, Leonard distinctly apologizes and makes a conscious effort to reform himself. The two scarred 30 companions reconcile only superficially and suffer perceptible losses of intimacy. The plot is complicated by the appearance of Maria's inebriated and disgruntled husband who attacks Leonard. After a crushing blow to his genitals, Leonard unleashes a shocking display of malice and murders and mutilates his assailant. 35

When Leonard callously forces himself onto Maria, we see his capability for harsh insensitivity, resulting in severe damage. But when Leonard slaughters Otto, and severs all his limbs, in order to fit the body into a suitcase, with the intent of eschewing penalty, it is all but too clear that Leonard Marnham is no longer the shy, unripe innocent the author 40 introduced us to.

In reference to Leonard's inhumanity the author uses irony to convey the idea that human actions during this time period were largely inhumane. McEwan's assessment of humanity and essentially his thesis by writing The Innocent is that man is inherently evil, requiring only the slightest 45 corruption (such as Leonard's entrance into manhood and the decadence exemplified by society) to unveil his intrinsic iniquity.

This essay is within the midrange parameters for the following reasons:

- Clearly understands the prompt and has a clear voice.
- Uses specifics from the text to illustrate points (paragraphs 2 and 3).
- Organization builds to a strong conclusion.
- Adheres to topic well.
- Demonstrates a willingness to stretch with regard to syntax and diction.
- Exhibits instances of awkward word choice (lines 7, 12, 37).
- Exhibits instances of awkward sentences (lines 9–11, 25–27).
- Does not provide a balanced characterization of Leonard.
- Does not provide proof of Leonard's innocence other than his sexuality.
- Veers dangerously close to plot summary.

It is obvious that this is an eager, intelligent, and thoughtful reader and writer. However, the results of the transformation on Leonard are not as fully developed as the prompt demands. It is only at the end of the essay that the transformation is connected to theme.

PART V

"AFTER WORDS"

A Suggested Reading Guide

As you probably know, a standard curriculum for AP Lit does not exist. Instead, teachers are urged to present material that will be appropriately challenging and enlightening while providing the opportunity for literary analysis. There are several ways of organizing the literature you study in an AP Literature and Composition course. Regardless of specifics, a broad selection of literature, covering many centuries and many styles, should be offered. Be confident that your teacher and course will meet the needs of the AP requirements.

We've developed several ways for you to reflect upon your own background. Once you have a clear overview of what you *do* know, you will be able to assess your particular strengths and weaknesses. You will also see the interrelationships of the literature you've studied and the commonalities and differences you will draw on to write your essays.

One approach to organizing your studies is chronological. This is the traditional survey of literature from "Beowulf to Virginia Woolf." This broad-based study provides you with many samples from different time periods and offers a context grounded in history. Another approach is the thematic one. Works are grouped by common ideas and are variations on a theme through time and genre. Often, it is obvious that certain works share a common sensibility. Generally, these characteristics are classified together as a literary movement. By connecting form and function, this type of reflection will broaden your understanding and analysis.

What follows is a bibliographic overview of literary movements.

CLASSICISM

The classical writer generally exhibits or is concerned with the following:

- Universality
- Noble ideas
- Dignified language
- Restraint
- Clarity

- Objectivity
- The importance of structure
- An edifying purpose

Suggested classical works and authors:

Homer	*The Iliad, The Odyssey*
The Bible	"Genesis," "Exodus," "Matthew"
Sophocles	*Antigone, Oedipus Rex*
Euripides	*Medea*
Aristotle	"On the Nature of Tragedy"
Plato	"The Apology," "The Allegory of the Cave"
Moliere	*Tartuffe, The Misanthrope*
Racine	*Phaedra*
John Milton	"L'Allegro," "Il Penseroso," "On His Blindness," *Paradise Lost* (excerpts)
Alexander Pope	"An Essay on Man," "An Essay on Criticism," "The Rape of the Lock"
Jonathan Swift	*Gulliver's Travels*
Voltaire	*Candide*

 Make a list of classical works you have read: Cite title, author, and major thoughts about each.

_____

_____

_____

_____

_____

REALISM

The realistic writer generally exhibits or is concerned with the following:

- Truth and actuality
- Detail
- Character portrayal
- Psychology
- Objectivity
- Lack of sentimentality

Suggested realistic works and authors:

Chaucer	*The Canterbury Tales*
Fyodor Dostoyevsky	*Crime and Punishment*
Leo Tolstoy	*Anna Karenina*
Anton Chekov	*The Cherry Orchard*
Ernest Hemingway	*The Sun Also Rises*
Henrik Ibsen	*Hedda Gabler, A Doll's House*

✓ Make a list of realistic works you have read: Cite title, author, and major thoughts about each.

_____

_____

_____

_____

_____

ROMANTICISM

The romantic writer generally exhibits or is concerned with the following:

- Emotions and passion
- Imagination and wonder
- The variety and power of Nature
- The individual
- Freedom and revolution
- Dreams and idealism
- Mystery and the supernatural
- Experimentation with form
- Spontaneity

Suggested romantic prose works and authors:

Anonymous	*Beowulf*
Bocaccio	*The Decameron*
Rabelais	*Gargantua*
Cervantes	*Don Quixote*
Shakespeare	*Hamlet, King Lear*
Goethe	*Faust*
Hawthorne	*The Scarlet Letter*
Bronte	*Jane Eyre*
Hugo	*Les Miserables*

Suggested romantic poetic works and authors:

Shakespeare	The Ballads—Scottish and British Sonnets
Robert Burns	"To a Mouse," "John Anderson, My Jo," "A Red, Red, Rose"
William Blake	"A Poison Tree," "The Sick Rose," "London," "The Chimney Sweep"
William Wordsworth	"Tintern Abbey," "My Heart Leaps Up," "London, 1802," "The World Is Too Much With Us," "I Wondered Lonely As a Cloud," "Ode on Intimations of Immortality," Preface to the Lyrical Ballads
Samuel Taylor Coleridge	"Kubla Khan," "The Frost at Midnight," "The Rime of the Ancient Mariner"
Lord Byron	"Sonnet on Chillon," "When We Two Parted," "Maid of Athens," "The Isles of Greece," "She Walks in Beauty"
Percy Bysshe Shelley	"Ode to the West Wind," "To a Skylark," "Ozymandias"
John Keats	"On First Looking Into Chapman's Homer," "Ode to a Nightingale," "Ode on a Grecian Urn," "When I Have Fears That I May Cease to Be"
Alfred, Lord Tennyson	"Ulysses"
Robert Browning	"My Last Duchess," "Pippa's Song," "Soliloquy of the Spanish Cloister"

✓ Make a list of romantic works you have read: Cite title, author, and major thoughts about each.

_____

_____

_____

_____

_____

IMPRESSIONISM

The impressionist writer generally exhibits or is concerned with the following:

- Appeals to the senses
- Mood and effects
- Vagueness and ambiguity
- Momentary insights
- Impressions of setting, plot, and character
- Emphasis on color and light
- Emotions and feelings
- Sensations into words

Suggested impressionistic works and authors:

Henry James	*The American*
Joseph Conrad	*Heart of Darkness, The Secret Sharer*, "The Lagoon"
Katherine Mansfield	"Bliss"
Kate Chopin	"Story of an Hour," *The Awakening*

 Make a list of impressionist works you have read: Cite title, author, and major thoughts about each:

_____

_____

_____

_____

_____

EXPRESSIONISM

The expressionist writer generally exhibits or is concerned with the following:

- Subjective responses
- Inner reality
- Abstract and mystical idea
- Symbols and masks
- Man and society in chaos
- Creation of new worlds

Expressionistic works and authors:

James Joyce	*Dubliners*
Eugene O'Neill	*Desire Under the Elms, The Hairy Ape, The Iceman Cometh*
T. S. Eliot	"The Hollow Men," "The Love Song of J. Alfred Prufrock"
Franz Kafka	*The Metamorphosis, The Trial*

✓ Make a list of expressionistic works you have read: Cite title, author, and major points about each:

_____

_____

_____

_____

_____

NATURALISM

The naturalist writer generally exhibits or is concerned with the following:

- Realism to its extreme
- Fact and detail
- Social awareness and reform
- A broad spectrum of subjects, both positive and negative
- Man as animal in society
- Scientific impartiality

Expressionistic works and authors:

Tennessee Williams	*A Streetcar Named Desire, Cat on a Hot Tin Roof*
Frank Norris	*The Octopus*
Stephen Crane	*Maggie, A Girl of the Streets*
Upton Sinclair	*The Jungle*

Make a list of naturalist works you have read: Cite title, author, and major thoughts about each:

_____

_____

_____

_____

_____

A note about literary movements: These are the movements you will find emphasized in the Western canon of literature. However, be aware that there are other literary movements that are currently recognized. Among them are the:

- Symbolist—an outgrowth of romanticism
- Existentialist—concern with man's alienation
- Absurdist—takes existentialism one step further into the realm of fractured reality

General Bibliography

Recommended Poets

 In addition to those referred to throughout this book, the following poets are representative of the poets you will encounter on the exam.

Matthew Arnold

W. H. Auden

Elizabeth Bishop

Gwendolyn Brooks

e e cummings

T. S. Eliot

Lawrence Ferlinghetti

Robert Francis

Robert Graves

Donald Hall

Seamus Heaney

Galway Kinnell

Maxine Kumin

Pablo Neruda

Sharon Olds

Wilfred Owen

Linda Pastan

May Swenson

Edna St. Vincent Millay

Dylan Thomas

Recommended Authors

Chinua Achebe: *Things Fall Apart*

Aeschylus: *Orestia*

Margaret Atwood: *The Handmaid's Tale*

Jane Austen: *Pride and Prejudice, Sense and Sensibility*

James Baldwin: *Go Tell It on the Mountain*

Charlotte Bronte: *Jane Eyre*

Emily Bronte: *Wuthering Heights*

Albert Camus: *The Stranger*

Willa Cather: *My Antonia, One of Ours, Death Comes to the Archbishop*

Anton Chekhov: *The Cherry Orchard*

Kate Chopin: *The Awakening*

Sandra Cisneros: *The House on Mango Street*

Joseph Conrad: *Heart of Darkness, Lord Jim, The Secret Sharer*

Stephen Crane: *The Red Badge of Courage*

Don Delillo: *White Noise*

Charles Dickens: *Great Expectations, A Tale of Two Cities*

Fyodor Dostoyevsky: *Crime and Punishment*
Theodore Dreiser: *An American Tragedy, Sister Carrie*
George Eliot: *Silas Marner, Middlemarch*
Ralph Ellison: *Invisible Man*
Euripedes: *Medea*
William Faulkner: *As I Lay Dying, The Sound and the Fury*
Henry Fielding: *Tom Jones*
F. Scott Fitzgerald: *The Great Gatsby*
Gustave Flaubert: *Madame Bovary*
E. M. Forster: *A Passage to India*
Thomas Hardy: *Jude the Obscure, Tess of the D'Ubervilles*
Nathaniel Hawthorne: *The Scarlet Letter*
Joseph Heller: *Catch-22*
Ernest Hemingway: *The Sun Also Rises*
Homer: *The Iliad, The Odyssey*
Zora Neale Hurston: *Their Eyes Were Watching God*
Aldous Huxley: *Brave New World*
Henrik Ibsen: *A Doll's House, Ghosts, Hedda Gabler*
Kazuo Ishiguro: *The Remains of the Day*
Henry James: *The Turn of the Screw, The American*
James Joyce: *A Portrait of the Artist as a Young Man*
Franz Kafka: *Metamorphosis, The Trial*
Ken Kesey: *One Flew Over the Cuckoo's Nest*
Maxine Hong Kingston: *The Woman Warrior*
D. H. Lawrence: *Sons and Lovers*
Gabriel Garcia Marquez: *One Hundred Years of Solitude*
Herman Melville: *Moby Dick, Billy Budd*
Arthur Miller: *Death of a Salesman, The Crucible*
Toni Morrison: *Beloved, Song of Solomon*
V. S. Naipul: *A Bend in the River*
Eugene O'Neill: *Desire Under the Elms, Long Day's Journey into Night*
George Orwell: *1984*
Tim O'Brien: *The Things They Carried*
Alan Paton: *Cry, the Beloved Country*
Jean Rhys: *Wide Sargasso Sea*
Jean Paul Sartre: *No Exit, Nausea*
William Shakespeare: *Hamlet, King Lear, Macbeth, Othello, Twelfth Night*
George Bernard Shaw: *Major Barbara, Man and Superman, Pygmalion*
Mary Shelley: *Frankenstein*
Sophocles: *Antigone, Oedipus Rex*
John Steinbeck: *The Grapes of Wrath, Of Mice and Men, Cannery Row*
Tom Stoppard: *Rosencrantz and Guildenstern Are Dead*
Jonathan Swift: *Gulliver's Travels*

Amy Tan: *The Kitchen God's Wife*
Leo Tolstoy: *Anna Karenina*
Mark Twain: *The Adventures of Huckleberry Finn*
Voltaire: *Candide*
Kurt Vonnegut: *Slaughterhouse Five*
Alice Walker: *The Color Purple*
Edith Wharton: *Ethan Frome, The House of Mirth*
Oscar Wilde: *The Importance of Being Earnest*
Thornton Wilder: *Our Town*
Tennessee Williams: *A Streetcar Named Desire,
    The Glass Menagerie*
Virginia Woolf: *To the Lighthouse*
Richard Wright: *Native Son*

Glossary of Terms

allegory A work that functions on a symbolic level.

alliteration The repetition of initial consonant sounds, such as "Peter Piper picked a peck of picked peppers."

allusion A reference contained in a work.

anapest A metrical pattern of two unaccented syllables followed by an accented syllable (˘ ˘ ´).

antagonist The force or character that opposes the main character, the protagonist.

apostrophe Direct address in poetry. Yeats's line "Be with me Beauty, for the fire is dying" is a good example.

aside Words spoken by an actor intended to be heard by the audience but not by other characters on stage.

aubade A love poem set at dawn which bids farewell to the beloved.

ballad A simple narrative poem, often incorporating dialogue that is written in quatrains, generally with a rhyme scheme of A B C D.

blank verse Unrhymed iambic pentameter. Most of Shakespeare's plays are in this form.

cacophony Harsh and discordant sounds in a line or passage of a literary work.

caesura A break or pause within a line of poetry indicated by punctuation and used to emphasize meaning.

catharsis According to Aristotle, the release of emotion that the audience of a tragedy experiences.

character One who carries out the action of the plot in literature. Major, minor, static, and dynamic are types of characters.

climax The turning point of action or character in a literary work, usually the highest moment of tension.

comic relief The inclusion of a humorous character or scene to contrast with the tragic elements of a work, thereby intensifying the next tragic event.

conflict A clash between opposing forces in a literary work, such as man vs. man; man vs. nature; man vs. God; man vs. self.

connotation The interpretive level of a word based on its associated images rather than its literal meaning.

convention A traditional aspect of a literary work such as a soliloquy in a Shakespearean play or a tragic hero in a Greek tragedy.

couplet Two lines of rhyming poetry; often used by Shakespeare to conclude a scene or an important passage.

dactyl A foot of poetry consisting of a stressed syllable followed by two unstressed syllables, / u u.

denotation The literal or dictionary meaning of a word.

denouement The conclusion or tying up of loose ends in a literary work; the resolution of the conflict and plot.

deus ex machina A Greek invention, literally "the god from the machine" who appears at the last moment and resolves the loose ends of a play. Today, the term refers to anyone, usually of some stature, who untangles, resolves, or reveals the key to the plot of a work. See the conclusion of Euripides's *Medea* for an example or the sheriff at the end of *Desire Under the Elms* by O'Neill.

diction The author's choice of words.

dramatic monologue A type of poem that presents a conversation between a speaker and an implied listener. Browning's "My Last Duchess" is a perfect example.

elegy A poem that laments the dead or a loss. "Elegy for Jane" by Roethke is a specific example. Gray's "Elegy in a Country Church Yard" is a general example.

enjambment A technique in poetry that involves the running on of a line or stanza. It enables the poem to move and to develop coherence as well as directing the reader with regard to form and meaning. Walt Whitman uses this continually.

epic A lengthy, elevated poem that celebrates the exploits of a hero. *Beowulf* is a prime example.

epigram A brief witty poem. Pope often utilizes this form for satiric commentary.

euphony The pleasant, mellifluous presentation of sounds in a literary work.

exposition Background information presented in a literary work.

fable A simple, symbolic story usually employing animals as characters. Aesop and La Fontaine are authors who excel at this form.

figurative language The body of devices that enables the writer to operate on levels other than the literal one. It includes metaphor, simile, symbol, motif, hyperbole, and others discussed in Chapter 8.

flashback A device that enables a writer to refer to past thoughts, events, episodes.

foot A metrical unit in poetry; a syllabic measure of a line: iamb, trochee, anapest, dactyl, and spondee.

foreshadowing Hints of future events in a literary work.

form The shape or structure of a literary work.

free verse Poetry without a defined form, meter, or rhyme scheme.

hyperbole Extreme exaggeration. In "My Love is Like a Red, Red Rose," Burns speaks of loving "until all the seas run dry."

iamb A metrical foot consisting of an unaccented syllable followed by an accented one; the most common poetic foot in the English language, $u\ /$.

idyll A type of lyric poem which extols the virtues of an ideal place or time.

image A verbal approximation of a sensory impression, concept, or emotion.

imagery The total effect of related sensory images in a work of literature.

impressionism Writing that reflects a personal image of a character, event, or concept. *The Secret Sharer* is a fine example.

irony An unexpected twist or contrast between what happens and what was intended or expected to happen. It involves dialogue and situation, and it can be intentional or unplanned. Dramatic irony centers around the ignorance of those involved while the audience is aware of the circumstance.

lyric poetry A type of poetry characterized by emotion, personal feelings, and brevity; a large and inclusive category of poetry that exhibits rhyme, meter, and reflective thought.

metaphor A direct comparison between dissimilar things. "Your eyes are stars" is an example.

metaphysical poetry Refers to the work of poets like John Donne who explore highly complex, philosophical ideas through extended metaphors and paradox.

meter A pattern of beats in poetry. (Answers to questions in poetry review: 5, 3, 2, 2, 4)

metonymy A figure of speech in which a representative term is used for a larger idea. ("The pen is mightier than the sword.")

monologue A speech given by one character. (Hamlet's "To be or not to be . . . ")

motif The repetition or variations of an image or idea in a work which is used to develop theme or characters.

narrative poem A poem that tells a story.

narrator The speaker of a literary work.

octave An eight-line stanza, usually combined with a sestet in a Petrarchan sonnet.

ode A formal, lengthy poem that celebrates a particular subject.

onomatopoeia Words that sound like the sound they represent (hiss, gurgle, bang).

oxymoron An image of contradictory terms (bittersweet, pretty ugly, giant economy size).

parable A story that operates on more than one level and usually teaches a moral lesson. (*The Pearl* by John Steinbeck is a fine example. See *Allegory*.)

parallel plot A secondary story line that mimics and reinforces the main plot. (Hamlet loses his father as does Ophelia.)

parody A comic imitation of a work that ridicules the original.

pathos The aspects of a literary work that elicit pity from the audience.

personification The assigning of human qualities to inanimate objects or concepts. (Wordsworth personifies "the sea that bares her bosom to the moon" in the poem "London, 1802.")

plot A sequence of events in a literary work.

point of view The method of narration in a work.

protagonist The hero or main character of a literary work, the character the audience sympathizes with.

quatrain A four-line stanza.

resolution The denouement of a literary work.

rhetorical question A question that does not expect an explicit answer. It is used to pose an idea to be considered by the speaker or audience. (Ernest Dowson asks, "Where are they now the days of wine and roses?")

rhyme/rime The duplication of final syllable sounds in two or more lines.

rhythm The repetitive pattern of beats in poetry. (Answer to question in poetry review: 74)

romanticism A style or movement of literature that has as its foundation an interest in freedom, adventure, idealism, and escape.

satire A mode of writing based on ridicule, which criticizes the foibles and follies of society without necessarily offering a solution. (Jonathan Swift's *Gulliver's Travels* is a great satire that exposes mankind's condition.)

sestet A six-line stanza, usually paired with an octave to form a Petrarchan sonnet.

sestina A highly structured poetic form of 39 lines, written in iambic pentameter. It depends upon the repetition of six words from the first stanza in each of six stanzas.

setting The time and place of a literary work.

simile An indirect comparison that uses the words "like" or "as" to link the differing items in the comparison. ("Your eyes are like stars.")

soliloquy A speech in a play which is used to reveal the character's inner thoughts to the audience. (Hamlet's "To be or not to be . . . " is one of the most famous soliloquies in literature.)

sonnet A 14-line poem with a prescribed rhyme scheme in iambic pentameter. (See Chapter 8 for a comparison between Shakespearean and Petrarchan sonnets.)

spondee A poetic foot consisting of two accented syllables, (/ /).

stage directions The specific instructions a playwright includes concerning sets, characterization, delivery, etc. (See *Hedda Gabler* by Ibsen.)

stanza A unit of a poem, similar in rhyme, meter, and length to other units in the poem.

structure The organization and form of a work.

style The unique way an author presents his ideas. Diction, syntax, imagery, structure, and content all contribute to a particular style.

subplot A secondary plot that explores ideas different from the main storyline. (In *Hamlet,* the main storyline has Hamlet avenging the death of his father. The subplot has Hamlet dealing with his love for Ophelia.)

symbol Something in a literary work that stands for something else. (Plato has the light of the sun symbolize truth in "The Allegory of the Cave.")

synecdoche A figure of speech that utilizes a part as representative of the whole. ("All hands on deck" is an example.)

syntax The grammatical structure of prose and poetry.

tercet A three-line stanza.

theme The underlying ideas that the author illustrates through characterization, motifs, language, plot, etc.

tone The author's attitude toward his subject.

tragic hero According to Aristotle, a basically good person of noble birth or exalted position who has a fatal flaw or commits an error in judgment which leads to his downfall. The tragic hero must have a moment of realization and live and suffer.

understatement The opposite of exaggeration. It is a technique for developing irony and/or humor where one writes or says less than intended.

villanelle A highly structured poetic form that comprises six stanzas: five tercets, and a quatrain. The poem repeats the first and third lines throughout.

Websites Related to the Advanced Placement Exam

There are thousands of sites on the Web that are in some way related to the study of college-level English. This is not a comprehensive list of all of these Websites. It is a list that is the most relevant to your preparation and review for the AP Literature and Composition Exam. It is up to you to log on to a site that may be of interest to you and to see for yourself just what it can offer and whether or not it will be of specific benefit to you.

- Since you are preparing for an Advanced Placement exam, go to the source as your first choice:

  http://www.collegeboard.org/ap

  http:www.collegeboard.org/ap/english

- For AP exam links:

  http://maxpages.com/aptest

- For free practice multiple-choice questions:

  http://aphelp.com

- For an interesting AP test club and chat room:

  http://clubs.yahoo.com/clubs/aptests

- For practice with essay questions:

  http://cbweb6.collegeboard.org/writewellCB/student/ap/html/apintro.html

Each of these Websites will lead you to others. There are just too many to list here; in fact, there are hundreds of thousands of sites listed on the web.

If you have any questions or comments you would like to share with the authors and/or readers of this text, you can go to the following website. There, you will find more information about the current AP English Literature and Composition prep, references of interest to AP Literature and Composition students, helpful hints for the AP Literature and Composition student, and a way to personally contact the authors. <http://clearestideas.com>

We suggest you use your favorite web server or search engine and type in ADVANCED PLACEMENT ENGLISH (AP), or ADVANCED PLACEMENT (AP) LITERATURE. (Our favorite search engine is www. google.com/ From that point on you can "surf the net" for those sites that suit your particular needs. You will have to take the time to explore these various domains and to make your own evaluation of their value to you and your expectations. Perhaps, you might even decide to set up your own AP Lit Website or chat room.

About the Authors

Estelle Rankin taught AP Literature at Jericho High School in Jericho, New York, for over 25 years. She was honored with the AP Literature Teacher of the Year award by the College Board in 1996. Estelle also received the Long Island Teacher of the Year award in 1990. She was the recipient of the Cornell University Presidential Scholars' award and has been recognized by the C. W. Post Master Teachers Program.

Ms. Rankin earned her bachelor's degree from Adelphi University and her master's from Hofstra University. She has pursued further graduate work in the field of creative studies at Queens College and Brooklyn University.

Ms. Rankin has done extensive work in the research and development of film, drama, and creative writing curricula. She has participated in numerous AP Literature conferences and workshops. In addition, she pioneered a "senior initiative mentoring program" based on internships and service. Her finest teachers were her parents, Edward and Sylvia Stern.

Barbara Murphy taught AP Language and other college level courses at Jericho High School in Jericho, New York for over 26 years. She has been a reader of the AP Language and Composition exam since 1993 and is a consultant for the College Board's AP Language and Composition and its Building for Success divisions for whom she has conducted workshops, conferences, and summer institutes. Ms. Murphy is currently on the faculty of Syracuse University's Project Advance in English.

After earning her bachelor's degree from Duquesne University and her master's degree from the University of Pittsburgh, Ms. Murphy did her doctoral course work at Columbia University. In addition, she holds professional certifications in still photography and motion picture production and is one of the founding members of the women's film company Ishtar Films.

Ms. Rankin and Ms. Murphy are the coauthors of the McGraw-Hill's *5 Steps to a 5: AP English Language*.